CW01184141

Outrageous Yachts

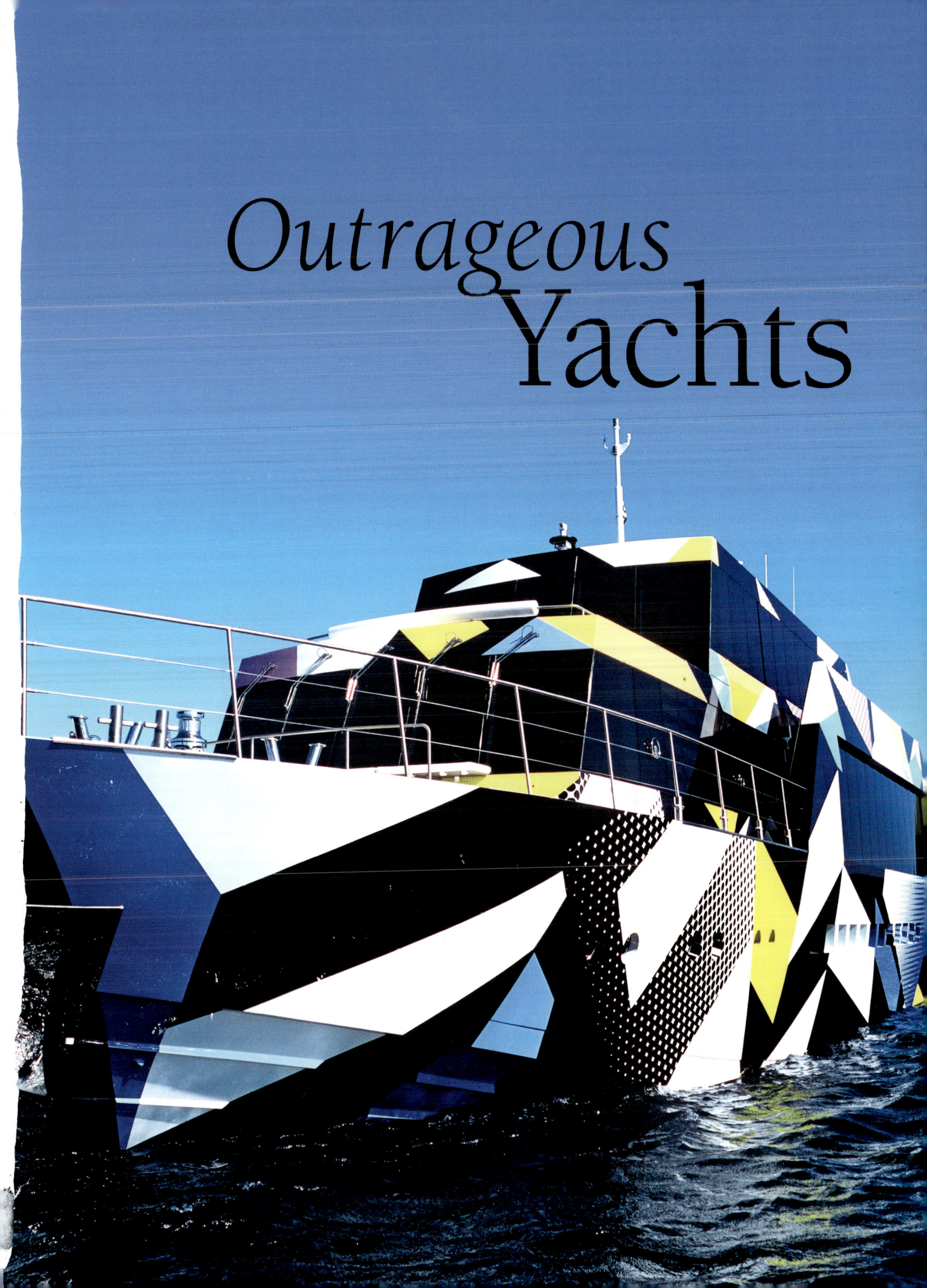

Outrageous Yachts

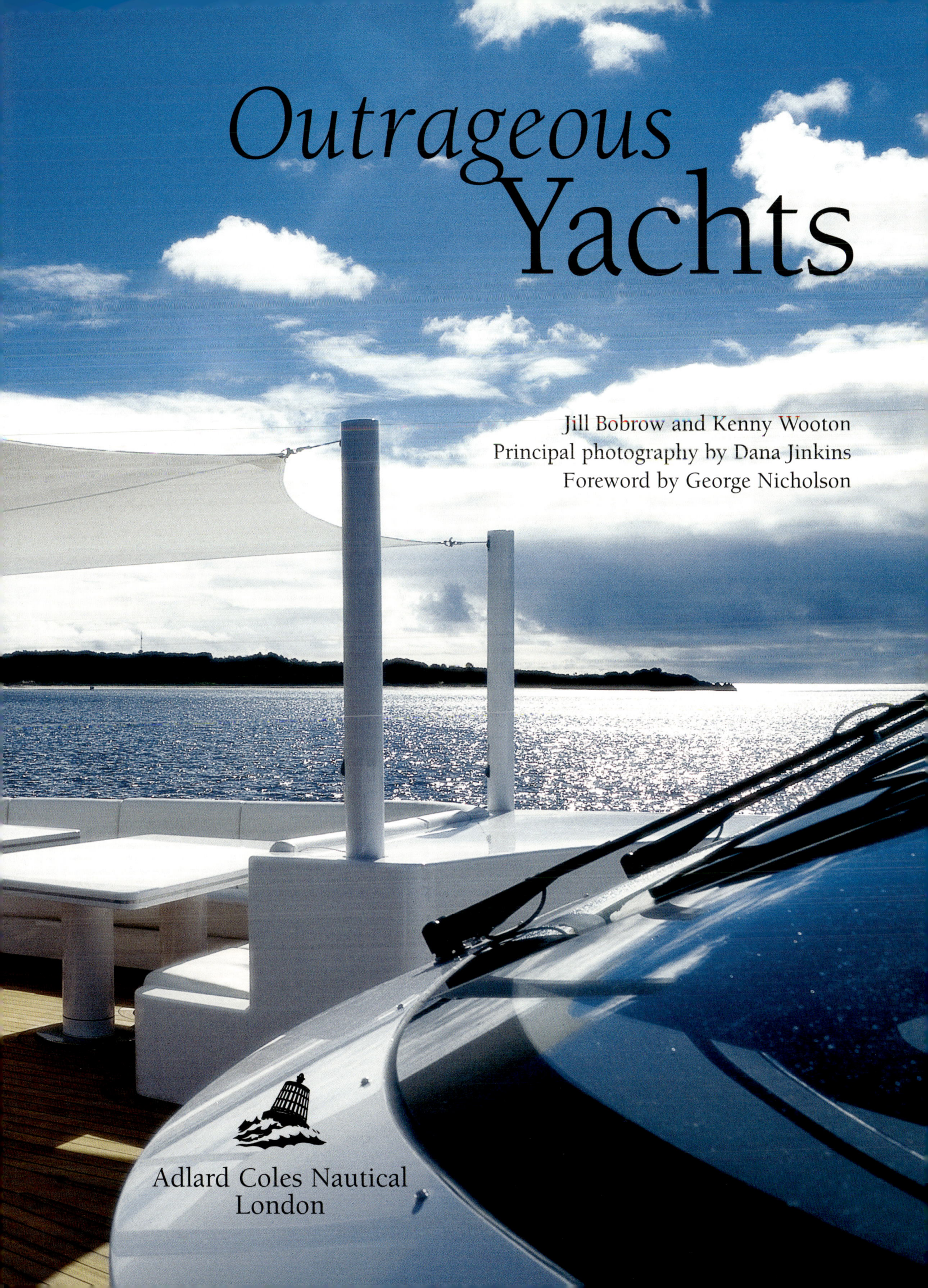

Jill Bobrow and Kenny Wooton
Principal photography by Dana Jinkins
Foreword by George Nicholson

Adlard Coles Nautical
London

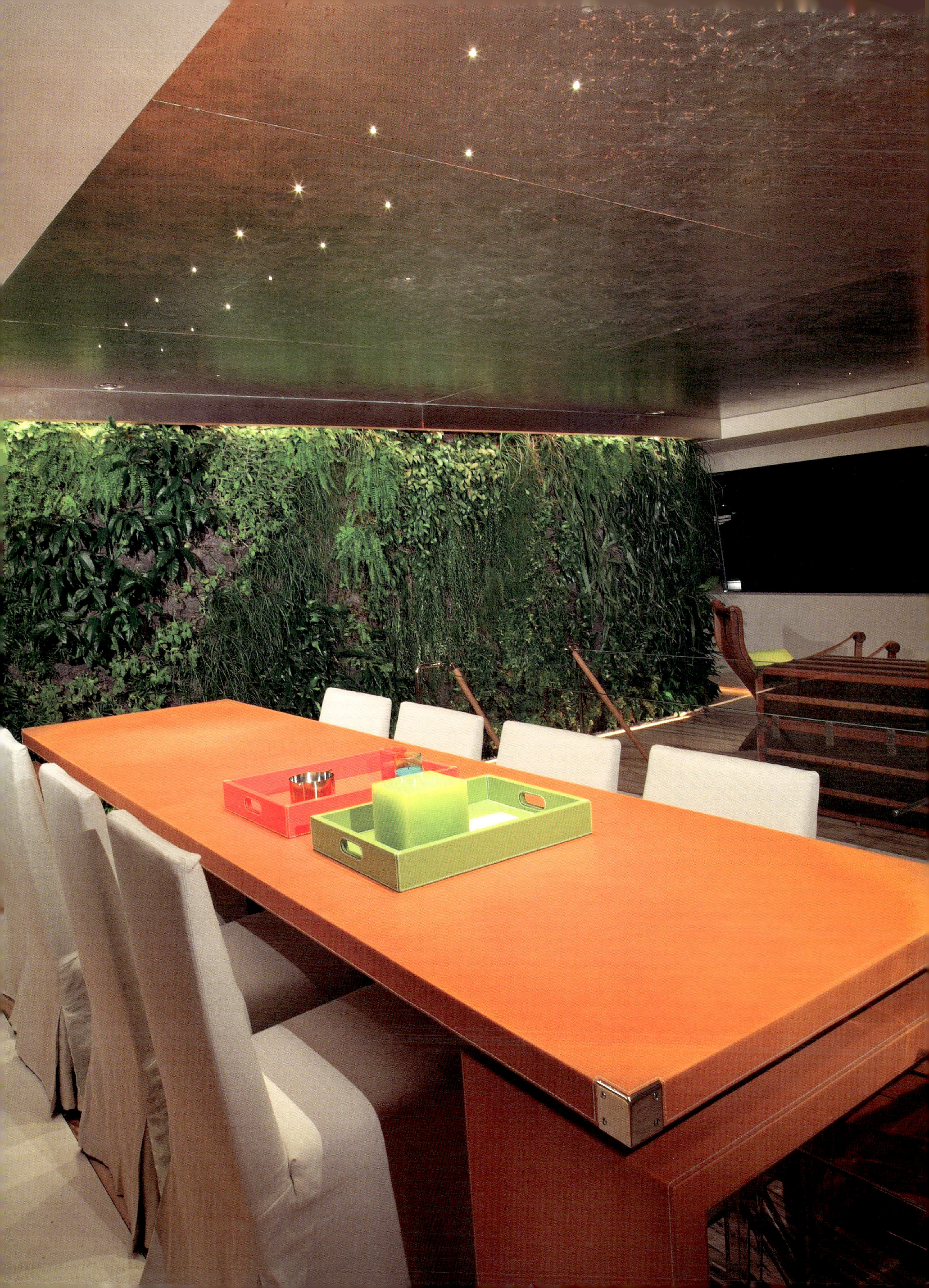

Contents

Foreword by George Nicholson 7

Introduction 8

The Yachts
Christina O 32
Mirabella V 42
Predator 5
Norwegian Queen 64
The Maltese Falcon 74
Alysia 84
Lulworth 94
Guilty 104
Alfa Nero 114
Hyperion 124
Martha Ann 130
Mr. Terrible 138
Nina J 148
Wally 143 Esense 158
S.S. Delphine 166
Allure Shadow 174
Sea Force One 182
Ranger 196
Silver 20
118 WallyPower 210
On the Horizon 222

Acknowledgements 232

PAGE ONE: Guilty…until proven innocent.

PRECEDING PAGES: Late afternoon on a forward deck of Silver.

OPPOSITE: A vertical garden of tropical plants and orchids graces Nina J's main saloon.

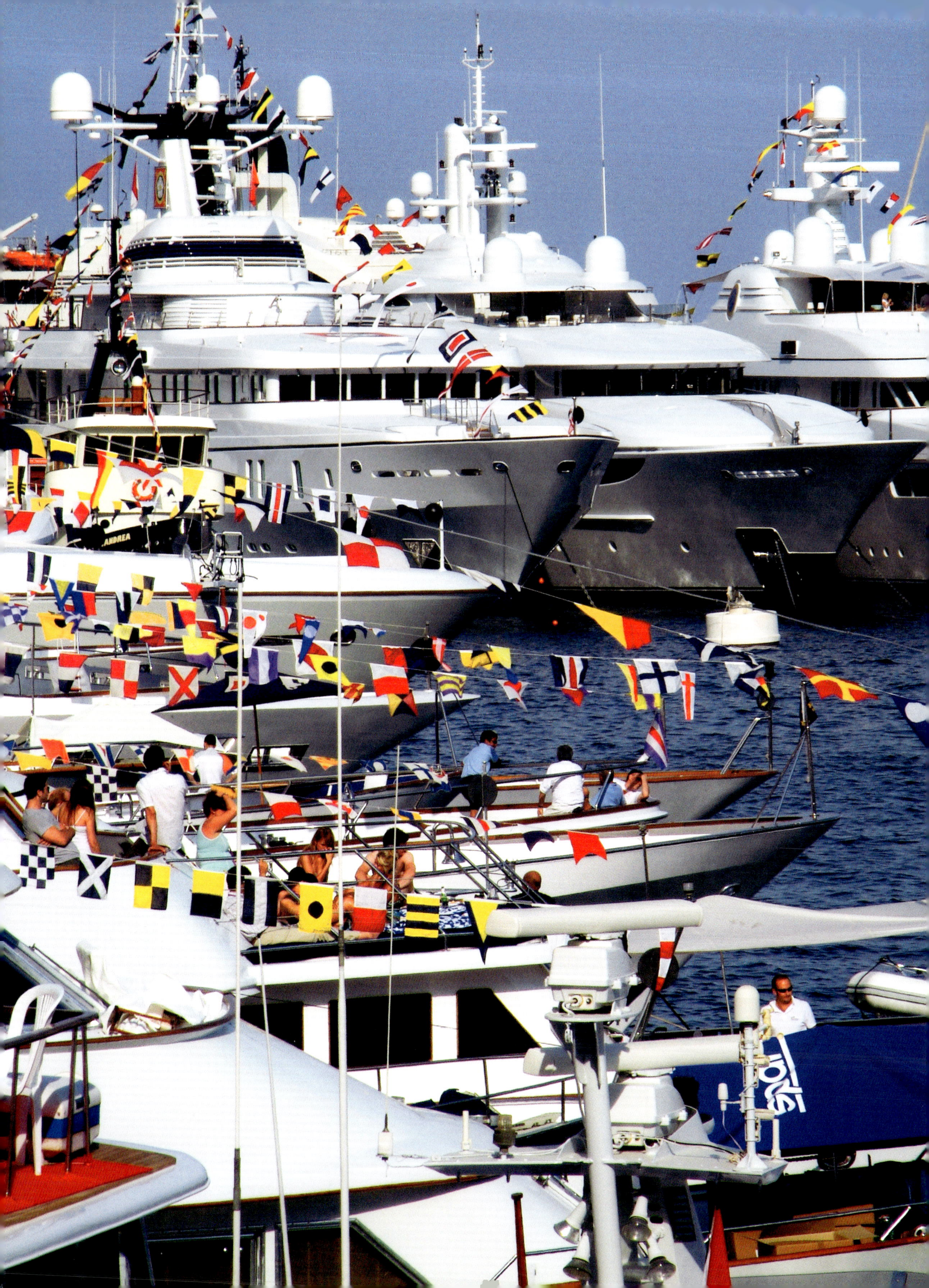
ANDREA

Foreword

The last decade has seen an unprecedented expansion of yachting in all its aspects: design and new construction in both power and sail; restoration and the renaissance of classic sailing yachts; racing; and the infrastructure that allows it all to happen. Yachting without all the new ports and marinas would be like driving without highways or flying without modern airports.

Yacht design and construction epitomize the very essence of "custom building," and unite a greater number of technical and artisanal skills than any other product. Jon Bannenberg, the designer who launched the modern era of yacht design, once said to me that designing and building a modern large yacht was like building a prototype Boeing 747 every time.

It would be impossible to cover every interesting yacht in a single book. They are all interesting. Yet for this volume choices had to be made, and no one could be better qualified to make that selection than authors Jill Bobrow—whom I have know for more years than I care to recall—and Kenny Wooton, the editor in chief and executive editor, respectively, of the premier yachting magazine *Showboats International*. In 1985 I wrote the Foreword to another book authored by Jill Bobrow and photographed by Dana Jinkins entitled *The World's Most Extraordinary Yachts*. What has transpired in the last 25 years in yachting is outrageous indeed!

This book covers a number of notable yachts, each demonstrating the ideas and determination of their owners, who, in some cases, must have prevailed over the hesitation of the designers to achieve their goals. I wonder what was said to Joe Vittoria, the owner of *Mirabella V* with her 300-foot+ (90-metre+) mast, and to Tom Perkins when he suggested the rig for *The Maltese Falcon*. Matching the interior of *The Maltese Falcon* to the external appearance was a work of genius on the part of designer Ken Freivokh.

I have had the good fortune to have visited personally many of the yachts featured in the book. In the 1980s I very nearly became the owner of *Christina O*, with the intention of making her into a private club and restaurant in New York. It is better that she is still flourishing as a fully functional yacht, although no longer steam driven. Steam has always been a weakness of mine, so I am delighted that the authors have included *S.S. Delphine* in their selection. I saw *Delphine* in Marseilles just after she had arrived from the United States, and before her restoration. The current owners are to be congratulated on a great rebuild—and for keeping the steam engines.

I am glad that both the Royal Huisman and Perini Navi yards have yachts of their build included in this book. They are both flagships of build quality and innovation in their respective countries, as well as in the wider yacht-building industry. Both have brought much to ease the burden of handling large sailboats. Lucca Basani and his Wally yachts have brought style, glamour, and performance to the world of coastal sailors and racers. These days Les Voiles de Saint-Tropez, the old Nioulargue race, would not be complete without four or five Wally yachts moored together, with their attendant quayside admirers. *Lulworth* is an extraordinary achievement in the classic yacht world. I saw her when she first arrived in Italy for her restoration. She was a pitiful sight; hard to imagine when you see her today. She is a real tribute to all the skilled and dedicated artisans who worked on her resurrection, for resurrection it truly was.

And the fact that there are possibly four new J-Class yachts currently under construction underscores the great attraction these incredibly gracious large racing yachts still have on the yachting public today.

As I write this foreword, the whole world is in financial turmoil, and the yachting industry along with it. However the 1930s, the era of the Great Depression, was a major period of large yacht construction and innovation. I am confident that the unique attractions of yachting will pull the industry through this current storm, and judging by the designs for future yachts at the end of the book, there is fair sailing ahead.

Yachts "dressed" for the annual Monaco Grand Prix—a Côte d'Azur extravaganza, rivalled only by the Cannes Film Festival.

George Nicholson, Chairman
Camper & Nicholsons International
2009

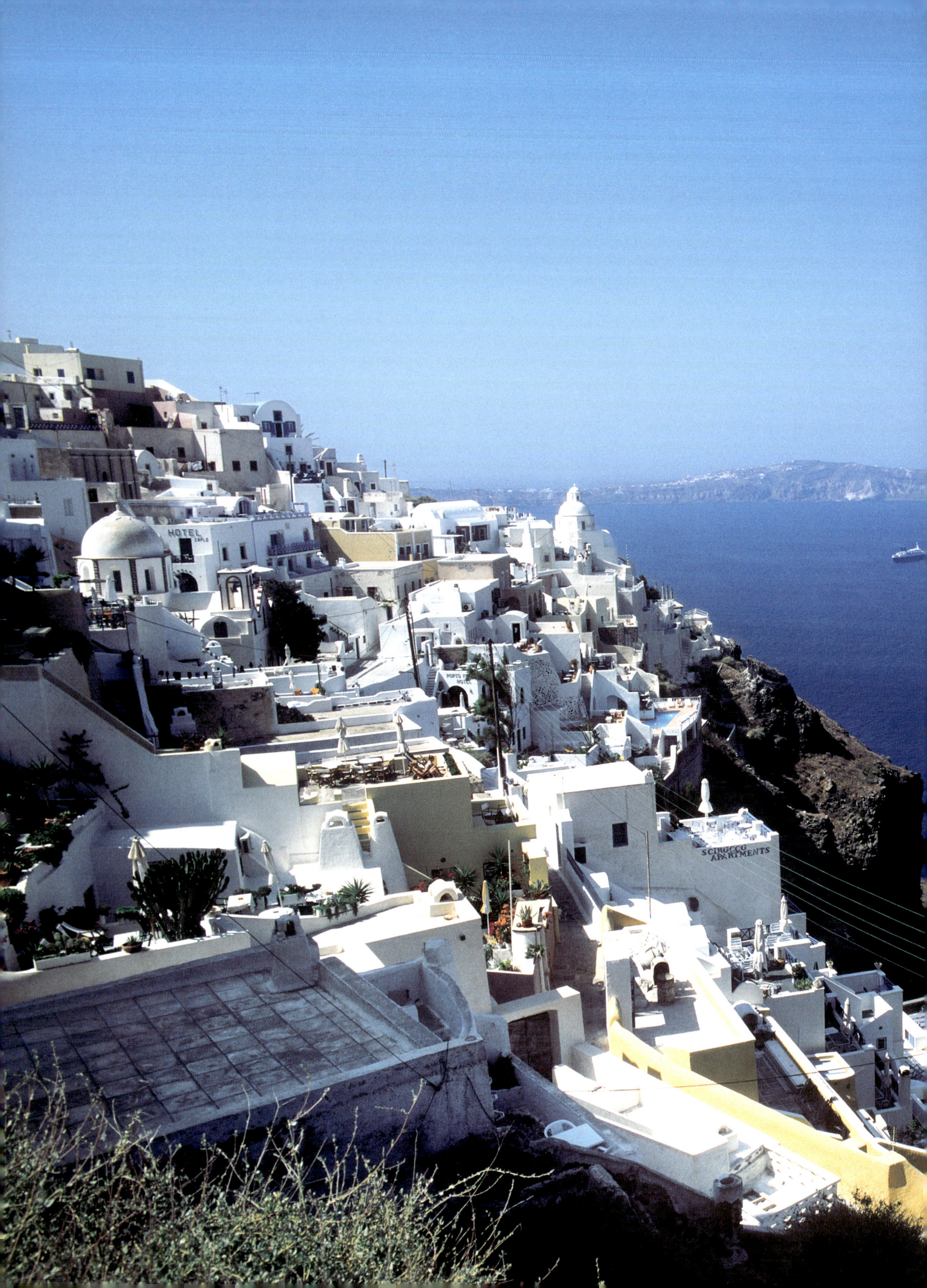
HOTEL
SCIROCCO APARTMENTS

Introduction

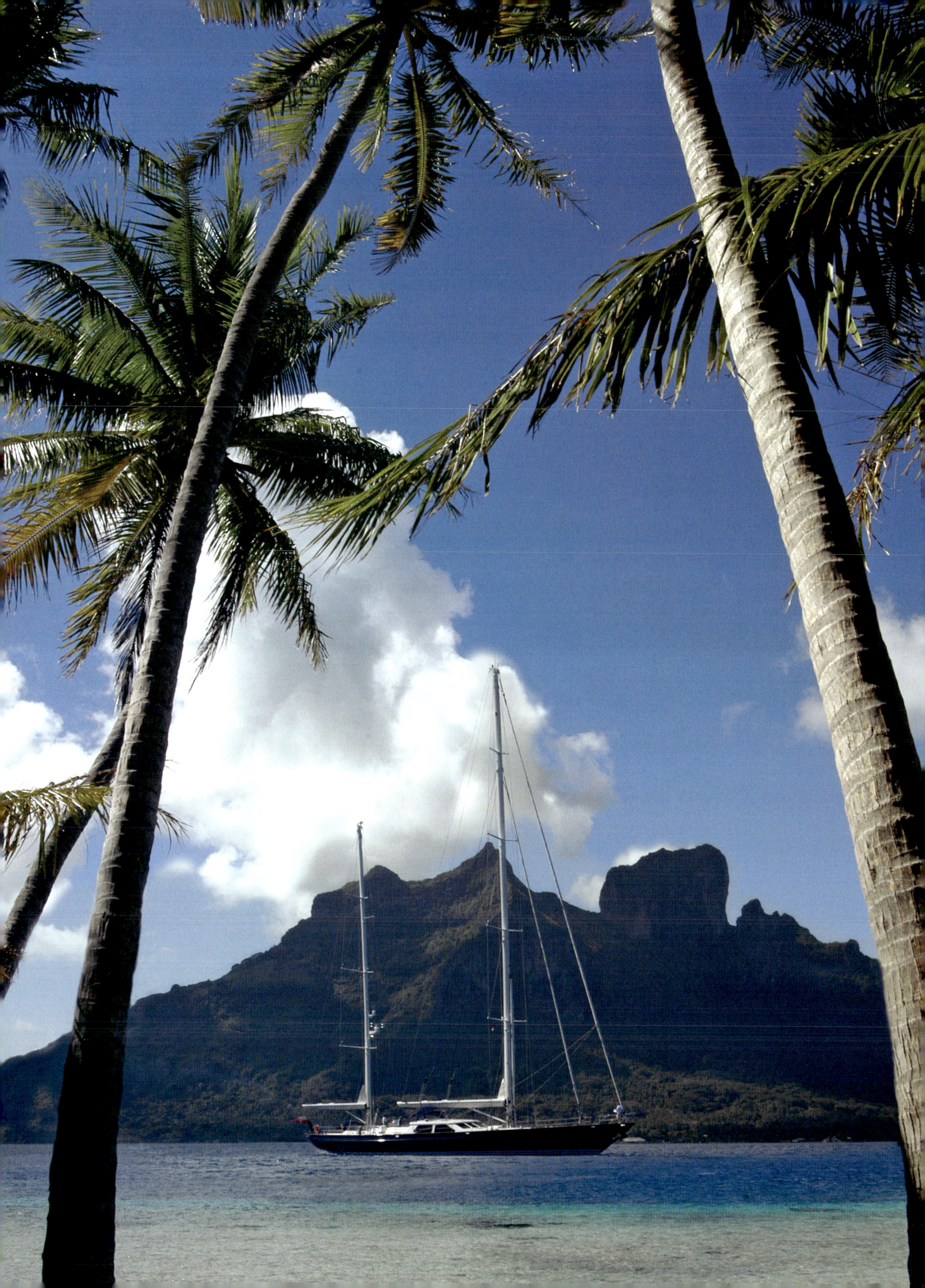

It could reasonably be argued that most yachts warrant the designation "outrageous." Yachts represent the ultimate expression of excess. They are created by sybaritic spirits operating firmly outside the realm of necessity and are adorned with exotic components and accoutrements aimed at producing the definitive waterborne luxury experience. But not all yachts are created equal. Unquestionably, some are more outrageous than others.

The yachts profiled in this book are, in our view, exceptional among a burgeoning class of dazzling peers. Some are manifestations of pure, ego-driven one-upmanship among people of formidable affluence. Others are creations of people who love the sea and want to share the joys of cruising or the thrill of discovery with family and friends. Still others are expressions of their owners' creative compulsions and deeply individual sensibilities. Some are the product of people who are drawn to the sensual lines of classic yachts and have spared no expense to painstakingly restore or re-create the spirit embodied in them. The yachts in this book are not necessarily the biggest, the most expensive, or the most opulent, but each represents a unique example of a type or class that has broken ground in some way. Each has a special element, or elements, that sets it apart from the ever-expanding universe of larger and larger yachts.

The examples in this book range from breathtaking restorations such as the 152-foot (46.3-metre) *Lulworth* (see pages 94–103), built in 1920 and relaunched in pristine condition in 2006, to *The Maltese Falcon* (see pages 74–83), a 288-foot (87.8-metre), high-tech take on the square-rigged sailing ships of old, commissioned by Silicon Valley venture-capital legend Tom Perkins; from the 257-foot (78.3-metre) *S.S. Delphine* (see pages 166–73), commissioned in 1918 by automobile magnate Horace Dodge and fully restored and kept healthy by a passionate Belgian family, to the 177-foot (54-metre) *Sea Force One* (see pages 182–95), a modern motoryacht that embodies the profoundly nontraditional tastes of a dynamic young Italian businessman. Also included are *Christina O* (see pages 32–41), arguably the most famous yacht in the world, once owned by Aristotle Onassis, and the quirky, 115-foot (35-metre) yacht *Guilty* (see

PRECEDING PAGES: *The 325-foot (99-metre)* Christina O *anchored off Santorini, in the Cyclades, Greece.*

OPPOSITE: Charlatan, *a 110-foot (33.5-metre) Ron Holland–designed sailing yacht, anchored off Bora Bora.*

TOP AND ABOVE: *Snorkelling, kayaking, the best seat in the house—yachting has it all.*

pages 104–13), owned by a contemporary art collector who commissioned Jeff Koons to paint the exterior.

The cost of building the largest and most lavish yachts in the world has surpassed the $300 million mark, making yachts by a wide margin a) the most expensive luxury goods on earth and b) the most expensive vacation retreats on the planet. And the outflow of cash doesn't stop when the Champagne bottle breaks on the bow. A rule of thumb in the yachting industry is that an owner should expect to pay between 10 and 15 percent of a yacht's build cost annually for crew, maintenance, and basic operations.

Large yachts are the quintessence of unrestrained opulence and extravagance. Designers, owners, and builders scour quarries around the world for exotic marble, onyx, and granite to cover floors and bathroom surfaces. Gold-plated fixtures are commonplace—not just doorknobs and taps, but even toilet-brush handles and tissue holders. Upholstery and carpets are woven from silks spun by worms found in a single place on earth. Attention to detail is astonishing in lighting, furnishings, and all other aspects of decor. Masterworks hang on the bulkheads and in the living areas and staterooms.

It's not uncommon to find exceedingly rare woods incorporated into today's yacht interiors. Although traditional yacht woods such as teak, mahogany, and oak remain popular, solid woods and veneers made from trees with highly exotic names are appearing more and more frequently. For example, the joinery on the 154-foot (47-metre) Delta Mr. Terrible (see pages 138–47) is fashioned out of more than a dozen different woods with beguiling grains, including koa, which is indigenous to Hawaii, bubinga, cerejeira, makoré, and wenge. Brilliant book-matched veneers, impossibly swirly burls, and mesmeric inlays are part and parcel of the modern yacht interior. Furniture is often custom made for the yacht; manufactured pieces tend to be gallery grade.

When does a boat become a yacht? Or for that matter, a megayacht, a superyacht, or a gigayacht? In Great Britain, the word *yacht* is synonymous with a sailboat of almost any size. For the rest of the world, the term *yacht* encompasses both sail- and motor-powered boats and usually connotes vessels of size. There are many opinions on what defines a yacht. The simplest is that a yacht is a watercraft used for leisure or pleasure. The words *megayacht, superyacht,* and *gigayacht* suggest vessels of progressively larger size, but in fact there are no meaningful distinctions among these terms.

Some marine historians claim that Cleopatra cruised around in a barge for pleasure. But it's generally agreed that the first yachts appeared on the scene in the six-

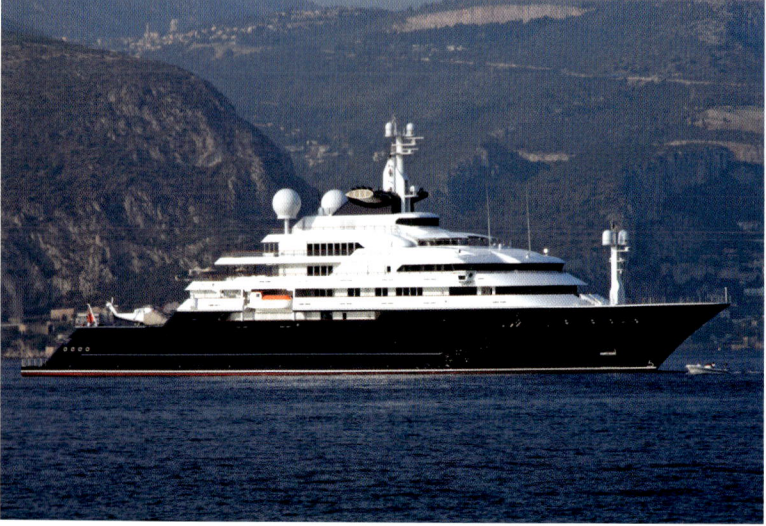

TOP: *Launched as* Eco, *this 244-foot (74.4-metre) Martin Francis–designed yacht was originally built for late Mexican communications magnate Emilio Azcárraga. Later she was sold to Larry Ellison of Oracle, who renamed her* Katana. *She is now British owned and called* Enigma.

ABOVE: *The 414-foot (126-metre)* Octopus, *owned by Paul Allen, co-founder of Microsoft, carries two helicopters, a submarine, and a small fleet of tenders.*

12 / OUTRAGEOUS YACHTS

teenth century, when the Dutch built fast-sailing ships called *jaghts* to wage war against their overseas ruler, King Philip of Spain. By the middle of the seventeenth century, these sailing ships had proliferated. The nature of men and their inherent proclivity for one-upmanship spawned rival *jaghts* and races were initiated. In 1660 the Dutch East India Company presented King Charles II of England with the yacht *Mary*. Apparently he was so delighted with her that he commissioned the building of more and more yachts, as did his brother James, Duke of York. The two brothers' competitive spirit led to the first documented yacht race in 1661. It ran from Greenwich to Gravesend and back.

Then, as now, yachting was a wealthy man's game. As with any sport, it was inevitable that people of like minds would band together to form clubs to celebrate their shared passion. The Irish claim that the first yacht club was the Cork Water Club (today still thriving as the Royal Cork Yacht Club), which was established in 1720. The Russians, however, maintain that the first club was the Flotilla of the Neva, started by Peter the Great in 1718.

Yacht clubs began proliferating in the late eighteenth century. Traditionally, they were all-male, ethnically homogeneous bastions of old money. Indeed, even well into the second half of the twentieth century, the membership

ABOVE: *Suntans and five-star service on the aft deck of the 246-foot (75-metre)* Mirabella V.

BELOW: *Refreshments are served on* Alfa Nero's *retractable balcony.*

ABOVE: A back flip and a free fall from the bow of the sailing superyacht Mirabella V in the Tobago Cays, St. Vincent and the Grenadines.

LEFT: Water toys such as jet skis and trampolines, are perfect charter accoutrements for kids aboard the 140-foot (42.7-metre) Four Wishes.

BELOW: *Charter yachts such as the 170-foot (51.8-metre)* Midlandia *store their water toys in a "garage" to keep the decks clear of clutter.*

of the moat prestigious old-line clubs was restricted to men. Today, most yacht clubs remain elite organizations, but they do not exclude anyone on the basis of race, gender, or creed, and they welcome young people who share a passion for the sport, offering them discounted initiation fees and dues.

Yacht owners are difficult to pigeonhole. They're an eclectic, international group that includes everyone from royalty, film stars, music moguls, star athletes, and venture capitalists to small business owners, real estate developers, restaurateurs, pig farmers, and car dealers. People buy and build yachts for many reasons, among which status is perhaps paramount. As clichéd as it may sound, to many, owning a yacht is the ultimate symbol of wealth. A passion for the sea certainly is a common denominator among yacht owners. A yacht provides those who can afford it with privacy, security, and a level of luxury sometimes hard to match ashore. It is a magic carpet upon which to travel the world, a moving portal from which to explore the countless miles across the globe where land and sea meet.

Some owners are into yachting simply to express their creativity, albeit on a titanic scale. These owners order custom yachts from the world's leading builders, remain intimately involved in their design and construction, then promptly put the boats up for sale, sometimes even before they are launched, and move on to the next project.

Time was, a yacht's supplemental gear consisted of a tender for getting guests to and from shore and maybe

INTRODUCTION / 15

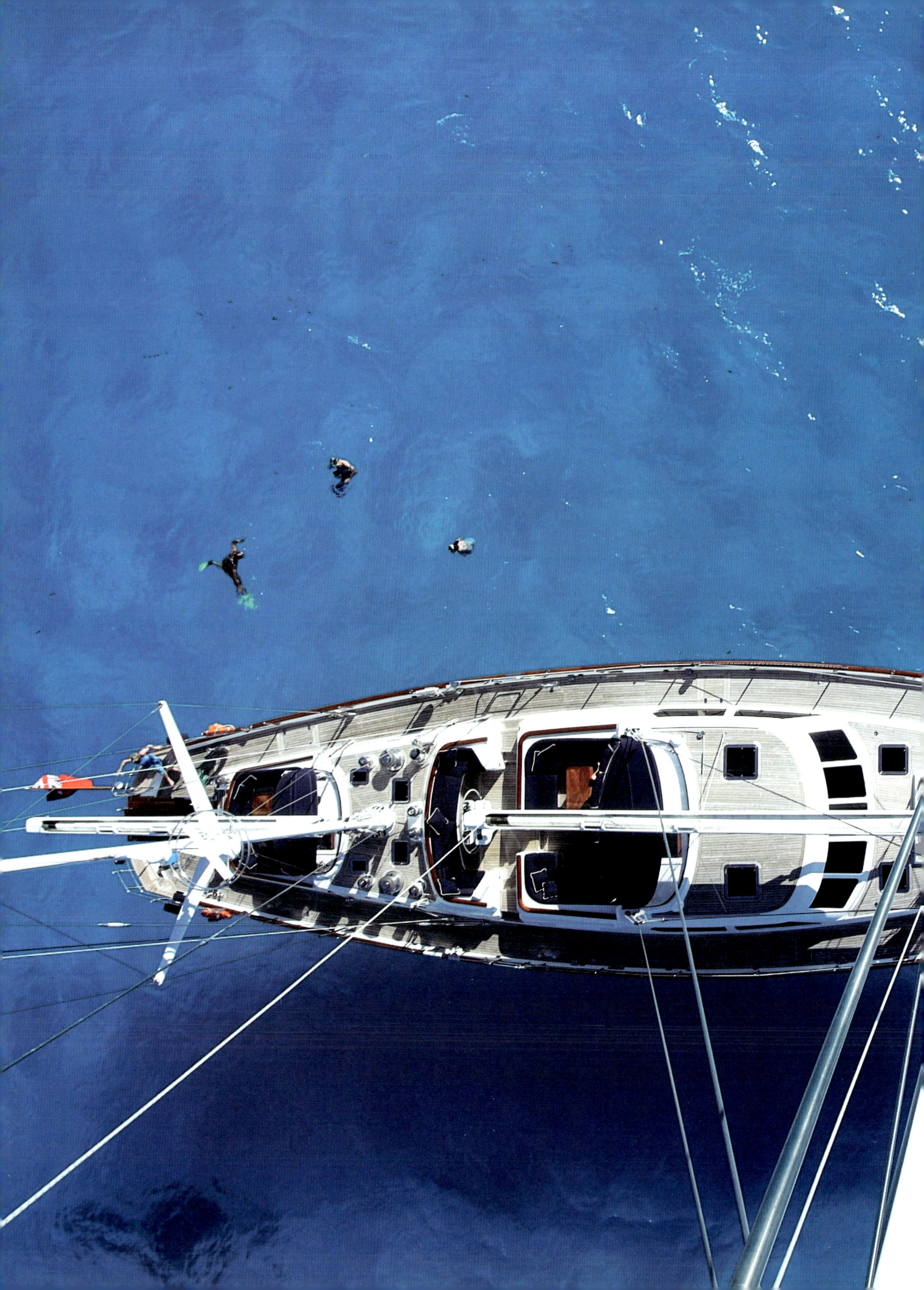

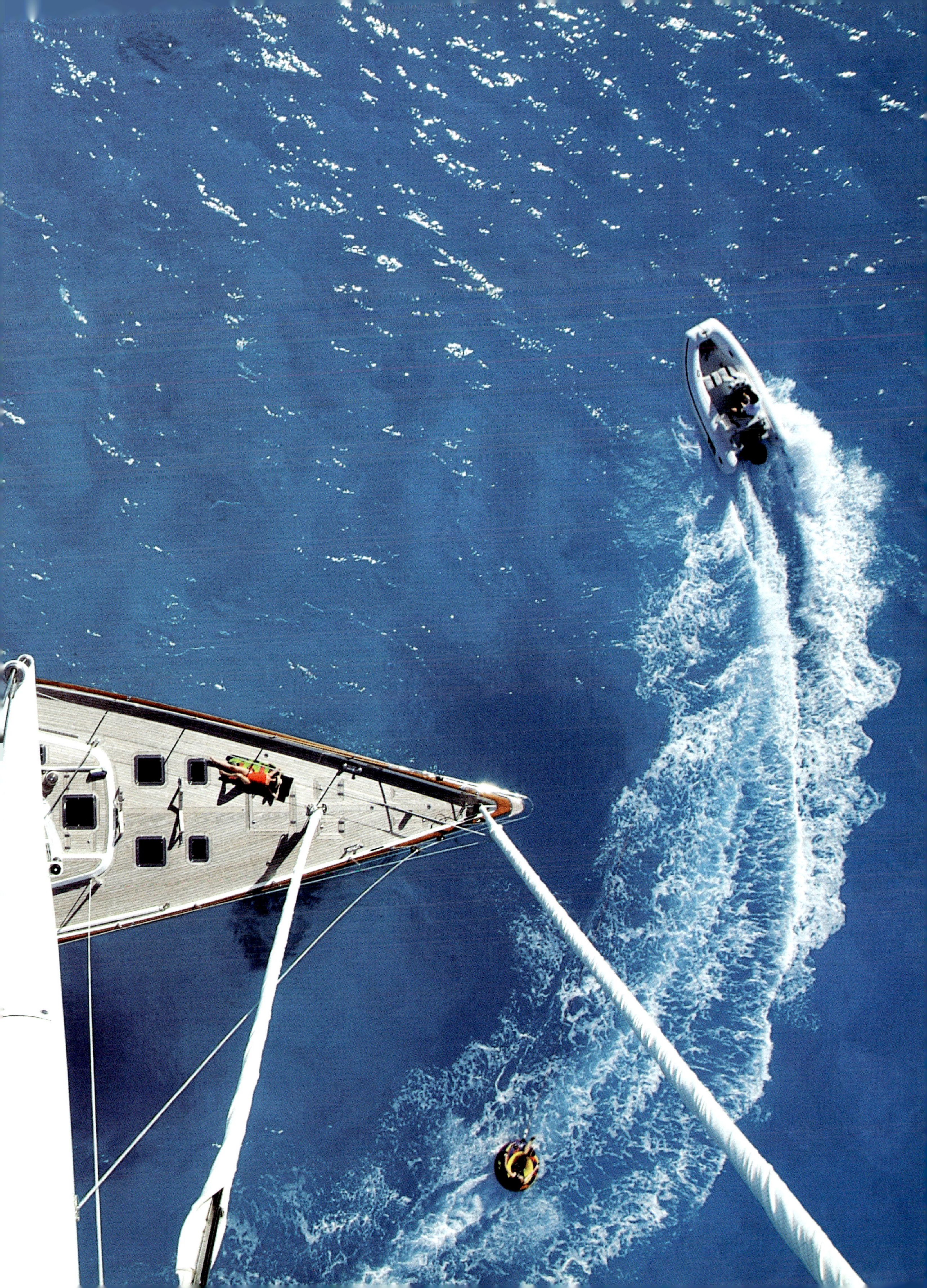

a ski boat and some skis. Yachts today are equipped for aggressive playing. In addition to the standard tow-behind toys, most modern motoryachts carry multiple personal watercraft, kayaks, small sailboats, bicycles, and on the odd occasion, even a small car for use ashore. Many yachts are equipped with dive gear and compressors. Some even have portable decompression chambers. Paul Allen's 414-foot (126.2 metre) *Octopus* boasts seven tenders, including one that is 69 feet (21 metres) long, and a submarine.

Submersibles have begun appearing on yachts in recent years. Allen's $12 million, ten-person submarine is reportedly capable of staying submerged for two weeks.

Helipads are increasing in popularity as well, as harbours in popular destinations on the Riviera and in the Caribbean become more crowded. If a yacht is anchored offshore, guests can be ferried directly to the boat from the nearest airport. Helicopters can be used for sightseeing or for collecting fresh flowers and provisions from distant islands. *Octopus* can accommodate two helicopters, one of which can be housed in a hangar in the superstructure. To manage the yacht and its toys, *Octopus* carries a crew of sixty.

There's no end to the amenities on the largest yachts today: saunas, gyms, theatres, recording studios, squash courts, spa tubs, and swimming pools. The 269-foot (82-metre) *Alfa Nero* (see pages 114–23) has a swimming pool that in a few minutes can be drained and converted into a helipad.

Contrary to common perceptions, many yachts don't stray far from home. They stay tied to the dock in a marina and are used as a party venue, or they revisit owners' favourite destinations season after season. The glamour ports of the Mediterranean—Monaco, Cannes, St. Tropez, Portofino, Palma de Mallorca, Porto Cervo in Sardinia, and Mikonos and Santorini in Greece—remain top draws in summer. Newport and Nantucket serve as summer headquarters for U.S. East Coast yachting. The Caribbean is the epicentre of the winter yacht charter industry. The region offers great cultural, social, and geographic diversity and a reliably perfect climate. The glamour islands are St. Barth's in the French West Indies and Mustique in the St. Vincent Grenadines, both of which are frequented by celebrities and the ultra-wealthy.

Some owners use their yachts to escape the pressures of their busy lives, while others are attracted to where the action is. Being on the dock in Monte Carlo for the Monaco Grand Prix, in the port in Cannes for the film festival, or in Gustavia in St. Barth's for New Year's

PRECEDING PAGES: *A bird's-eye view from the top of the mainmast of* Charlatan *in Bora Bora.*

BELOW: *Relaxing by the spa pool on the sundeck of* Christina O.

BOTTOM: *Like many yachts today,* Princess Marianna *is equipped for helicopter operations.*

OPPOSITE, TOP: *Every March, during the annual St. Barths Bucket Regatta, the port of Gustavia in St. Barths teems with sailing superyachts, while during the Christmas and New Year's holidays, the harbour is more apt to be filled with motoryachts.*

OPPOSITE, BOTTOM LEFT: *Sunset in Newport, Rhode Island—one of the world's classic yachting destinations.*

OPPOSITE, BOTTOM RIGHT: Centurion's *guests take kayaks for a closer glimpse of South Sawyer Glacier, Alaska.*

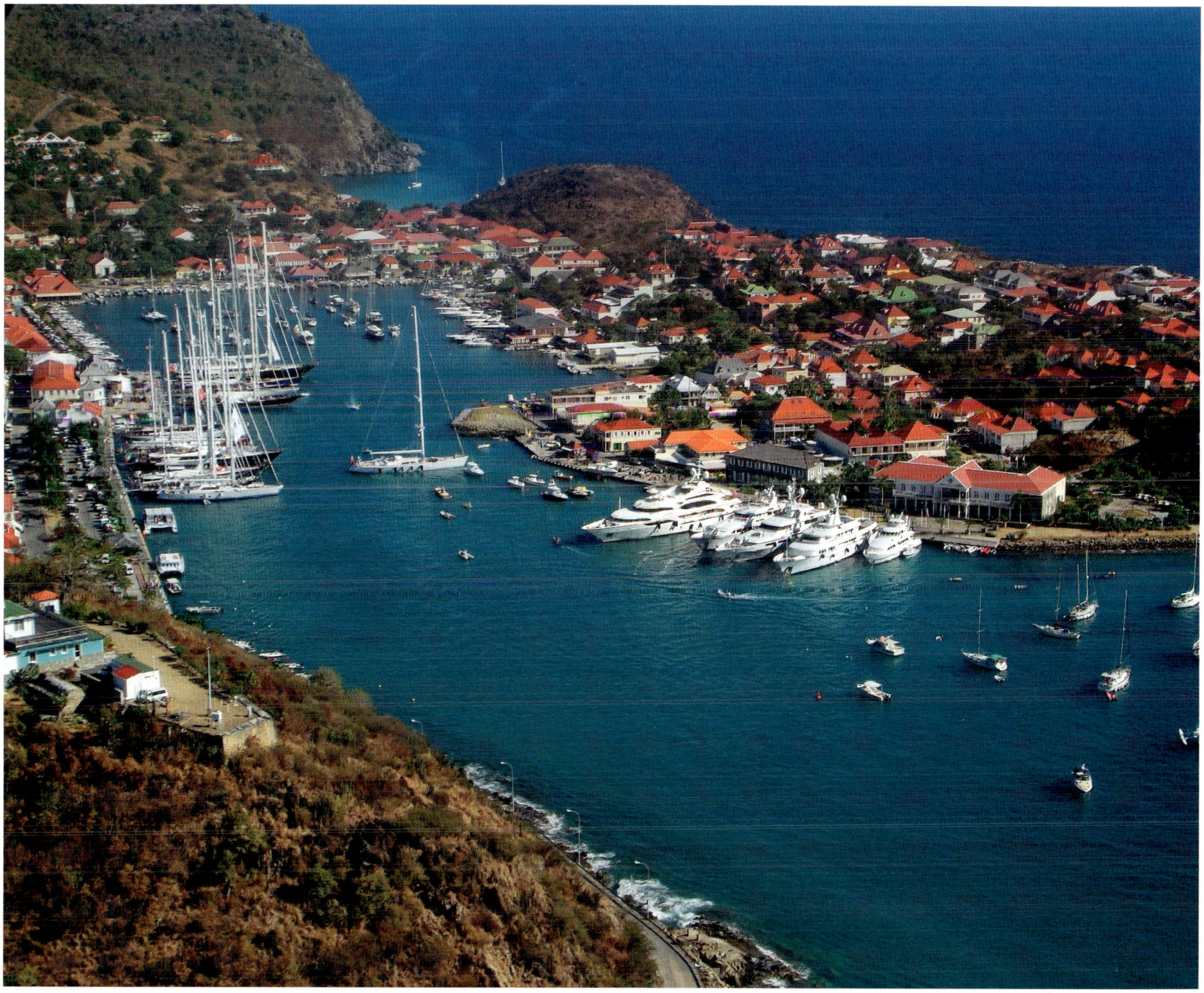

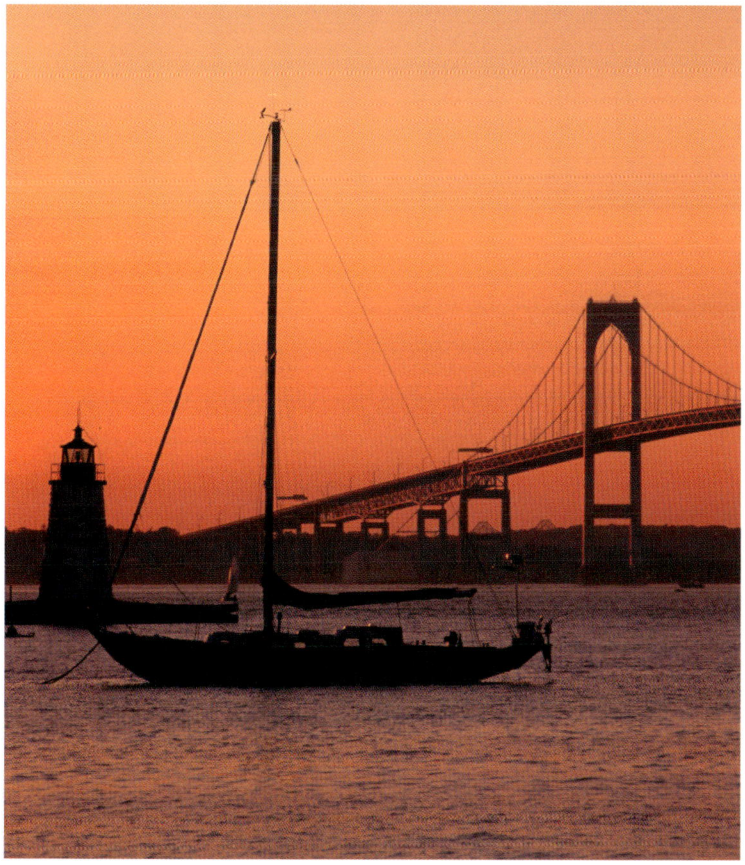

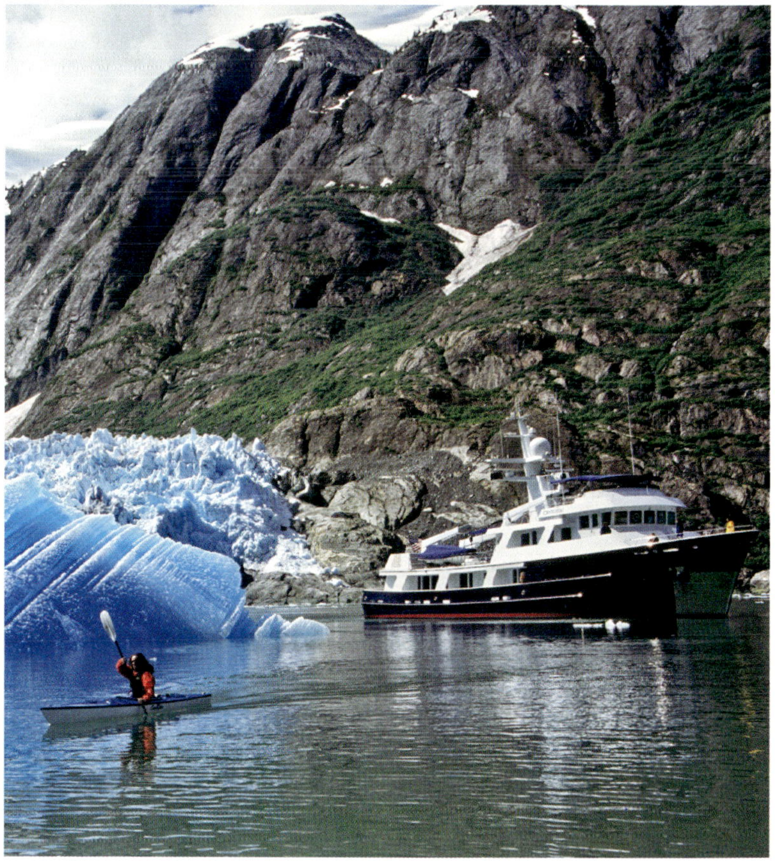

ABOVE: *The gaff riggers are neck and neck during Les Voiles de Saint-Tropez Regatta for both modern and classic yachts.*

ABOVE RIGHT: *Large yachts racing in the St. Barths Bucket Regatta. The square-rigged Maltese Falcon leads the pack.*

LEFT: *Restored or re-created J-class yachts Ranger, Velsheda, and Windrose compete in the Antigua Classic Regatta.*

Eve—these are the pantheon of yachting's see-and-be-seen events—and the toughest tickets to acquire.

While some yachting people prefer to be part of the scene, others use their yachts to stay as far from the scene as they can. As yachts have grown in size, their range and versatility have increased. Most yachts over 150 feet (46 metres) in length have transatlantic range. Many owners who've already experienced the mainstream yachting destinations start venturing off the beaten path. They'll send their crews on the long offshore passages to deliver the boat to a given destination, and then they'll fly in for a few weeks of cruising. Some yachts even circumnavigate the globe and the owner simply pops in for the highlights.

The compulsion to explore has spawned a new class of pleasure craft called "expedition" or "explorer" yachts. Some earlier versions were converted naval or commercial vessels retrofitted with luxury interiors. These vessels typically have extended range and fortified hulls that might be able to break through ice. As nice as some of the conversions were and are, they can still feel a bit rough around the edges. In recent years, expedition yachts have been designed from scratch. Their construction and systems may be heavy-duty, but their interiors are luxurious. Not unlike SUVs, they are designed to cruise off track without support and without forgoing any creature comforts.

A recent phenomenon is the "shadow" or "escort" boat. Often converted commercial workboats, these vessels tag along with the owner's main yacht, carrying its toys, boats, and vehicles. Keeping toys and gear aboard an escort vessel frees up living space on the primary yacht without forcing the owner to leave his favourite toys behind. In some cases over 200 feet (61 metres) long, escort boats typically have hangars and are capable of serving as bases for heavy helicopters. The hangars and decks can hold just about anything a compulsive yachtsman never wants to leave home without: offshore fishing boats, Range Rovers, submarines, pilots, security people, and nannies. Shadow Marine's 220-foot (67-metre) *Allure Shadow* (see pages 174–81) has nearly 100,000 gallons of fuel capacity with facilities for diesel, gasoline, and aviation fuel. The escort boat's extra fuel can extend the primary yacht's range, enabling exploration of remote locales.

Sailing yachts, which comprise a relatively small percentage of the overall yachting fleet, have always had long-range capability. Although many large sailing yachts often cruise under power—in part because of compro-

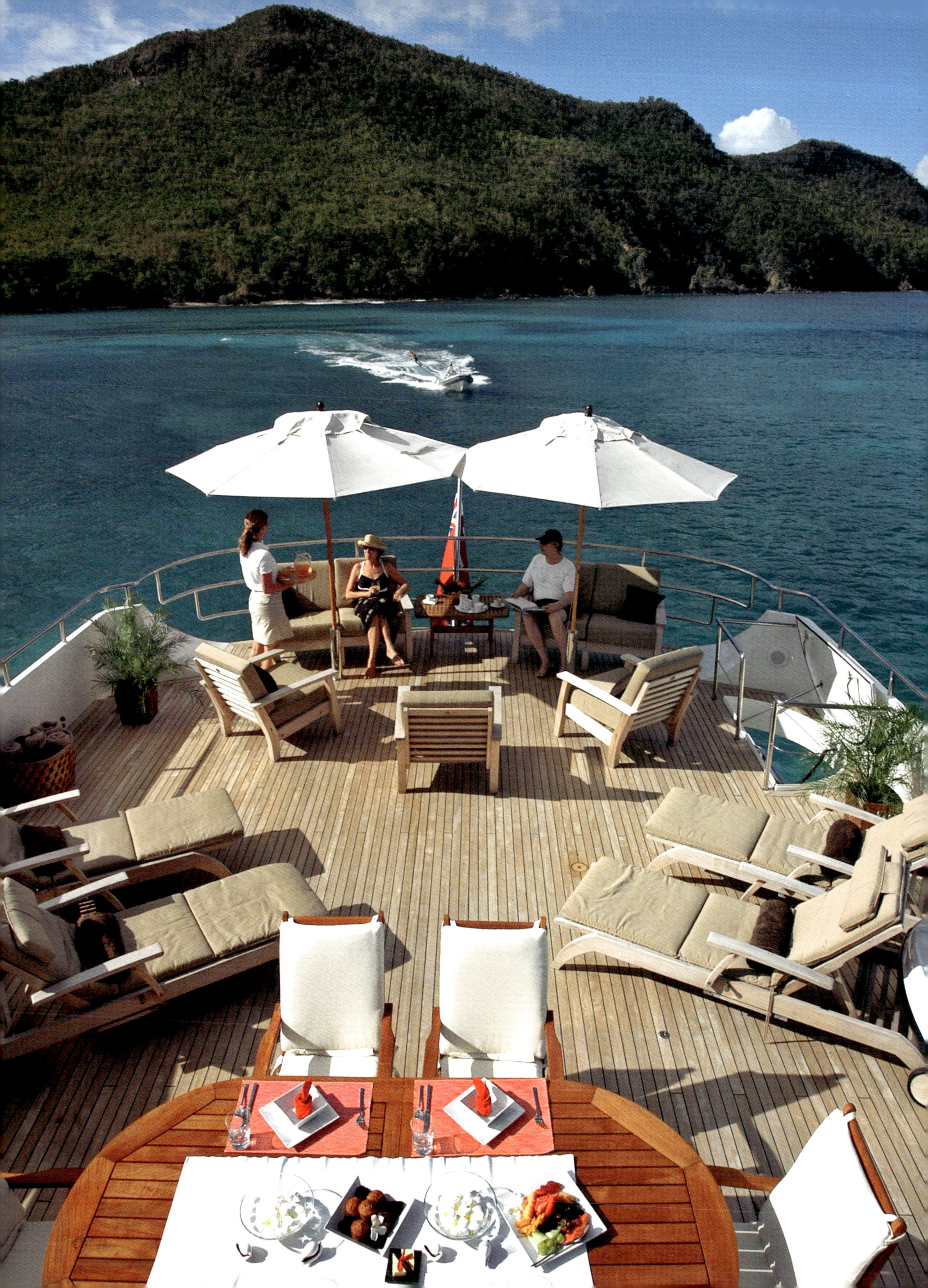

mises made in sailing performance to accommodate living space—in theory there are few destinations a sailing yacht can't reach. Cruising the polar regions to view wildlife has become popular in recent years and has taken power and sailing yachts to the very ends of the earth.

One common personality trait among yachtsmen is competitiveness. Sailors, even those who just cruise, find it difficult to turn down a drag race into port with another yacht. Some, such as Larry Ellison, founder of software giant Oracle, take their competitive compulsions to extraordinary lengths, investing hundreds of millions of dollars chasing the America's Cup—yacht racing's most coveted prize. An increasing number of sailing yachts today are being designed for better performance so their owners can race them. The Wally *Esense* (see pages 158–65) is an example. Racing modern super-size sailboats has grown in popularity in recent years, as more have come on line. Special events such as the Bucket regattas in Newport and St. Barth's and the Superyacht Cup regattas in various venues around the world offer owners of large yachts a way to flex their competitive muscles. The difficulty of accurately handicapping yachts of widely diverse design usually results in the races being held in good-spirited fun rather than cutthroat competition. Camaraderie rules the day—at least the end of it, when the rum starts to flow.

OPPOSITE: Guests aboard Lionshare *live the life off Union Island in the Grenadines.*

ABOVE: ReJoyce *readies for an alfresco dinner in the British Virgin Islands.*

Over the past two decades, classic yacht racing has grown in popularity. The sight of a fleet of gaff-rigged, wooden sailboats racing to windward on a white-capped tropical sea is sublime. An awareness of the fast-disappearing fleet of older yachts and an appreciation of their beauty has resulted in a spate of classic-yacht restorations. The dwindling supply of restorable classics, particularly larger ones like *Lulworth*, combined with the intrinsic beauty of the "old ladies," has triggered a surge in the construction of new classics or "spirit of tradition" yachts. These usually have their own class at classic regattas in deference to the fragility and lesser performance of the original classics.

Perhaps the grandest example of the revival of classic and spirit-of-tradition racing is the renewed interest in the majestic 130-foot (39.6-metre) J-Class yachts that competed for the America's Cup in the 1930s. Only three of the original ten J-Class yachts built during that decade remain, each after extensive renewals: *Endeavour, Shamrock,*

INTRODUCTION / 23

and *Velsheda*. In 2003 yachtsman John Williams took delivery on a J-Class recreation called *Ranger* (see pages 196–201). While mostly faithful to the lines of her namesake, built in 1937, she has modern sailing systems and electronics. She races with an appropriate handicap in the same class as the originals whenever possible. The sight of two or three J-Class yachts charging toward a mark takes the breath away. *Ranger* and the originals are promised more competition, as several more J-Class yachts are currently in build or in development.

Most yachts today are equipped with extensive communications equipment and are used by their owners as mobile offices. But in reality, few busy owners spend significant amounts of time aboard their boats. The average owner spends three to four weeks a year aboard his yacht. To mitigate operating costs, some owners make their yachts available for charter when they aren't using them.

Yacht charter dates back to the 1950s, when entrepreneurs in the Caribbean came up with the idea that northern tourists might pay good money to go cruising in the islands on the private yachts that sometimes just sat at the dock between visits by their owners. Yacht charter today is a sophisticated, growing industry, commanding prices that can easily make it the most expensive per-person holiday week in the world. But the level of service and luxury that charter yachts offer puts them in a class all their own.

Motoryacht charter with crew can range from roughly $70,000 to $1 million a week, depending, of course, on the length of the boat, the number of clients aboard, and a variety of other factors. Maritime laws and regulations regarding design and construction of the yachts that charter limit the majority of them to a maximum of twelve guests. On top of the basic rate, charterers also pay for fuel, food, alcohol, dockage, and gratuity for the crew. A rule of thumb is that the extras can add as much as 50 percent of the charter rate to the bill. These are imposing sums, but guests can expect five-star food, royal service, and a personalized itinerary. Sailing yachts are generally less expensive to charter than motoryachts, but at the highest ends of the market, the numbers begin to converge.

The most popular charter destinations are the Mediterranean in summer and the Caribbean in winter.

TOP: *Yachts often carry as many as ten different dinner services.*

BOTTOM: *The chef offers a spectacular Sunday buffet aboard* Mirabella V.

OPPOSITE: Charlatan *steers clear of the magnificent reefs off Bora Bora in French Polynesia.*

OVERLEAF: *Port Hercule in Monaco accommodates the crème de la crème of yachts during the summer season.*

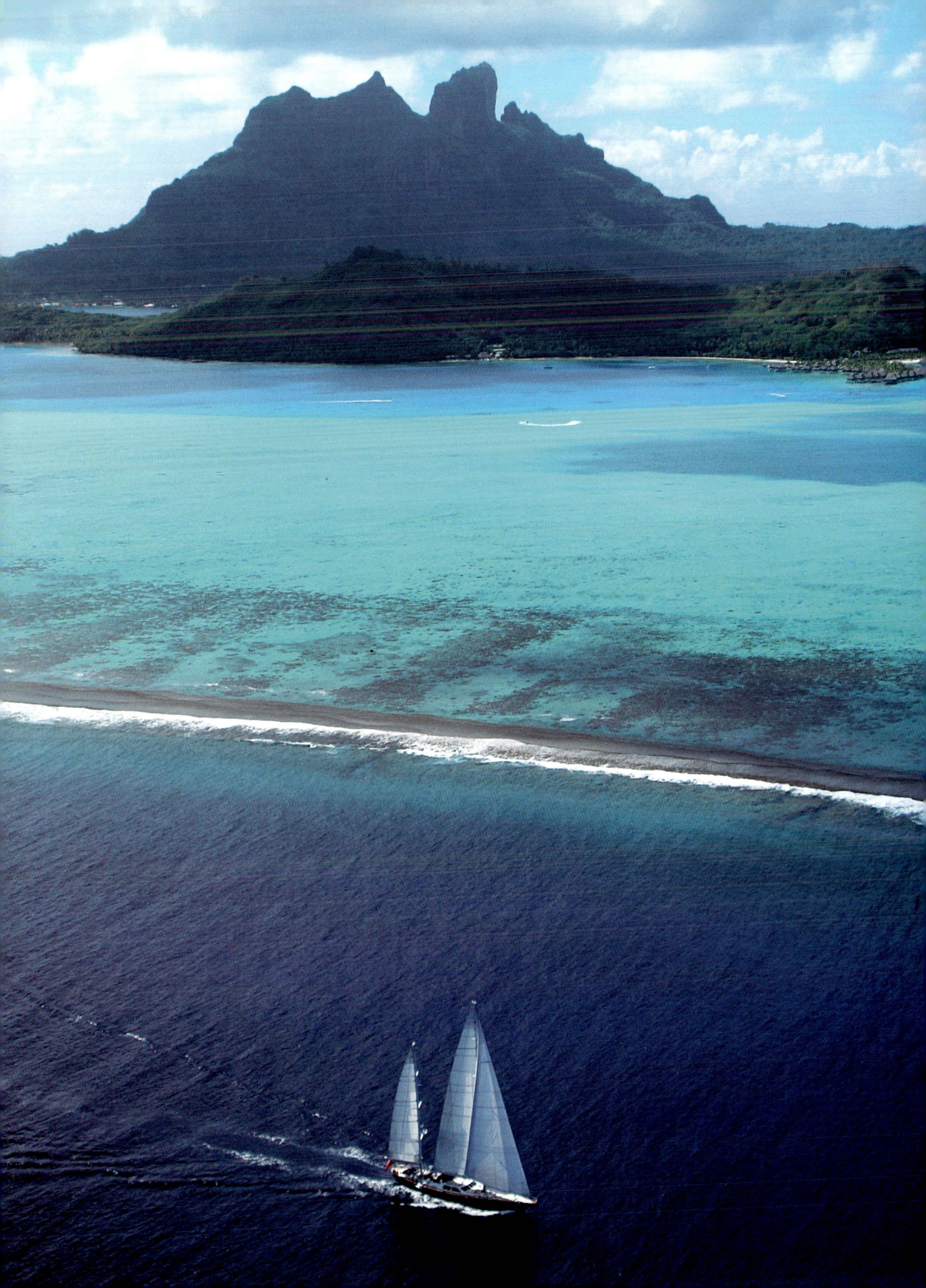

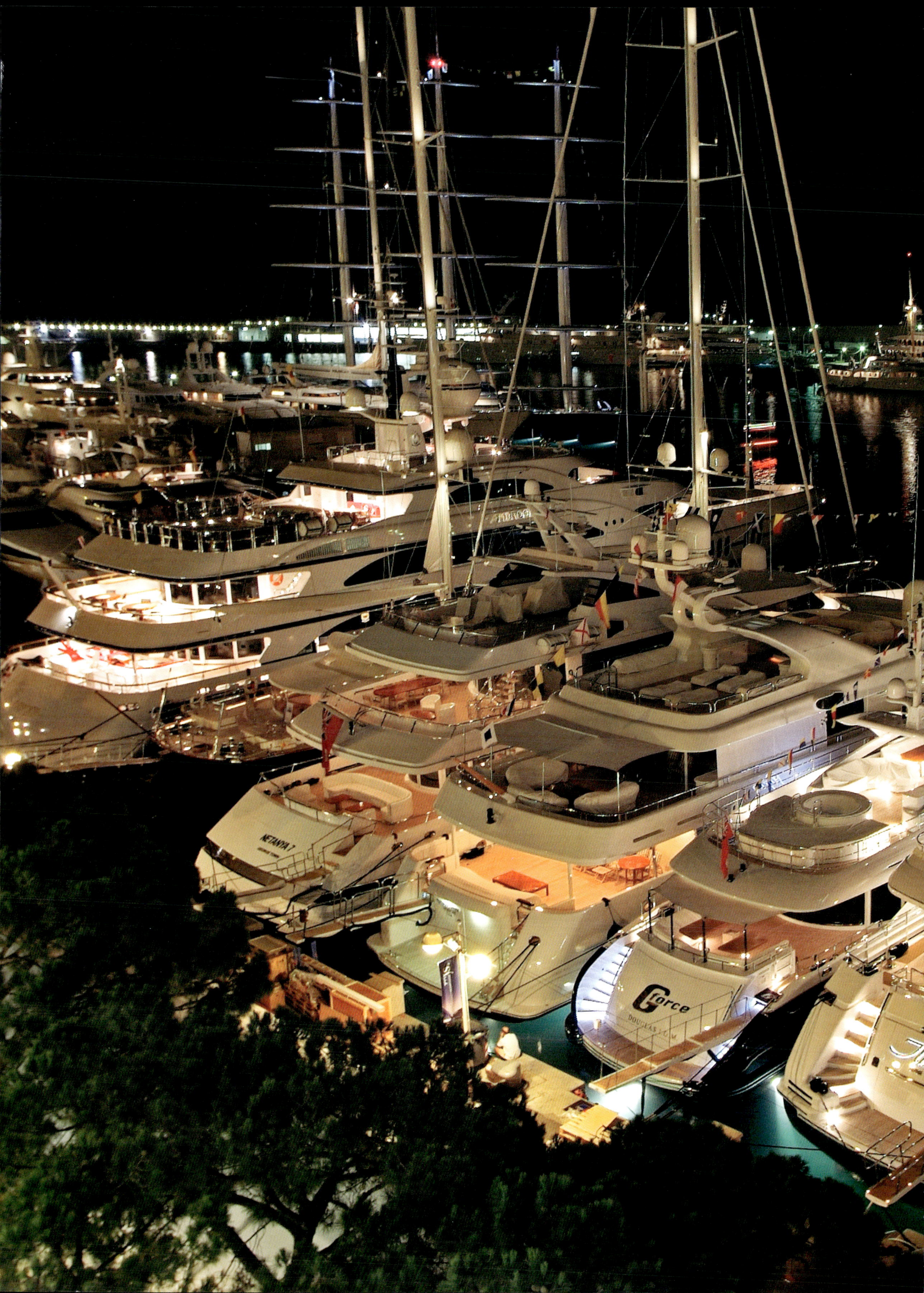
NETANYA 7
Gforce

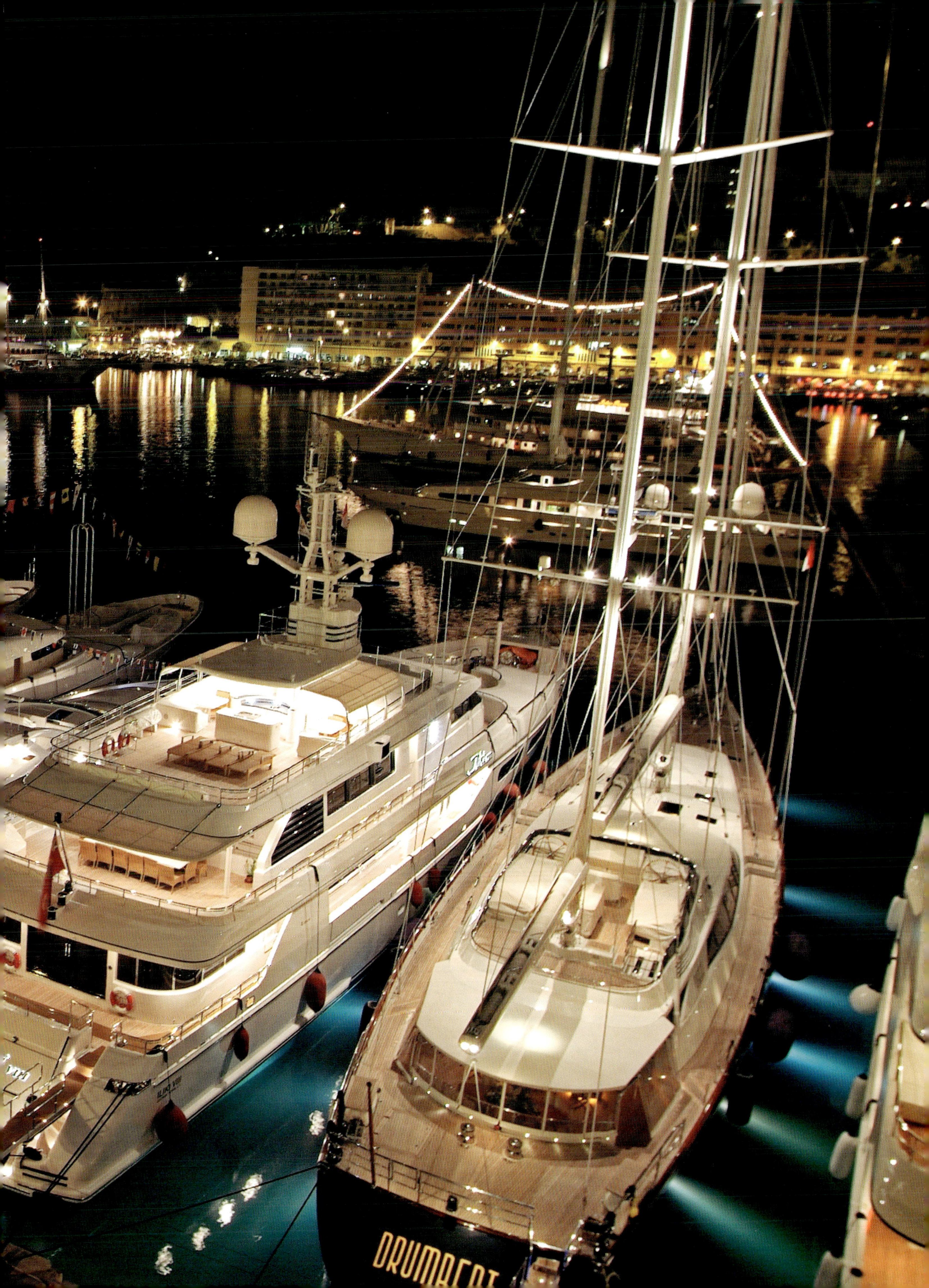

Princess Marianna, launched in 2003 at Danyard Allborg in Denmark, was designed by Espen Øino. She has a drydock for the custom tender, which, when flooded, converts into a 39-foot (12-metre) swimming pool.

Some yachts make the seasonal run back and forth between the two areas; others spend an occasional summer in New England or Alaska, depending on where the owner plans to take his holiday.

Adventurous owners, or those who are just bored with the standard destinations, occasionally will send their yachts far afield, to the South Pacific, Australia, New Zealand, or Southeast Asia, opening opportunities for charterers to experience places they might never have visited and certainly not on the level of luxury a yacht provides. The intimacy, privacy, security and geographic flexibility a yacht charter offers, appeal to affluent clients of all stripes and keep these magnificent machines on the move, as they were designed to be.

Some yacht owners like their boats to stand out in a crowd. Yachts can be outrageous for any number of reasons. The *Wall Street Journal* dubbed *A* the "ugliest yacht in the world." This 394-foot (120-metre) torpedo, designed by Martin Francis and Philippe Starck, is owned by Andrei Melnichenko, a Russian banker and oil tycoon in his mid-thirties. At 295 feet (90 metres), *Ice*, owned by Suleiman Kerimov, is considered one of the most environmentally friendly yachts. Luciano Benetton's *Tribu*, launched in 2007, also was built to standards aimed at reducing the impact yachts have on the environment. Other notable yachts include Roman Abramovich's 375-foot (114-metre) *Pelorus,* which is equipped with bullet-proof glass, a missile detection system, two helicopters, and a submarine.

There are many undeniably outrageous yachts that do not appear in our book for one reason or another, the most common being their owners' desire for privacy, but that bear mentioning. For instance, the series of yachts *Carinthia V, VI,* and *VII,* owned by German supermarket magnate Helmut Horton, were all trendsetters in terms of styling, speed, and technology.

Trendsetters beget trendsetters and in 1997, Leslie Wexner, CEO of The Limited, was so taken with the *Carinthia* series that he modelled his lovely 352-foot (107-metre) yacht *Limitless* after them. Despite all the yachts that have been built since *Limitless,* she is still a head turner in any harbor.

Another pioneering design was the 344-foot (105-metre) *Lady Moura,* launched in 1990 by Blohm & Voss

Flush decks, such as this one on the Wally 143 Esense, *are all the rage on sailing superyachts.*

and belonging to Nasser Al-Rashid, of Saudi Arabia. She has unusually large volume and is the only yacht to carry a heavy Sikorsky 576 helicopter with a seating capacity of thirteen. She was a pioneer in storing tenders in garages instead of having them piled on deck.

Yachts exceeding 300 feet (91.5 metres) in length are not a new phenomenon. Witness yachts such as *Savarona*, the 446-foot (136-metre) classic built in 1931 for American heiress Emily Roebling Cadwalader, whose family business constructed both the Brooklyn and Golden Gate bridges. *Savarona* underwent a $35 million rebuild in 1992 and now belongs to a Turkish shipbuilder. The 323-foot (98.4-metre) *Christina O* has had a few lives, originally built as a patrol vessel in 1943 but converted into a yacht by Onassis. The *Christina O* that appears on the pages of this book had a $50 million refit in 2001.

Through the '80s and '90s and into the twenty-first century, the number of yachts afloat and their average lengths have steadily increased. This aquatic arms race has now driven the overall length of the largest yachts to more than 500 feet (152.4 metres). The recent boom has been fuelled largely by silicon and oil. Competitors for the largest yachts in the world now include high-tech billionaires such as Allen and Ellison, as well as the new cadre of young Russian oligarchs such as Abramovich and the perennial players from the Arab world. These massive vessels have begun to encroach on the province of cruise ships in both size and amenities. Their full-time crew can number in the thirties or forties, sometimes to serve no more than a dozen guests.

In 2000 the McCaw brothers, Craig and John, U.S. telecommunications barons, built two gigayachts; the 301-foot (91.7-metre) *Tatoosh* was built at Nobiskrug and the 370-foot (112.8 metre) Kusch-designed *Le Grand Bleu* at the Vulcan yard in Germany. For various economic reasons, *Tatoosh* was acquired by Allen and *Le Grand Bleu* was sold to Abramovich, who in turn gave it to his friend Eugene Shvidler.

After Allen launched *Octopus* in 2003, Ellison upped the ante and built his 452-foot (137.8-metre) *Rising Sun*. He now co-owns the boat with David Geffen of Geffen Records. The yacht is so big that it can't dock at most marinas. It has five storeys and eighty-two rooms; the living area alone exceeds 86,111 square feet (8,000 square metres). Crown Prince Sultan bin Abdul Aziz, Defense Minister of Saudi Arabia, built a slightly larger yacht, *Al Salamah*, measuring 456 feet (139 metres), and in 2008 another Arab-owned yacht, *Al Said*, broke the 500-foot barrier at 508 feet (154.8 metres). Abramovich, who is the "big yacht" fleet admiral linked to five superyachts ranging from 162 to 377 feet (49.4 to 115 metres) in length, has more on the drawing board, including the mysterious *Eclipse*, which, at approximately 540 feet (164.6 metres), might be the largest yacht in the world, larger even than *Dubai*, the state yacht belonging to Sheikh Mohammed bin Rashid Al Maktoum of Dubai.

For some, one yacht simply is not enough. In 1983 the late Mexican media magnate Emilio Azcárraga Milmo commissioned twin 141-foot (43-metre) yachts, *Azteca* and *Paraiso*, from Feadship in the Netherlands. One was for the Mediterranean and the other for the Caribbean. They were designed by the late Jon Bannenberg, a creative force in large-yacht design. On occasion, if there was a spillover of family and friends and the yachts were in the same ocean, Azcárraga would cruise them in tandem, having breakfast on one and dinner on the other.

Azcárraga, a true yachting enthusiast and innovator, later commissioned the extraordinary groundbreaking gas turbine/water jet–propelled 244-foot (74.4-metre) *Eco*. After his death, *Eco* eventually was sold to Oracle's Ellison, who renovated it and renamed it *Katana*. Ellison kept *Katana* in the Atlantic and bought another boat, the 192-foot (58.5-metre) *Izanami*, and kept her in the Pacific. He has since sold both boats and now, as mentioned above, owns *Rising Sun*.

Classic yachts lined up for the Cannes Régate Royale, a race that takes place every fall in the glamorous French Riviera port.

Microsoft's Allen has owned multiple yachts simultaneously. At one point he owned the 198-foot (60.4-metre) *Meduse*, the 303-foot (92.4-metre) *Tatoosh,* and *Octopus*. In 2006 an American yachting couple, Doug and Linda Von Allmen, took delivery of two yachts in the same week: the 157-foot (47.9-metre) Trinity *Lady Linda,* and the 197-foot (60-metre) Lürssen *Linda Lou*. One has a dark interior; the other's is light. One has a deep draft; the other's is shallow.

In 2007 one yachtsman built twin 127-foot (38.7-metre) yachts, *Areti I* and *Areti II*, at Burger Boat Company, again with the intention of keeping one on either side of the Atlantic. In 2008 Ron Joyce, founder of the Canadian doughnut franchise chain Tim Hortons, built a 161-foot (49-metre) Trinity motoryacht called *Destination Fox Harb'r* to go along with his 134-foot (40.8-metre) alloy sailing yacht of the same name. He has painted both a distinctive metallic gray, which is the same colour as his private jet.

It is quite common for yacht owners who are big players and own many very big yachts to tinker as well with as many as a dozen smaller yachts, sportfishing boats, daysailers, picnic boats, and the like. For some, passion borders on obsession.

The very notion of yachts and yachting is outrageous, but they capture our imagination. They are the ultimate escape vehicle—the quintessential magic carpet. They may represent the most audacious and conspicuous use of wealth possible, but they are, at their root, an extension of the spirit that made capitalist societies great and ferried explorers to distant shores on voyages of discovery.

INTRODUCTION / 31

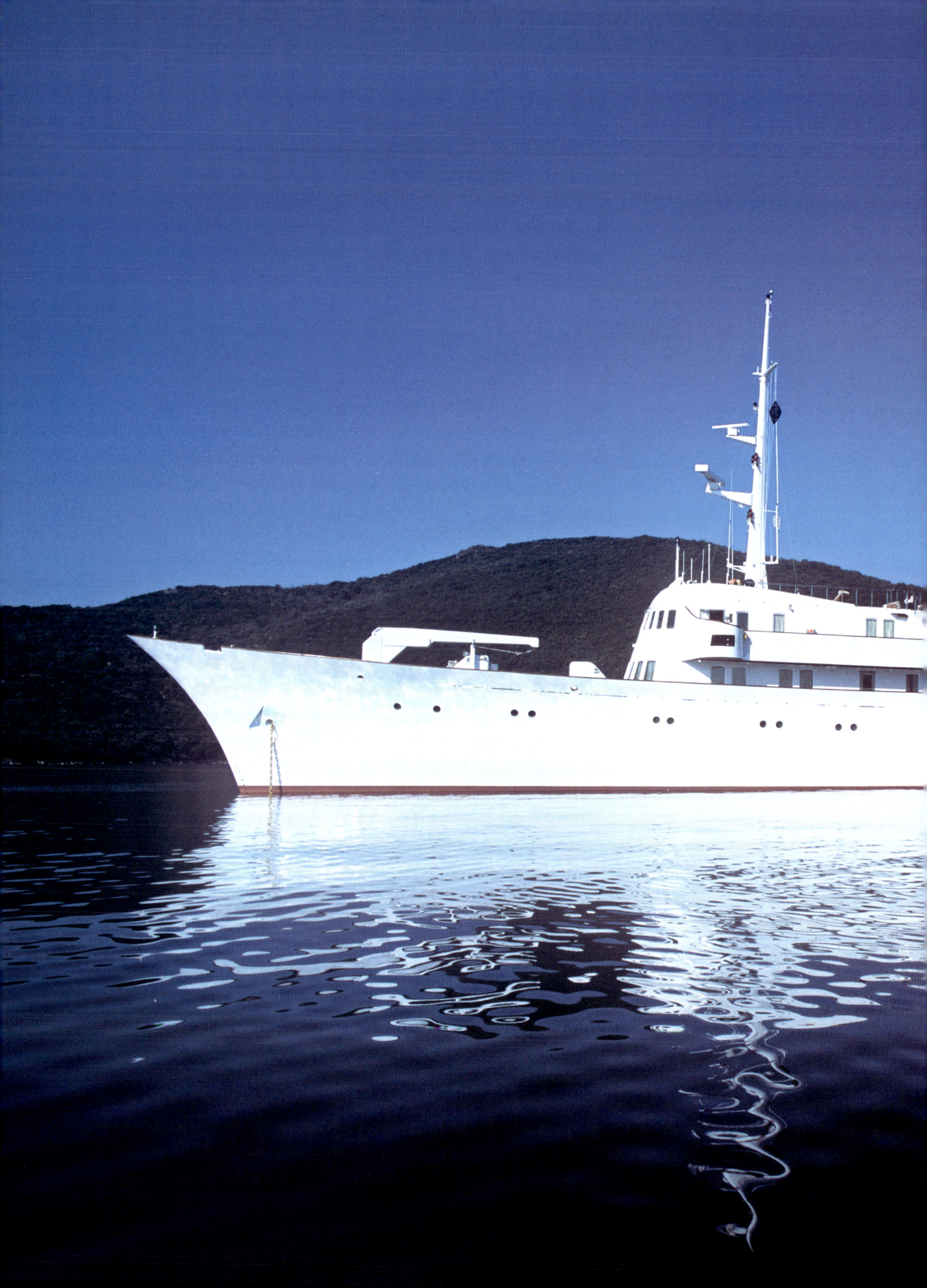

Christina O

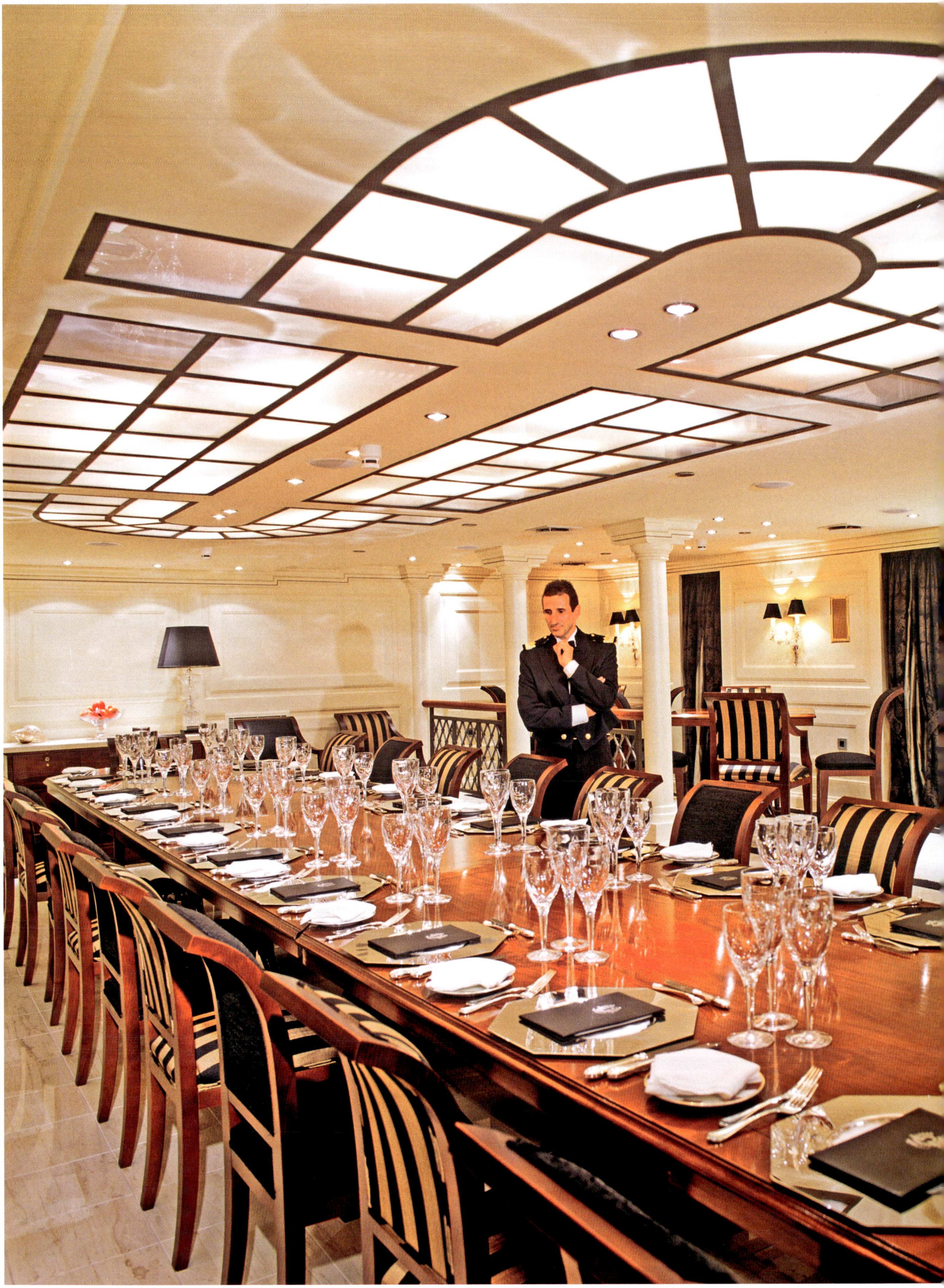

PRECEDING PAGES: Christina O rests at anchor off the town of Nidri, on the island of Lefkada, near Onassis's island of Skorpios. Her distinct yellow steam funnel now houses air-conditioning ducts.

LEFT: Her formal dining room seats up to forty guests, twenty-four at the main table and sixteen at four more intimate tables.

If you live in landlocked Nebraska, the Swiss Alps, or the outback of Australia, and you know the name or pedigree of only one historic yacht, chances are that that yacht is the legendary *Christina*, or *Christina O*, as she is now called. Built in 1943 by Canadian Vickers as the anti-submarine convoy frigate *HMCS Stormant*, she was sold at scrap value for $34,000 to self-made Greek shipping magnate Aristotle Onassis in 1948. He took her to the Howaldt Werke in Kiel, Germany, where he had her gutted and converted into an astonishing luxury yacht for the then princely sum of $4,000,000, which is mere peanuts by today's standards.

She emerged the belle of the Med. Onassis used *Christina* to attract heads of state, actors, actresses, divas—a virtual who's who of the '50s and '60s. Everyone from Winston Churchill to King Farouk, Rudolf Nureyev, Marilyn Monroe, JFK, and the Aga Khan. The wedding reception of Monaco's Prince Rainier and American actress Grace Kelly was held aboard the *Christina*. While Onassis was still married to his first wife, Tina Livanos, he had a passionate love affair with opera diva Maria Callas. Not destined to marry her, in 1968 Onassis married a different sort of diva, the widow of John F. Kennedy, Jacqueline Kennedy, whose nickname soon became Jackie O.

Upon Onassis's death in 1975, the yacht reverted to his daughter, Christina, but as her life was in turmoil, she donated it to the Greek government to be used as the presidential yacht. The boat was renamed *Argo*, but without the loving ownership of Onassis, care languished and she fell into disrepair. The government tried unsuccessfully to sell her in the early 1990s; she was finally purchased in 1998 by a consortium of investors and a former family friend of Onassis, John Paul Papanicolaou, another Greek shipping magnate, who had memories of the yacht from his childhood and had full intentions of restoring her to her former grandeur.

ABOVE: *The music room, a step above the dining room on the upper level, houses a grand piano and Maria Callas memorabilia.*

BELOW: *Christina Onassis aged three aboard the* Christina *in 1953.*

BOTTOM: *A handmade table in the Children's Room has eight individual compartments filled with art supplies. The walls are hand painted with an* Alice in Wonderland *theme.*

LOA: 325' 3" (99.14 m)
Beam: 36' 6" (11.13 m)
Draft: 14' (4.24 m)
Builder: Canadian Vickers / 1943 (as *Stormant*)
Rebuilt: 1954 (as *Christina*)
Refit yard / year: Viktor Lenac, Croatia / 2001
Naval architect: Costas Carabelas
Exterior styling: N/A
Interior design / refit: Apostolos Molidris, Decon
Top speed: 17 knots
Hull construction: Steel / Aluminium

ABOVE: *In Ari's bar, the footrests and handholds are made of whales' teeth and the bar stools are infamously upholstered in whale foreskin.*

BELOW: *At the base of the spiral staircase in the central atrium is a mosaic of Onassis's logo: an Omega and a garland of laurel.*

The boat was gutted and more than 50 percent of her hull was entirely renewed. Some 560 tons of steel were replaced, and 56 miles of new wiring were introduced, along with 140 tons of pipe work. The refit consumed 1.2 million man-hours and reportedly cost $50 million. The result is a highly successful luxury charter yacht that carries thirty-six passengers in eighteen staterooms and recaptures the ambience and wonder of her heyday.

With a 36½-foot (11.1-metre) beam and a length of 325 feet (99 metres), *Christina O* offers an exceptional amount of volume. She has five enclosed decks and plenty of on-deck space for guests. As on a cruise ship, each deck has a name. The top level is called the Compass Deck and features a ring of steamship-style teak sun loungers and a bar forward of the funnel. The next deck down is the Bridge Deck, domain of the captain. It houses the lifeboats, inflatable tenders, and twin varnished Hacker Craft launches, which are fitted in davits port and starboard. Next is the Promenade Deck,

OPPOSITE, TOP: *The show lounge has a raised stage with the original lapis balustrade. It doubles as a cinema room with a drop-down screen.*

OPPOSITE, BOTTOM: *The Onassis suite living room still boasts its original onyx fireplace and Aristotle's desk.*

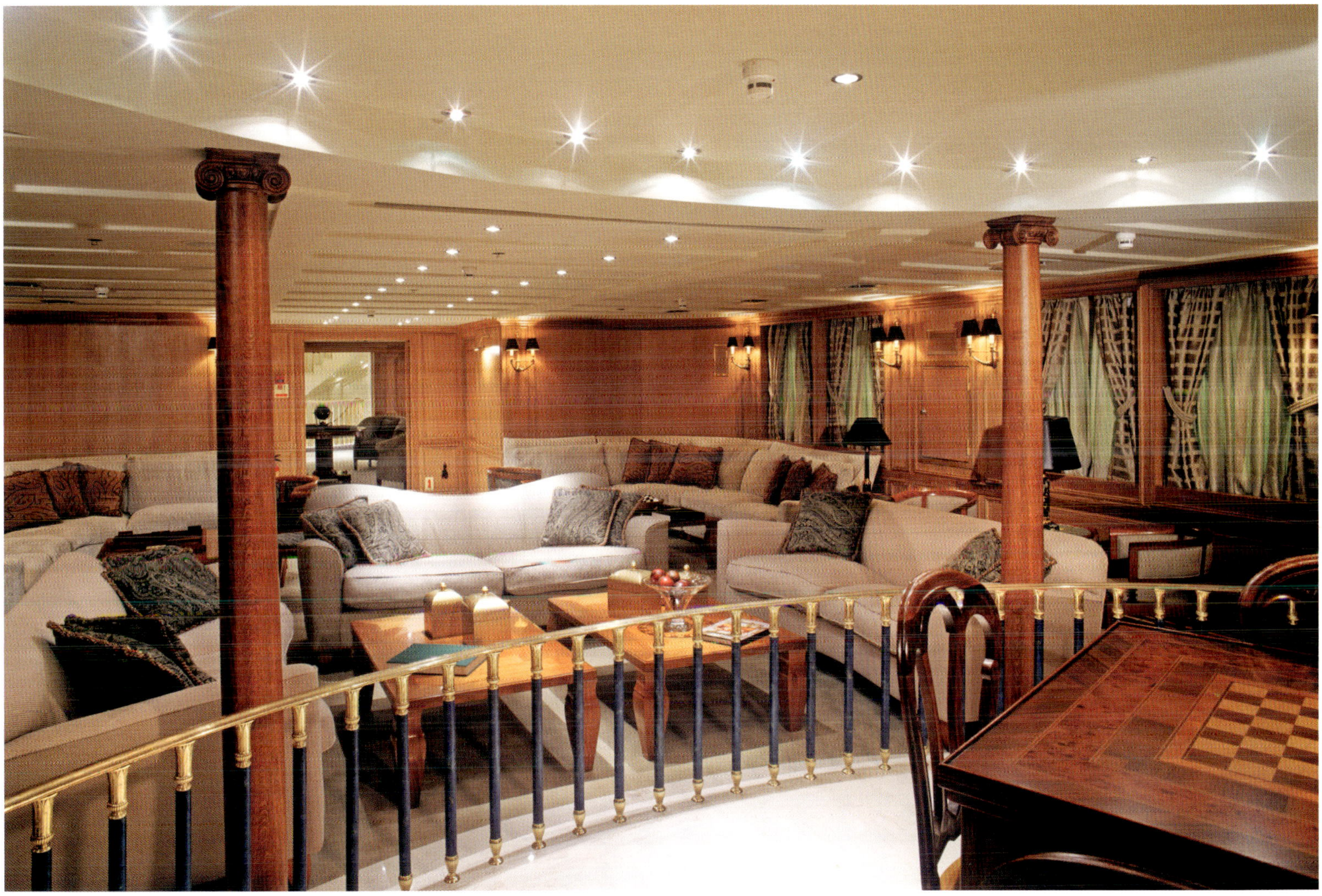

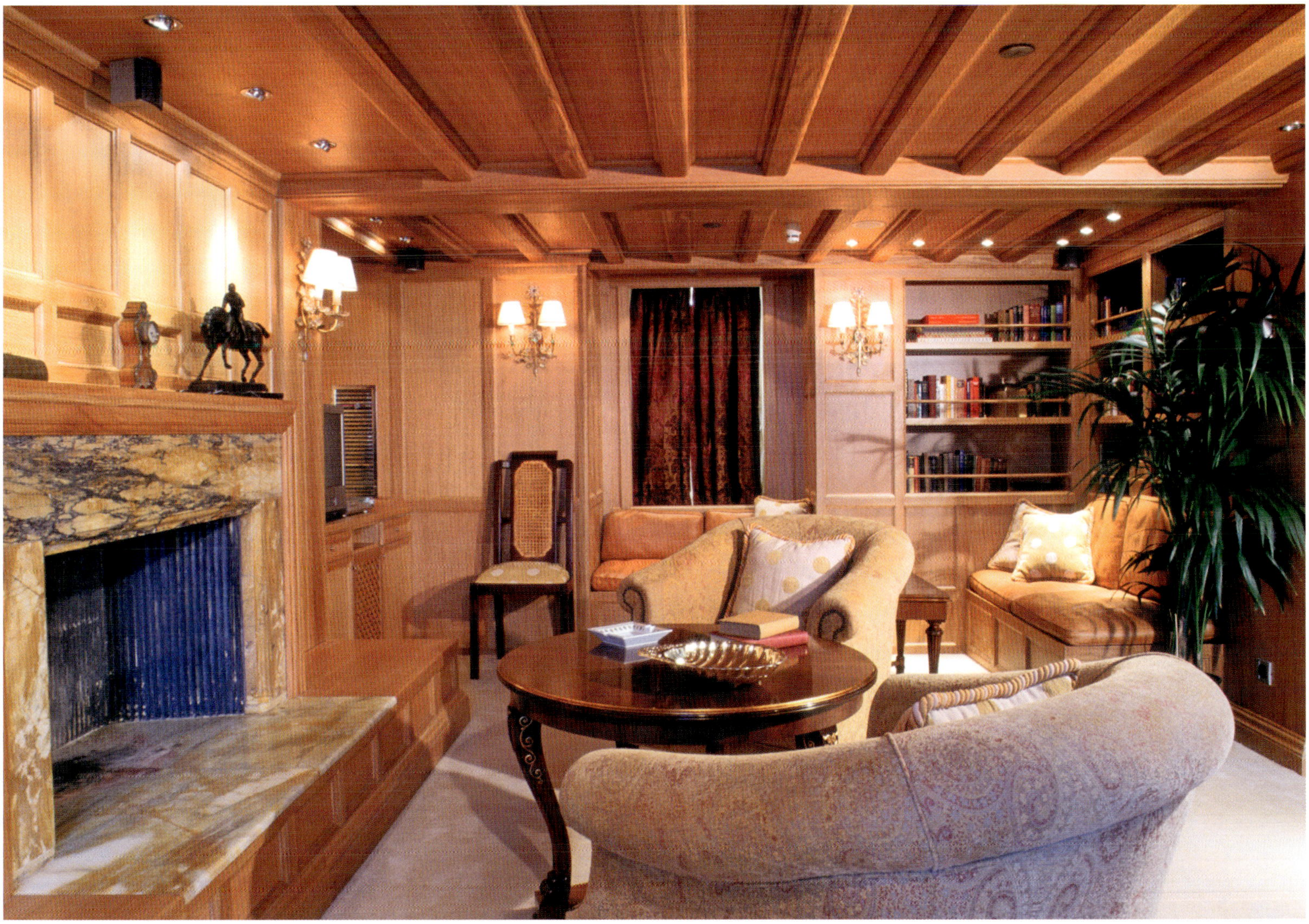

ABOVE: *A grand buffet luncheon is served on the semicircular bar aft on the promenade deck.*

on which you can circle the entire yacht. On this deck you will also find a spa pool, a large semicircular bar, and several tables for dining. Aft is the helipad. The main deck is home to a swimming pool with a mosaic floor that re-creates the renowned Minoan fresco depicting a young man vaulting over a bull from the Palace of Knossos in Crete. When the pool is empty, the mosaic can be raised flush with the deck to become a dance floor. It is one of *Christina O*'s most distinguishing features, along with her big yellow main funnel.

The yacht no longer sports a steam engine. Her technical platform has been completely modernized, so the funnel is now used for other purposes, such as housing air-conditioning ducts. Two new MAN diesel engines and three MAN generators were installed. She now has a cruising speed of 18 knots and a top speed of 22; Onassis cruised at 14 knots but could rev her up to 24 knots.

There are several areas on *Christina O* that are reminiscent of the original yacht, among them the Lapis Lounge, the Show Lounge, Ari's suite, Ari's Bar, the Music Lounge, the Sport Lounge, and the Children's Room. The Lapis Lounge, on the main deck, is handsomely panelled in oak and iroko. The centerpiece of the room is its lapis lazuli fireplace. On the walls are works by Renoir and De Chirico. Adjacent to this room is the infamous Ari's Bar. The semicircular, rope-covered bar is reputedly made from the timbers of a Spanish galleon. The bar's glass top covers a lighted relief of the sea, complete with tiny models showing the development of ships and shipping throughout history. On the wall is the original map that charted the daily position of the Onassis fleet. The bar's footrests and handholds are made of ornately carved and polished whales' teeth collected by Onassis's whalers. The barstools still sport their original seats, which are made of whale foreskin, although they now have protective leather covers. It is here that Onassis reportedly leaned over to Ava Gardner or some other female guest and said, "Madame, do you realize you are sitting on the biggest penis in the world?"

Forward of the bar, the main deck now houses a banquet-size, split-level formal dining room. With an enormous table for twenty-four and four more intimate tables around the edges, it seats up to forty guests. The ceiling has a backlit glass panel that mirrors the shape of

ABOVE: *The original mosaic swimming pool on the aft deck rises to become a dance floor.*

the table. The Baccarat crystal sconces are original to the room. On the upper level, a step above the dining room along the starboard passageway, is a music lounge with a baby grand piano and Maria Callas memorabilia, including her sole gold record.

The reconfiguration of the interior space opened up a cavernous area in the middle of the yacht, the size of a three-storey New York town house. The most imposing sight on *Christina O* is the central atrium with its spiral staircase, which spans all four decks and is handsomely fitted with onyx and brass handrails. The atrium floor at the base of the stairwell is decorated with a mosaic of Onassis's logo: an Omega and a garland of laurel.

Each of the guest cabins is named for a Greek island. They are meant to be of equal comfort, but because of the unusual shape of the hull, ten of the eighteen cabins are a bit larger and have sitting areas and desks. All can be configured as either queen-size or twin cabins, and all have lovely en suite marble bathrooms. The truly deluxe cabin is the Aristotle Onassis suite, the living room of which has an original onyx fireplace, walls lined with bookshelves, beamed ceiling, and classic armchairs and sofas. It opens to the master bedroom, which is fitted with a king-size bed, original Baccarat crystal fixtures, and brass-framed windows. There is also a new en suite marble bathroom.

In addition to the grand common rooms, the yacht boasts a children's playroom, a gymnasium, a beauty saloon, and a massage room. A newly created room on the Promenade Deck is the stately, oak-panelled library, which opens onto the Show Lounge. Furnished with three sofa-and-chair groupings and a raised stage enclosed by a rail with lapis balusters, this space doubles as a cinema room, complete with surround sound and a large drop-down screen.

Christina O is an eclectic yacht steeped in history. She combines the flavour of the Mediterranean with a touch of an Old World British manor house. Being aboard makes you feel like someone special. And if you want to charter her, you'd better be someone who wouldn't mind parting with a million dollars a week.

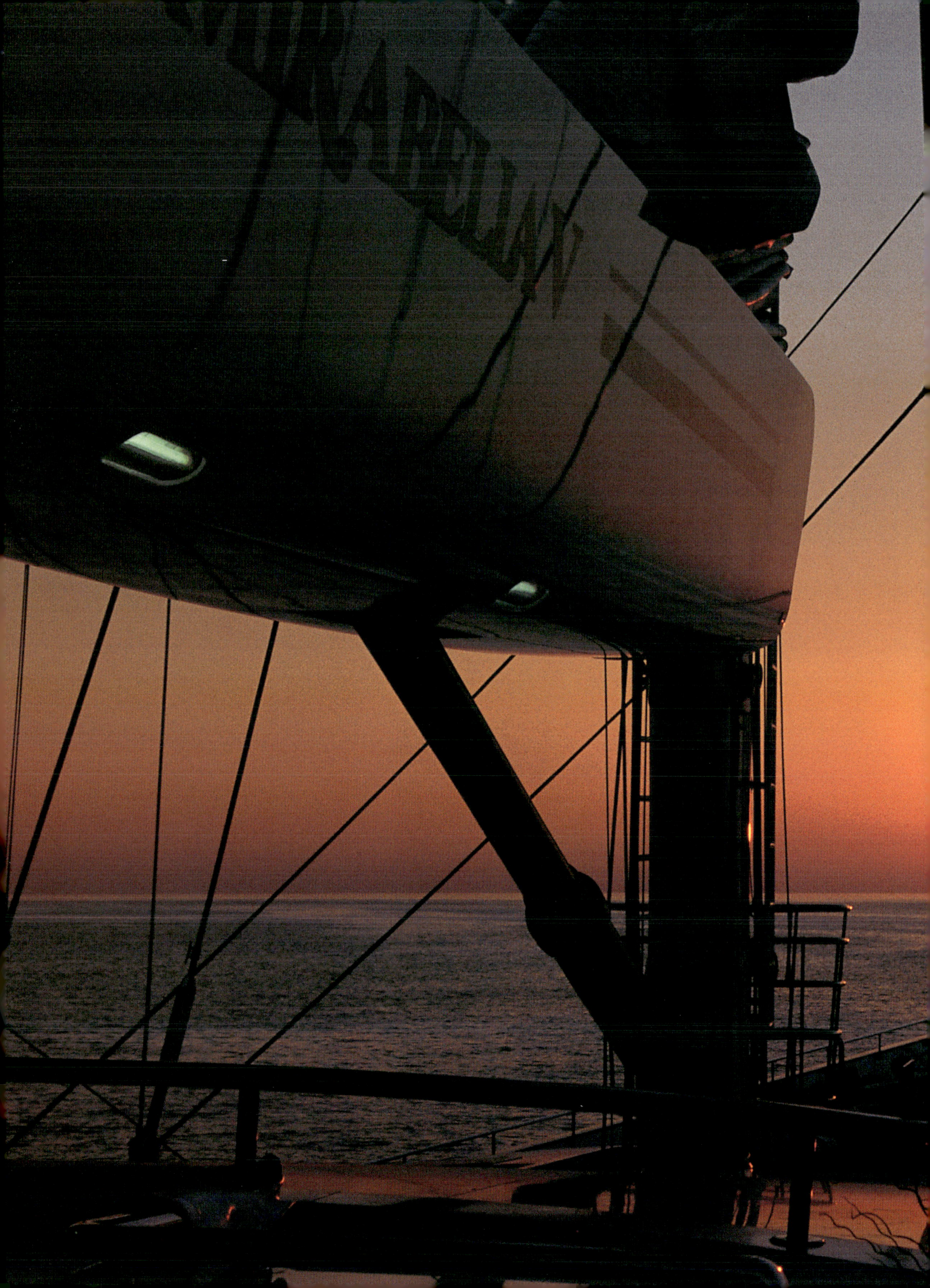

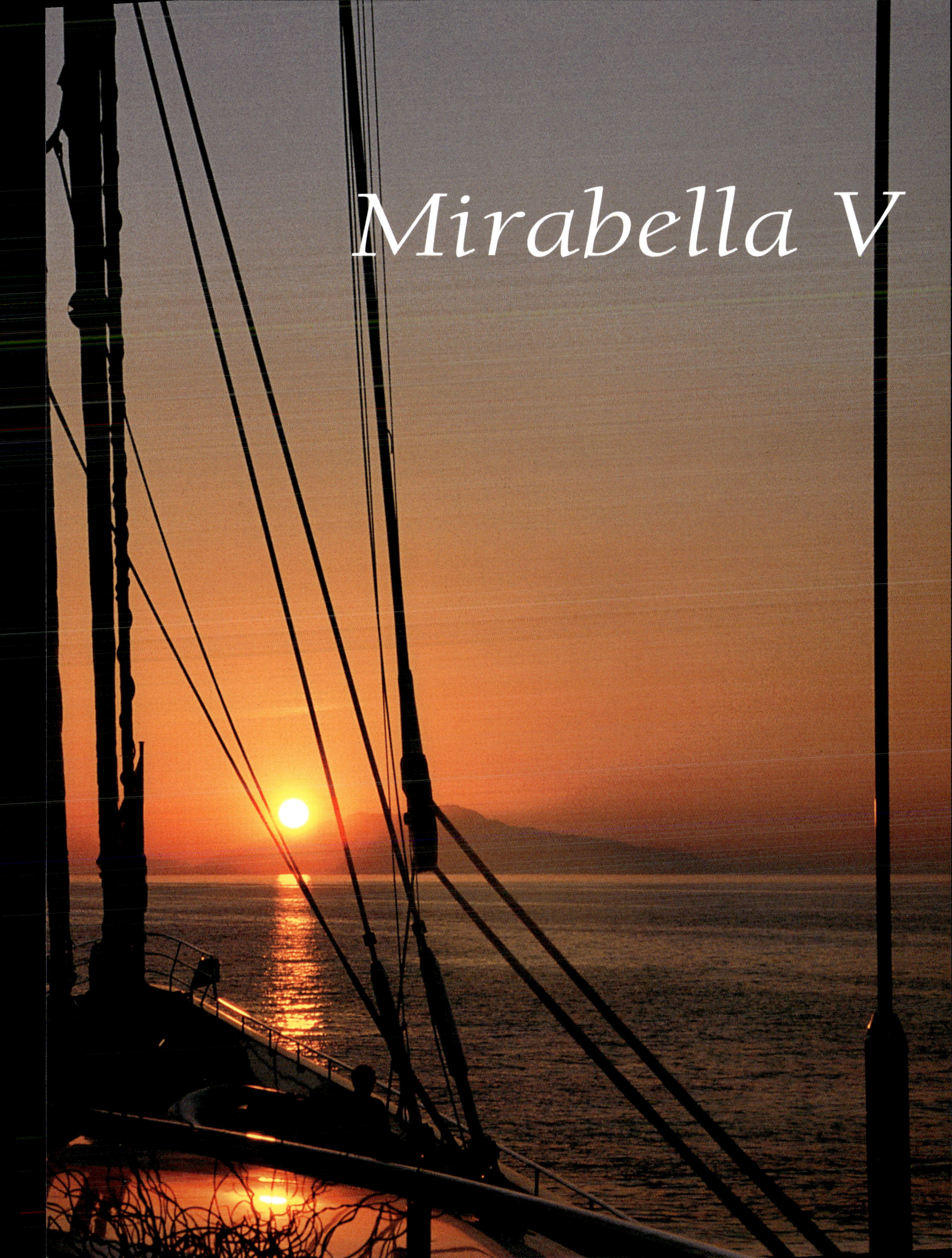

Mirabella V

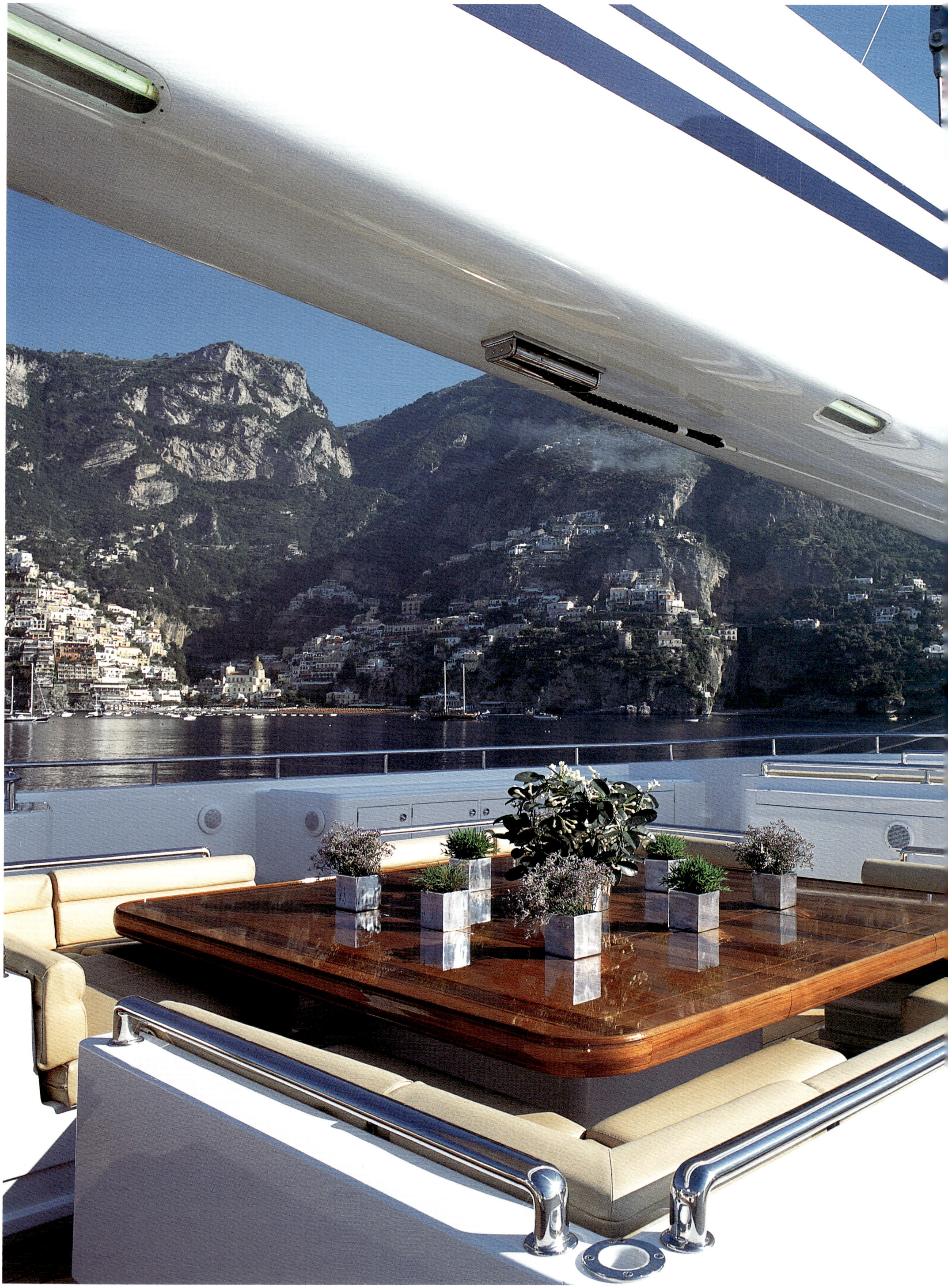

PRECEDING PAGES: *Sunset on the foredeck off the isle of Capri.*

LEFT: *The giant boom holds the massive mainsail. The fly bridge has port and starboard steering stations, a barbecue bar, and a large table for outdoor dining.*

BELOW: *Owner Joe Vittoria at the helm off the Amalfi Coast.*

Only superlatives suffice to describe Mirabella V. She is most likely the only yacht that appears in the Guinness Book of World Records. At 247 feet (75.2 metres) in length, she may not be the largest sailing yacht in the world, but she is the largest single-masted yacht, or sloop, with the tallest mast and the biggest sail. She is more than twice the length of the J-Class yachts of the 1930s. Her mast extends nearly 300 feet (91.4 metres) above the waterline; indeed, she is as tall as the Statue of Liberty from the bottom of the base to the top of the torch. With her keel fully lowered, Mirabella V's draft of 32' 10" (10 metres) is deeper than that of the QE2. At 19,730 square feet (1,833 square metres), her Genoa is the largest sail in the world. She is 60 percent longer and more than 2.5 times heavier than the next largest sloop.

Historically, yachts exceeding 80 feet (24.4 metres) in length were built with more than one mast to divide the vessel's sail area into smaller, more easily handled units. But today's technologies have improved the reliability of larger sails and spars and simplified their handling.

Mirabella V's mast is too tall to pass under the Bridge of the Americas in the Panama Canal, the Verrazano-Narrows Bridge in New York, or San Francisco's Golden Gate Bridge. Owner Joe Vittoria realized these limitations when he conceived his mega-sloop. He built her not to sail around the world like Tom Perkins and his *The Maltese Falcon,* but as a special charter yacht that would appeal to sporty guests who wanted luxury and liked to sail fast. She can clip along at 20 knots under sail. Her primary haunts are the Caribbean in winter and the Mediterranean in summer.

Launched at the end of 2003 and sea-trialled and delivered to Vittoria in the spring of 2004, *Mirabella V* was seven years in the making. During her construction, an image of a double-decker bus superimposed inside her hull was created to emphasize her height. Designed by renowned naval architect Ron Holland, she was controversial from her inception. In addition to her staggeringly tall rig, her boom is 90 feet (27.4 metres) long and her keel mechanism is extremely complex; the centreboard rises and lowers hydraulically, and the keel can be fixed in one of four positions: fully down for sailing, half-way down for motoring, just below the deck level, and all the way up, where it can be seen above the superstructure poking through the deck just aft of the mast. Vittoria has always loved boats, having started out working at a local yacht club when he was a teenager. A successful businessman, he finished up his corporate career as chairman and CEO of Avis, the car-rental company. In 1986 he helped to structure the management buyout of the company and led it until it was sold in 1996, which gave him the wherewithal to turn his avocation into a new business. Many private yachts are built expressly for the owner's private use and entertainment, but *Mirabella V* was intended as an addition to Vittoria's Mirabella charter fleet, which includes *Mirabellas I* and *III*—both 131-foot (40-metre) sloops.

Paramount in Vittoria's mind when conceiving *Mirabella V* was to think green. He wanted a sailing yacht that would have the comfort and performance of a motoryacht, yet be able to cruise long distances without the noise, pollution, and fuel costs of a motoryacht. *Mirabella*'s complex water system feeds both grey and black water through high-pressure membranes that filter out solids and other impurities and then pump the solids into a tanker instead of overboard. All oil is filtered and recycled. Garbage is separated into plastics, metals, and organic waste for recycling.

ABOVE: *Powerful stainless-steel mechanisms furl and unfurl the foresails.*

OPPOSITE: *The top of Mirabella V's mast is nearly 300 feet (91.4 metres) above the waterline—the tallest single sailboat mast in the world at the time she was built.*

LOA: 246' 8" (75.2 m)
Beam: 48' 7" (14.82 m)
Draft: board up / down 12' 8" (4 m) / 32' 10" (10 m)
Naval architect: Ron Holland Design
Exterior styling: Ron Holland Design
Interior design: Ron Holland / Luciana Vittoria
Builder / year: VT Shipbuilding, Woolston, Hampshire, England / 2003
Hull construction: Composite

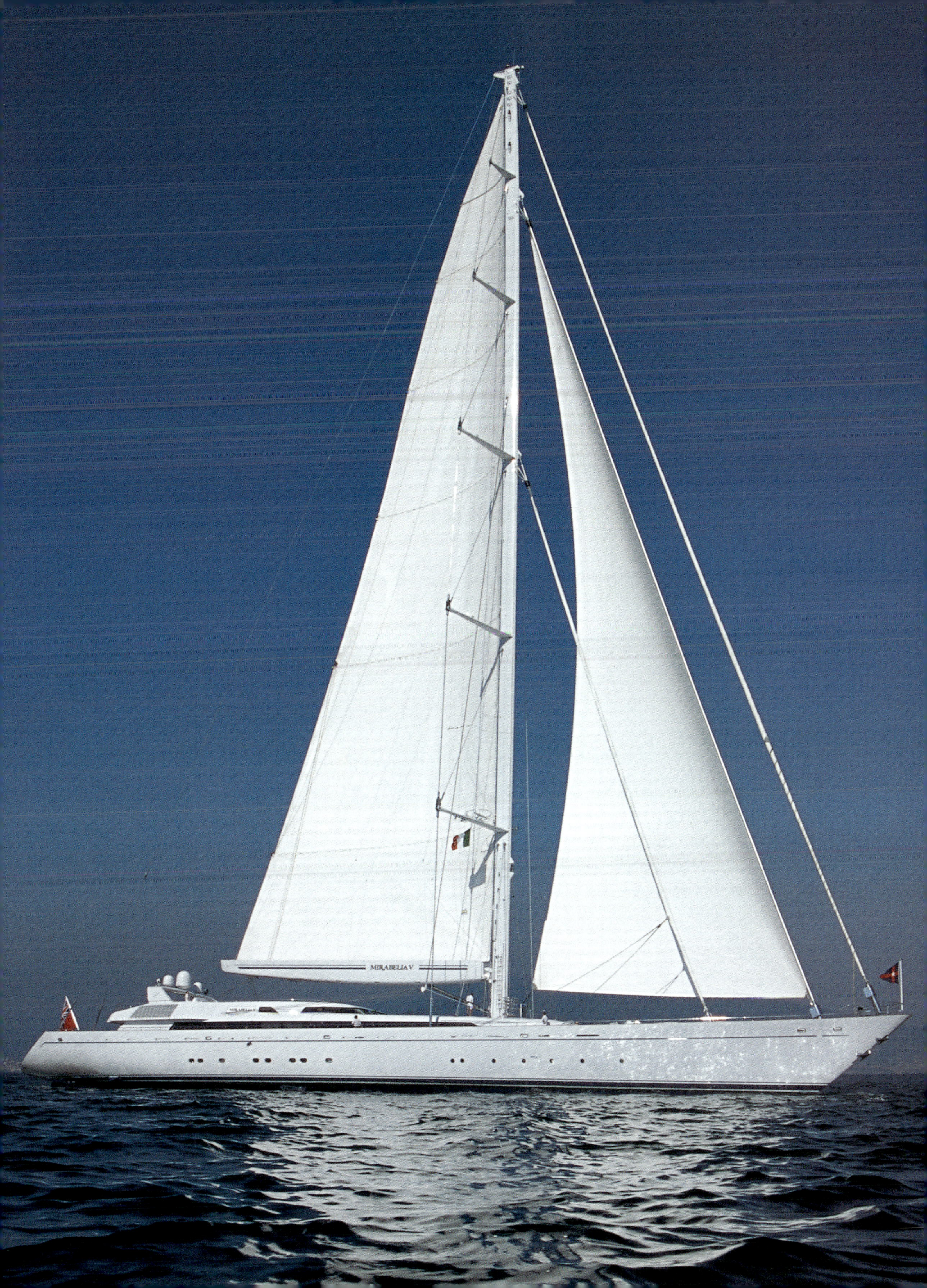
MIRABELLA V

ABOVE: *The covered aft deck has wraparound seating and two tables that can be expanded and swivelled to create various dining configurations.*

48 / OUTRAGEOUS YACHTS

BELOW, FROM TOP TO BOTTOM: The pilothouse has ample seating and a 180-degree view. The game table is forward in the open, airy main saloon. The aft deck table is set to receive guests.

MIRABELLA V / 49

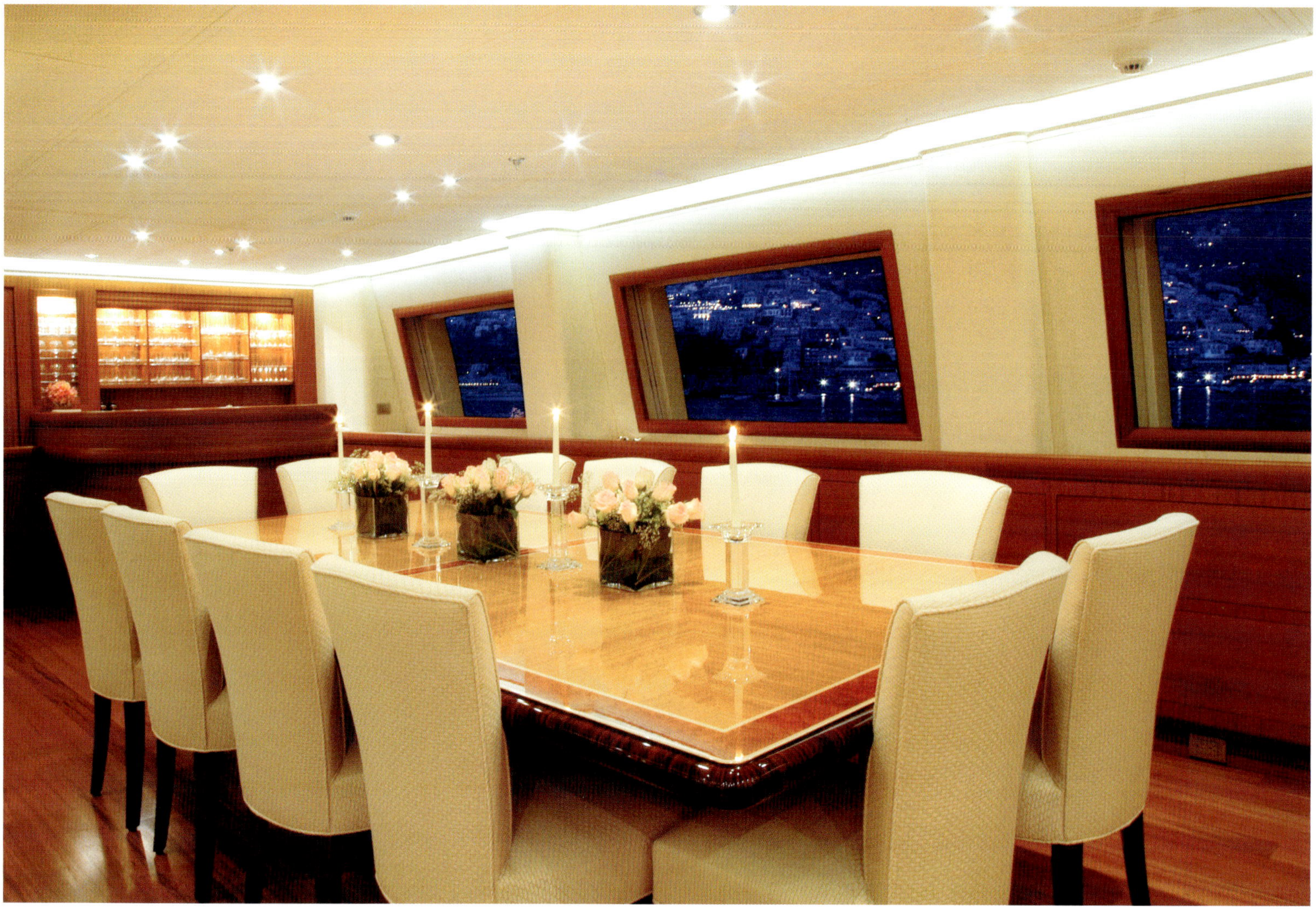

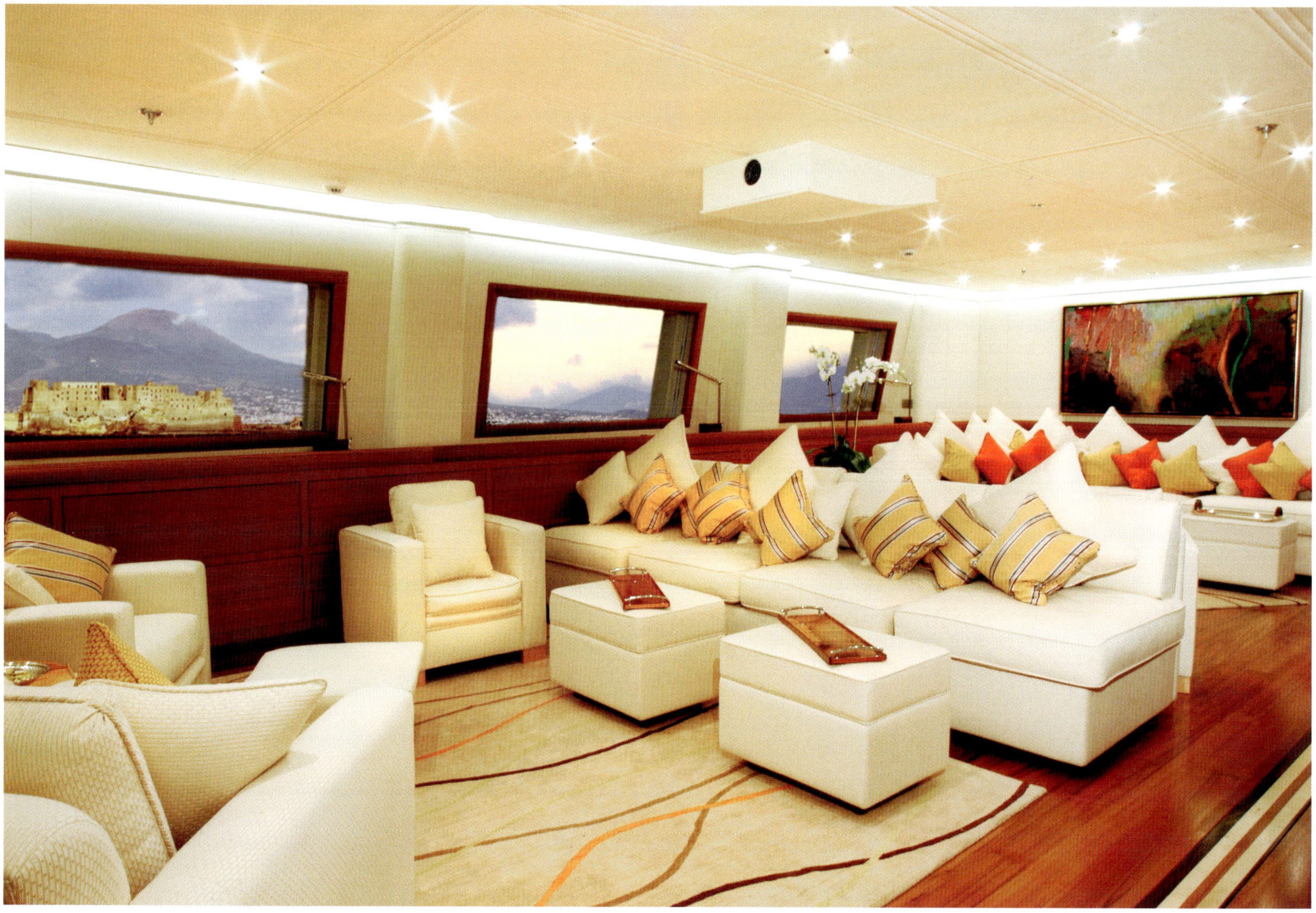

OPPOSITE, TOP: *The formal dining area is to starboard with the bar forward. The height and abundance of windows, combined with the soft vanilla and caramel hues of the space, creates a calming ambience and a direct connection to the outdoor scenery.*

OPPOSITE, BOTTOM: *The saloon seating area is to port. It is appointed with large, comfortable couches arranged in two groupings.*

RIGHT: *The sundeck doubles as an outdoor cinema at night.*

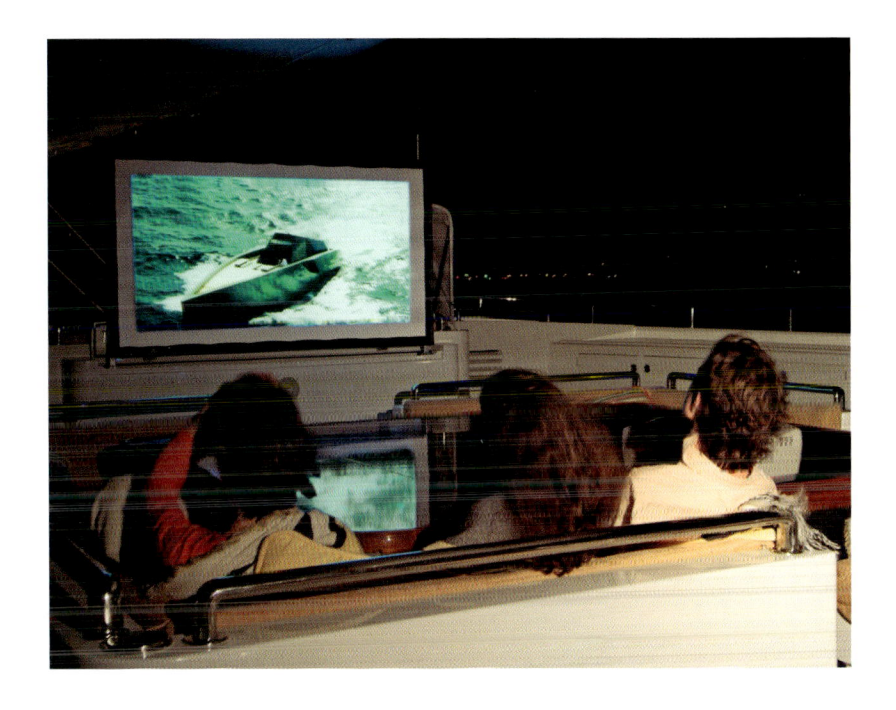

Vittoria originated the idea for Mirabella V with his good friend builder Bob Derecktor of Derecktor Shipyard. When Derecktor passed away, Vittoria turned to Ron Holland to help him carry out his dreams and schemes. After much discussion, the initial plans for a boat 60 metres in length had stretched to 76 metres. Mirabella V was constructed at the VT Shipbuilding (Vosper Thorneycroft) yard at Woolston, Hampshire, England. The Hamble-based firm High Modulus Europe Ltd., a subsidiary of a New Zealand company, supervised technical aspects of the composite construction of hull and rig. Doyle Sails was put to the test to create a new kind of sail and battens.

Vessels of Mirabella V's size are typically made of steel or aluminium, but in her case a composite material was chosen because it would accelerate construction, reduce maintenance (composite materials do not require regular repainting to inhibit corrosion), and improve thermal and acoustic insulation.

The interior was designed by Ron Holland, with considerable input from Vittoria and his wife, Luciana. The main saloon, which can be entered from the aft cockpit or through a side corridor, is vast. It is handsomely appointed with a large dining table, a bar, and various seating areas, including a custom-designed game table. The types of wood used for the floor, the wainscoting, and elsewhere in the room are teak and a light cherry. Forward of the main saloon are the wheelhouse and the master suite, which comprises a bedroom, a study and a large dressing room. Here, as throughout the boat, Oriental rugs and fine Georgian and Regency furniture, along with a number of custom-made pieces, add character and warmth. Designer and craftsman Sir David Linley was responsible for the decorative game table in the saloon as well as wardrobe doors inlaid with walnut charts and maps.

The six guest cabins—four doubles and two twins—are reached by a staircase leading down from the main saloon. Each of the cabins is named after a semiprecious stone and colour coordinated accordingly. All the cabins are equipped with a writing desk, en suite bathroom and full entertainment system. If you don't feel like staying in your cabin to watch a movie, you can take advantage of the outdoor cinema on the top deck of the yacht.

The deck areas offer fabulous outdoor-living amenities, including dining tables, sun pads, barbecue grills, and best of all, a bona fide twenty-person swimming pool on the foredeck. For spectacular views, a sky-lift elevator takes guests a third of the way up the mast.

Mirabella V charters for upward of $400,000–$425,000 a week. When she was conceived, that was a staggering amount of money. With yachts getting bigger and bigger, that fee is no longer as superlative as her other qualities.

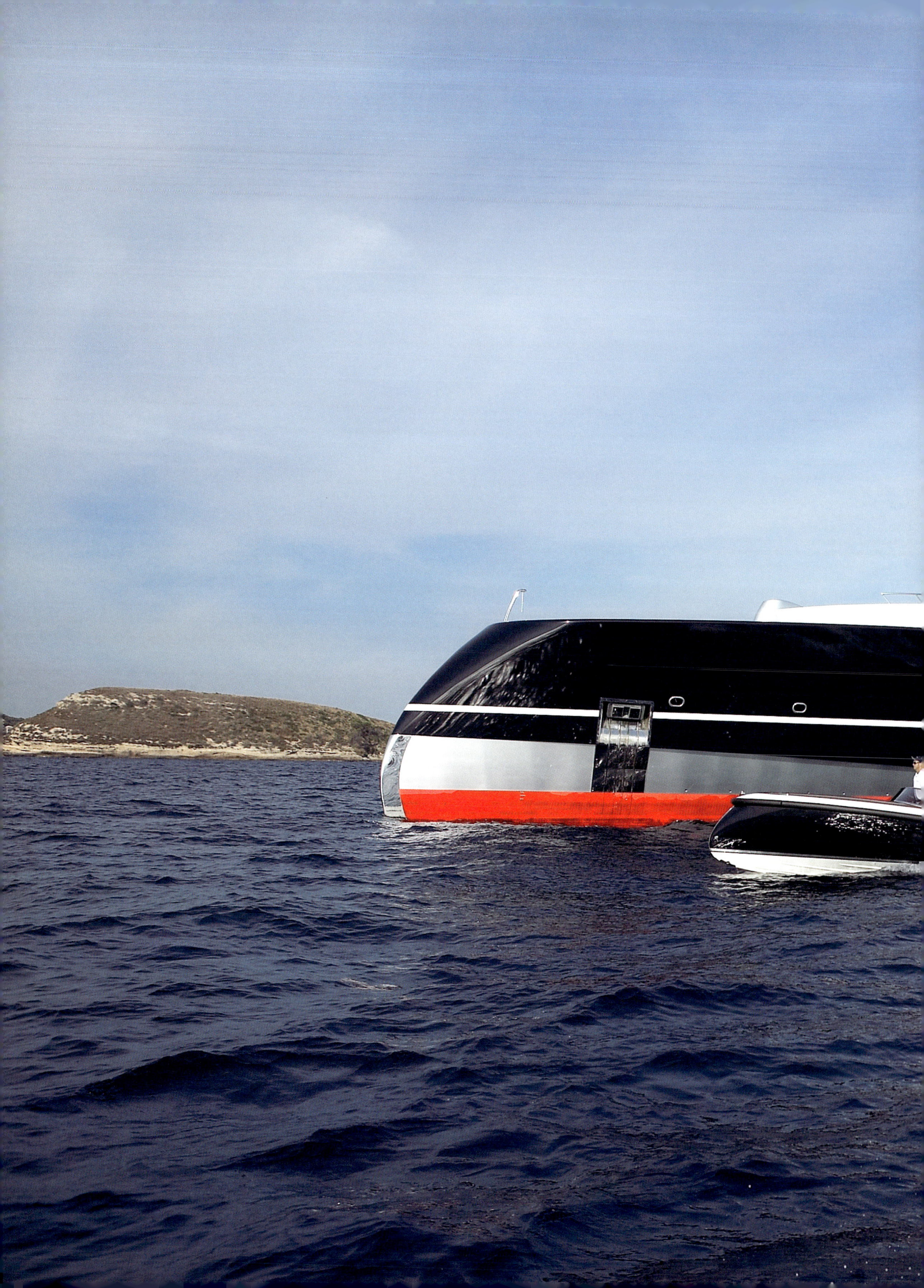

Predator

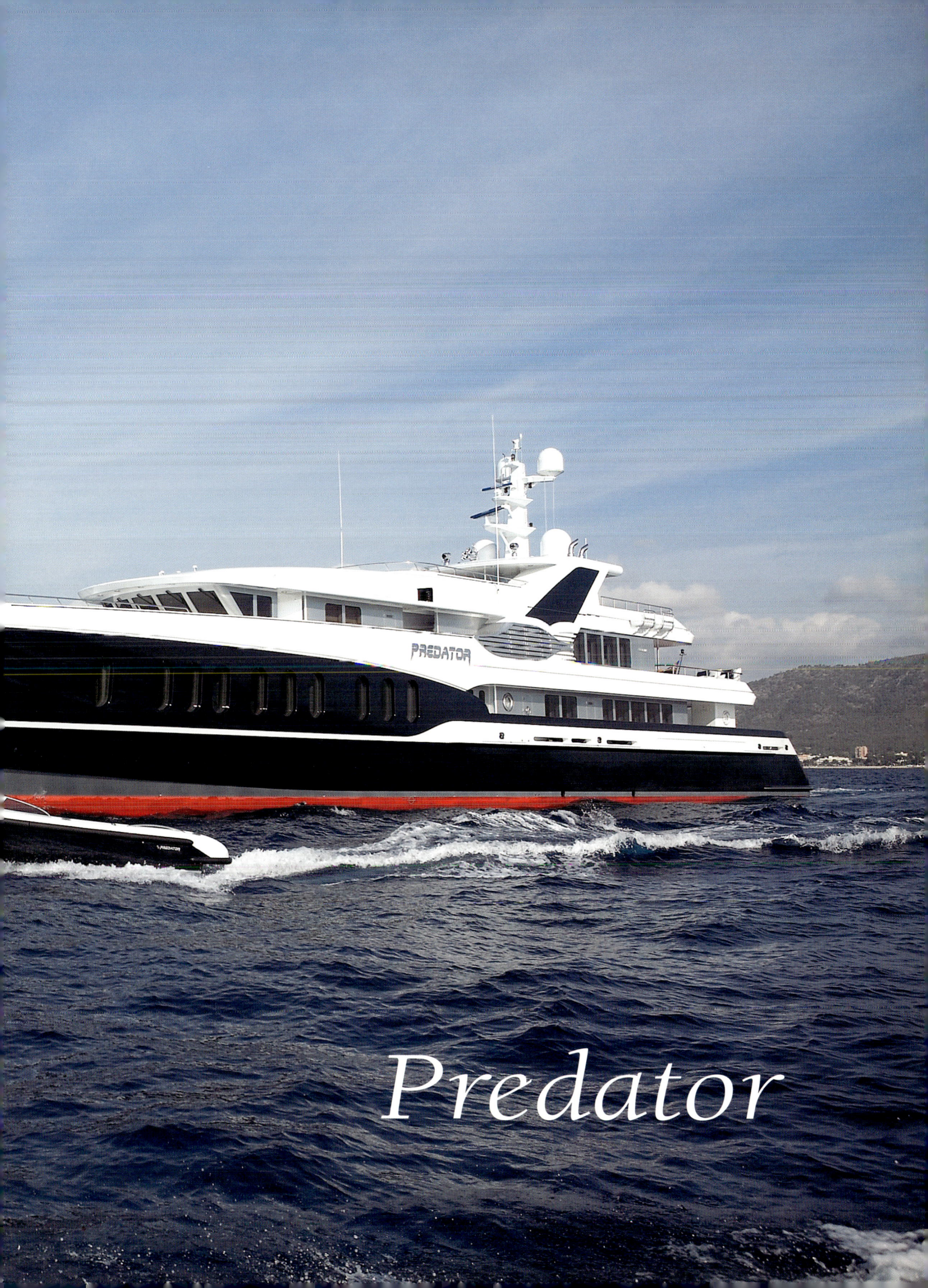

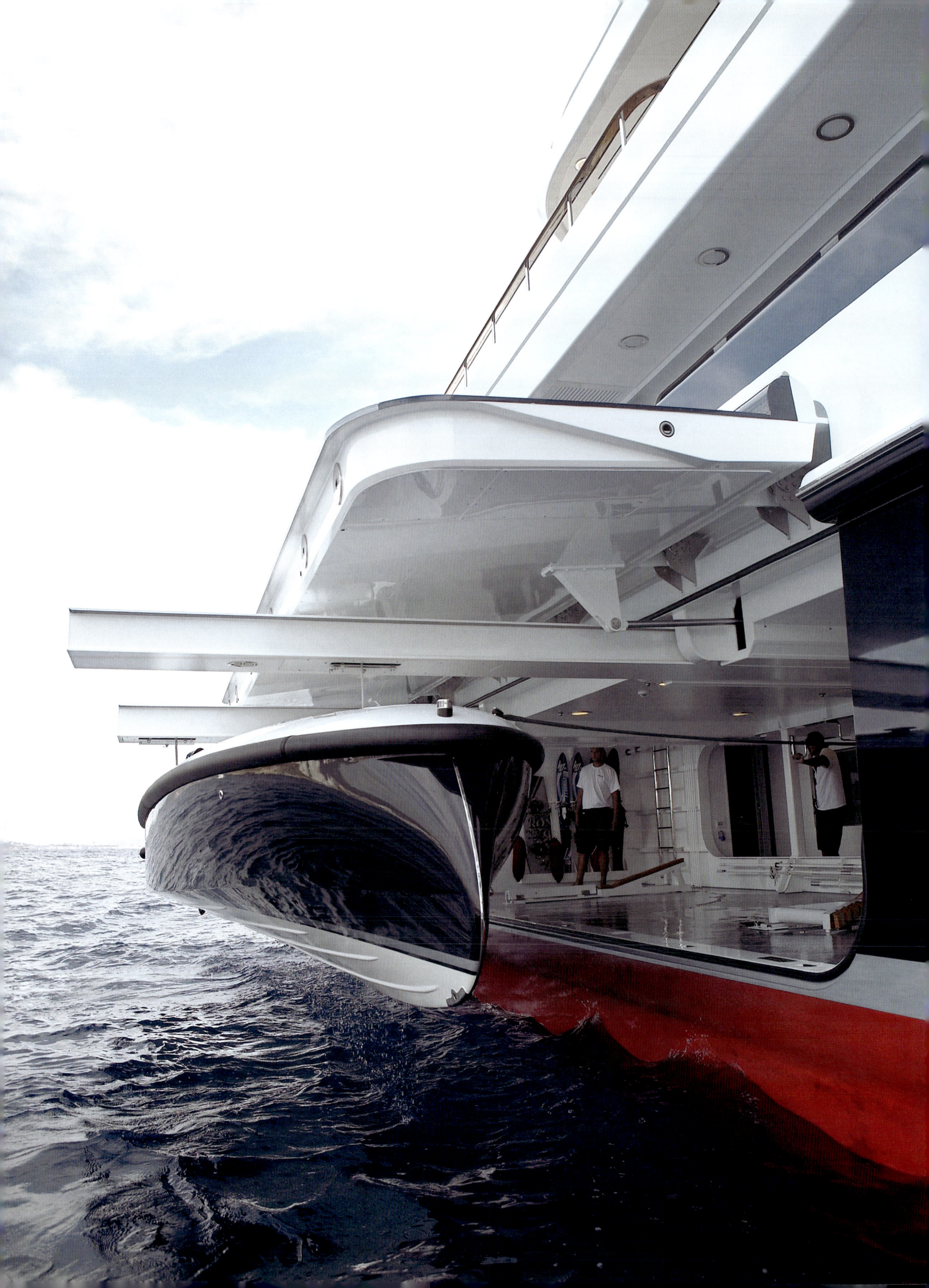

PRECEDING PAGES: *With her unusual axe bow, Feadship's* Predator *presents a striking profile.*

OPPOSITE: Predator's *custom tender, which mimics the axe bow of the mothership, and deploys from a bay on the side of the yacht.*

Predator. Rarely in the annals of yachting has a vessel's name been so in sync with her appearance. Her "axe" bow gives her an aggressive profile reminiscent of the warships of the late nineteenth and early twentieth centuries. She looks as if she is ready to hunt down enemy craft and sink them—while her guests relax on board in total luxury.

Launched in 2008, the 238-foot (72.8-metre) *Predator* is in the forefront of a shift in yacht design and naval architecture aimed at both greater comfort and more efficient performance, particularly among high-speed vessels. To date, few yachts with the axe-bow feature have been built, although many concept drawings exhibit the configuration, and commercial and naval vessels are beginning to appear with the unusual forward shape.

The genesis of *Predator*'s axe-bow design dates back to 2003, when a designer from outside the yachting industry asked the Dutch shipbuilding concern Feadship to investigate the feasibility of designing and building a superyacht based on the concept of a semi-submerged bow that cuts through the waves rather than riding over them. A cooperation between two shipyards and one design operation—Koninklijke De Vries Sheepsbouw, Royal Van Lent, and De Voogt Naval Architects—Feadship was created in the mid-twentieth century as an export association. Exhaustive technical research by the De Vries yard and De Voogt determined that the best solution would be to base the design of the hull on the axe-bow designs of the late 1800s. Models were tested, but the project was not taken further.

Enter the future owner of *Predator*. He came to Feadship with a request for a 70+-metre yacht capable of speeds in the 25-knot range, but not powered by jets or gas turbines. At such speeds, a conventional diesel-propeller propulsion package would generate high propeller-blade loads, resulting in excessive noise and vibration. To minimize the required propulsion power, Feadship proposed the low-resistance axe-bow configuration. The owner, who recognized the benefits and liked the aggressive, raked look, agreed and the project was a go.

Extensive seakeeping tests were performed at MARIN (Maritime Research Institute Netherlands) to perfect the hull shape, and De Voogt worked to refine and maintain the "yachtiness" of the profile. Unlike a traditional flared bow, which resists the forces that drive the nose of a vessel into the waves when the sea is rough, the axe bow slices through the waves, causing a significant reduction in pitching and, consequently, creating greater comfort aboard. The reduced pitching and slamming in rough seas also allows the yacht to run faster and steadier without extra power.

TOP: *The bridge is arranged as a social area with sofas and cocktail tables.*

BOTTOM: *The AV server room would be at home on the space shuttle.*

ABOVE: The custom dining table, designed by Sir David Linley, separates to provide unimpeded access to the main saloon through the dining saloon.

LOA: 238' (72.8 m)
Beam: 37' 11" (11.4 m)
Draft: 12' (3.7 m)
Naval architect: De Voogt Naval Architects
Exterior styling: De Voogt Naval Architects
Interior design: Bannenberg Designs Ltd.
Builder / year: Feadship–Koninklijke De Vries Scheepsbouw, Aalsmeer, The Netherlands / 2008
Top speed: 28.5 knots
Hull construction: Steel / Aluminium

If the bow presented great engineering and naval architectural challenges, the propulsion system offered the greatest technical challenge. *Predator* is fitted with four 16-cylinder MTU diesels, which produce a combined 23,000-plus horsepower. They run in tandem with two Renk reduction gears, which were developed for the *Predator* and are the only ones of their kind in the world. The gearboxes drive two Rolls Royce controllable-pitch propellers, each 10½ feet (3.2 metres) in diameter. Either two or four main engines can be engaged, depending on the required operation, and one- or three-engine modes are also possible. At maximum rpm, and depending on fuel load, the package can drive *Predator* to a top speed of 28.5 knots. The engine room, typically a tight space on a yacht packed with machinery, is a generous 14 feet (4.3 metres) high in some places. A

RIGHT: *An intimate lounge in the master suite.*

OVERLEAF: *The main saloon is designed for comfortable interaction among guests. The walls feature extensive use of Karelian birch, accented with Macassar ebony.*

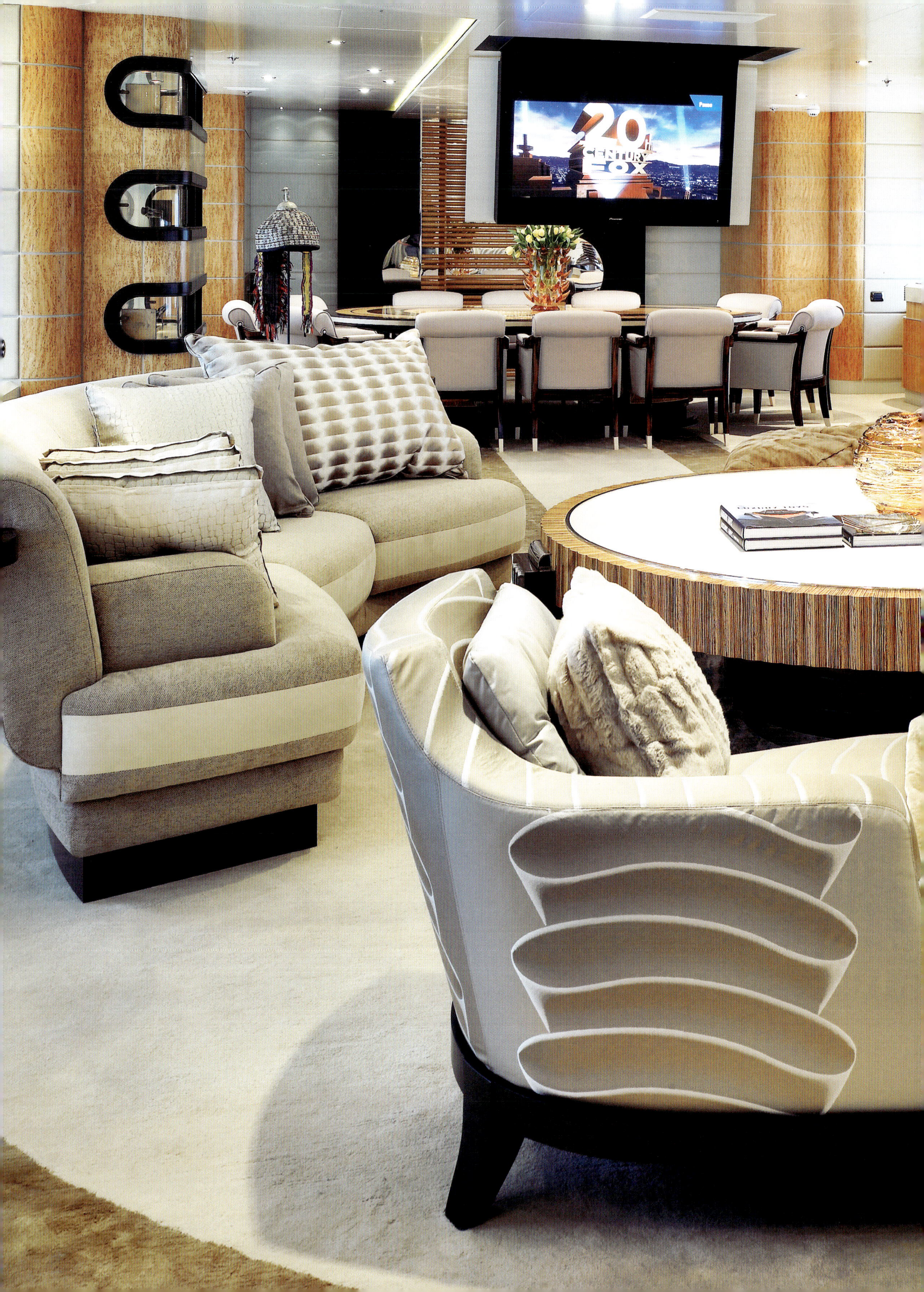
20th CENTURY FOX

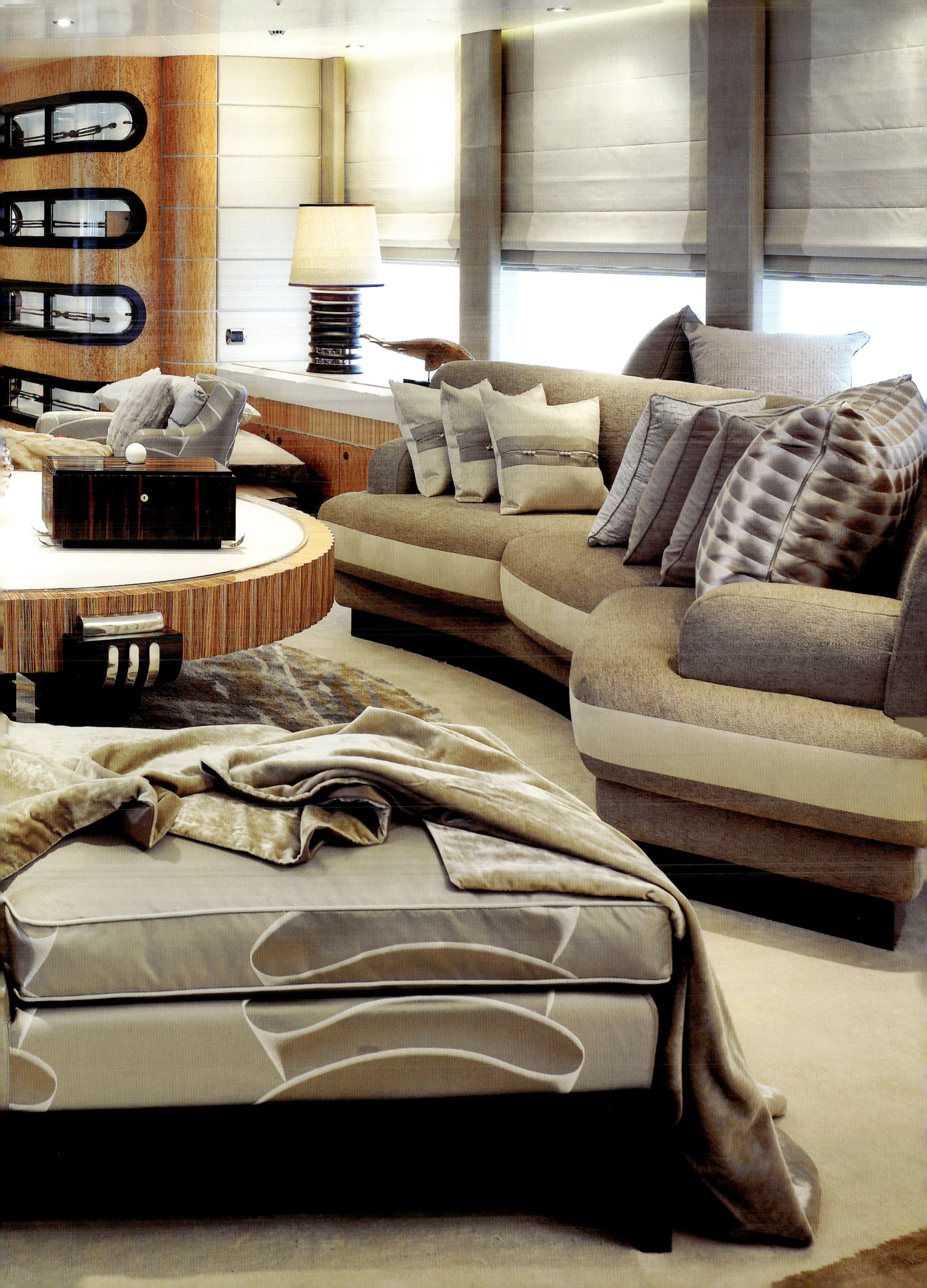

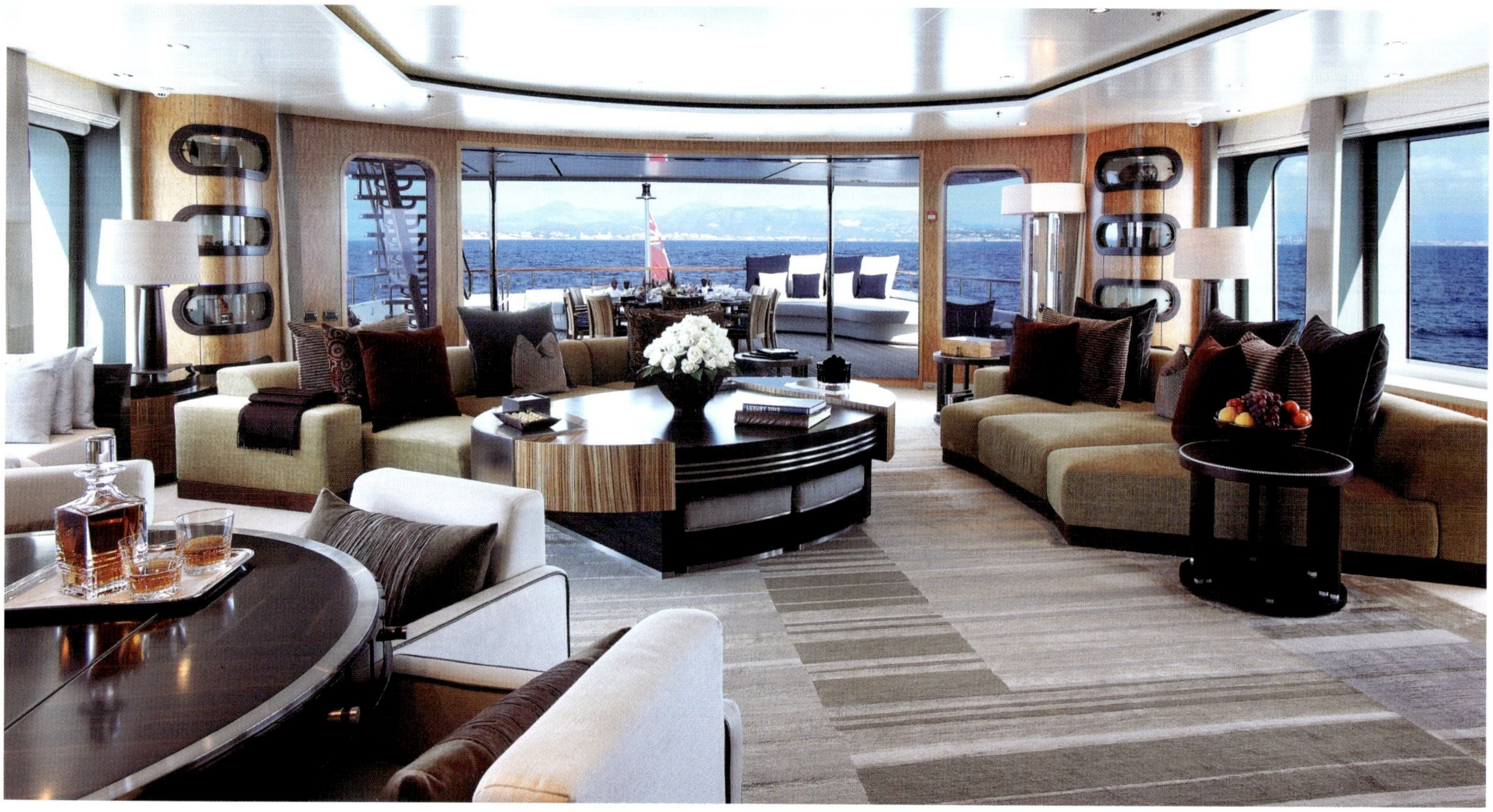

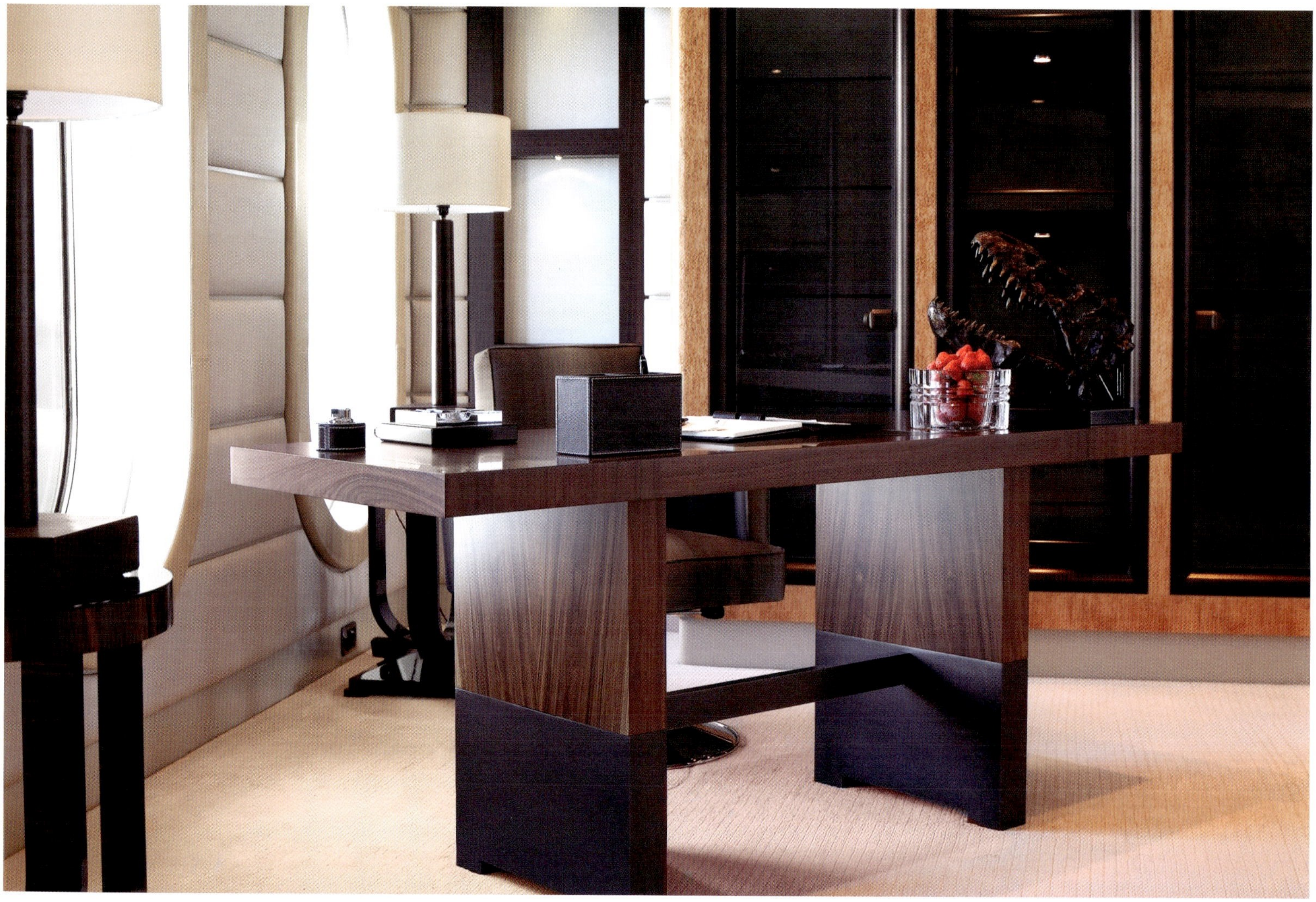

OPPOSITE, TOP: The bridge-deck lounge affords sweeping views. It is divided into a number of seating areas. The coffee table is made of nickel, Macassar ebony, and zebrano wood.

OPPOSITE, BOTTOM: The simple yet elegant study in the master suite.

ABOVE: The full-beam master suite is one of only three guest staterooms on the yacht. Its layout is open and airy, with pillars separating the spaces instead of bulkheads, and six large, elliptical windows on either side. A skylight above the bed floods the room with natural light.

RIGHT: The twin sinks in the master bath are also illuminated by a skylight.

TOP: *Predator's engine room is 14 feet (4.3 metres) high in some places. Her four 16-cylinder MTU diesels can power the yacht to a top speed of 28.5 knots.*

BOTTOM: *The tender storage bay in the hull side.*

238-foot (72.5-metres) steel-hulled yacht could not reach such speeds through brute force alone. Significant steps were taken to keep *Predator's* weight down. Her superstructure is made of aluminium, and composite materials were used for her topsides. In addition, her interior is constructed out of lightweight composite board and many of the wood and marble finishes are thin veneers mounted on honeycomb backing.

De Voogt designed the yacht's general accommodations, but the interior design was carried out by Bannenberg Designs with input from the owner's own decorator. The owner's one major request was for extensive use of Karelian birch, which is found only in Northern Europe. Because the birch has a light finish, accents were done in dark woods, including Macassar ebony and zebrano.

Surprisingly, *Predator* has sleeping quarters for only six guests in two VIP suites and one expansive master stateroom. The master is the largest single-level owner's stateroom Feadship has ever installed. Six large windows on either side of the room let in light and enhance the feeling of space. A skylight over the bed retracts upward.

Like the carpets in the VIP suites, the carpet in the master is made of Muga silk, which is extracted from a species of silkworm found only in Northeast India and is used to make monks' robes. The carpets were hand-stitched in Nepal. The architecture of the VIP suites is similar to that of the master and they are lavishly appointed as well.

Special attention was paid to sightlines on the main deck and other places on the boat. The owner wanted openness and *Predator* provides it. The formal dining table, which seats twelve, was made by Sir David Linley. The base, of Macassar ebony, is criss-crossed in a diamond pattern with faux ivory. The top incorporates Macassar ebony, zebrano, and nickel. The main saloon is bathed in natural light from its large windows. The entire yacht is equipped with a state-of-the-art AV system.

The real relaxing on the *Predator* takes place in the lounge on the bridge deck and in the outdoor spaces. The lounge features a bar, a large flat-screen television, and a custom casino table. The outside spaces are set up for sunbathing, alfresco dining, and entertaining. The yacht is equipped with a pair of custom tenders, personal watercraft, and a dive centre, complete with an inflatable decompression chamber.

The best seat in the house, however, resides way forward on the nose of the bow. There, where the yacht meets the sea, is a small hole into which a twin seat can be screwed into place. It is, of course, equipped with seat belts.

OPPOSITE: *In contrast to typical yacht helidecks, which are positioned aft close to the radar mast and antennae, Predator's pad is on the uncluttered foredeck.*

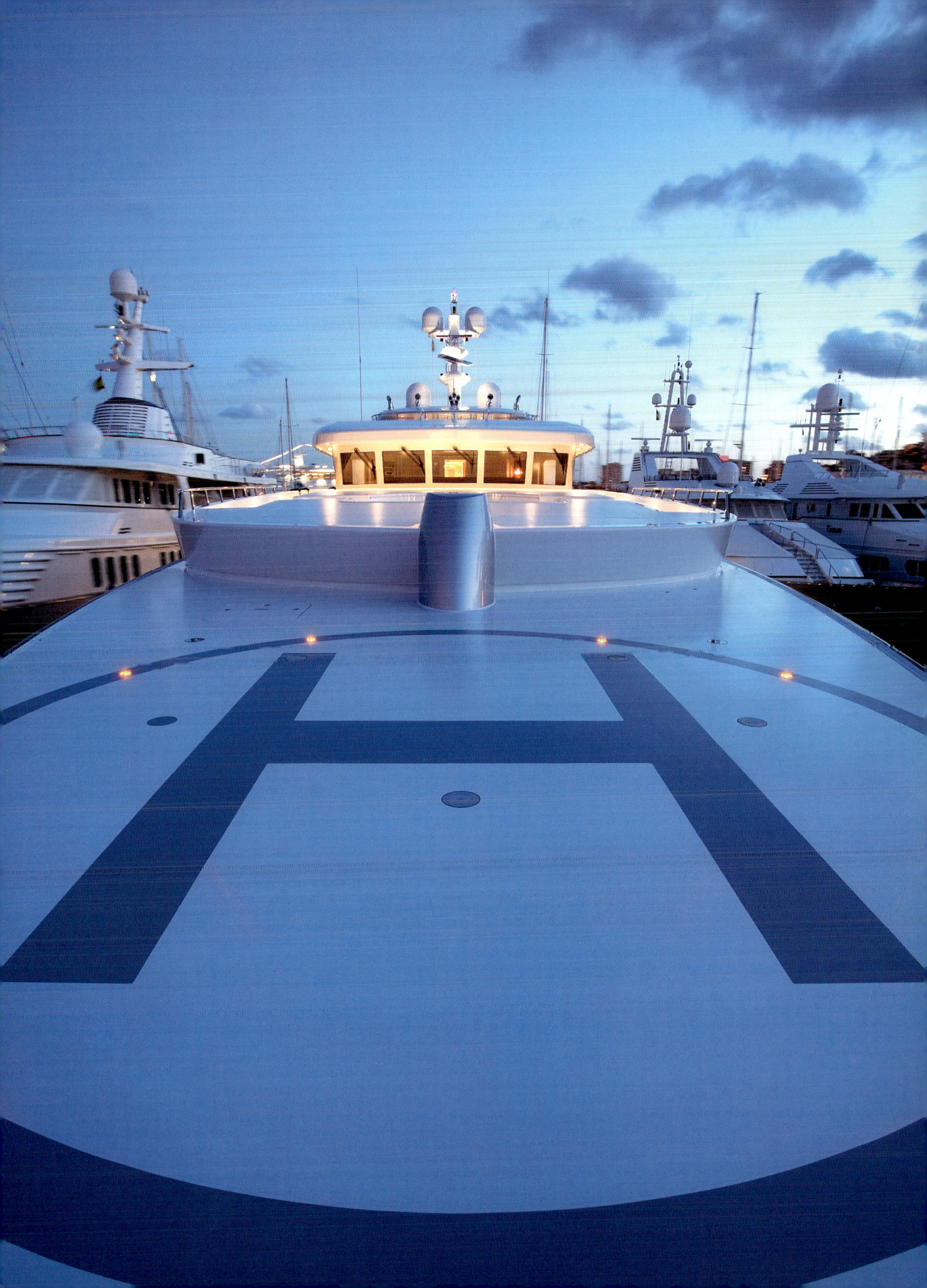

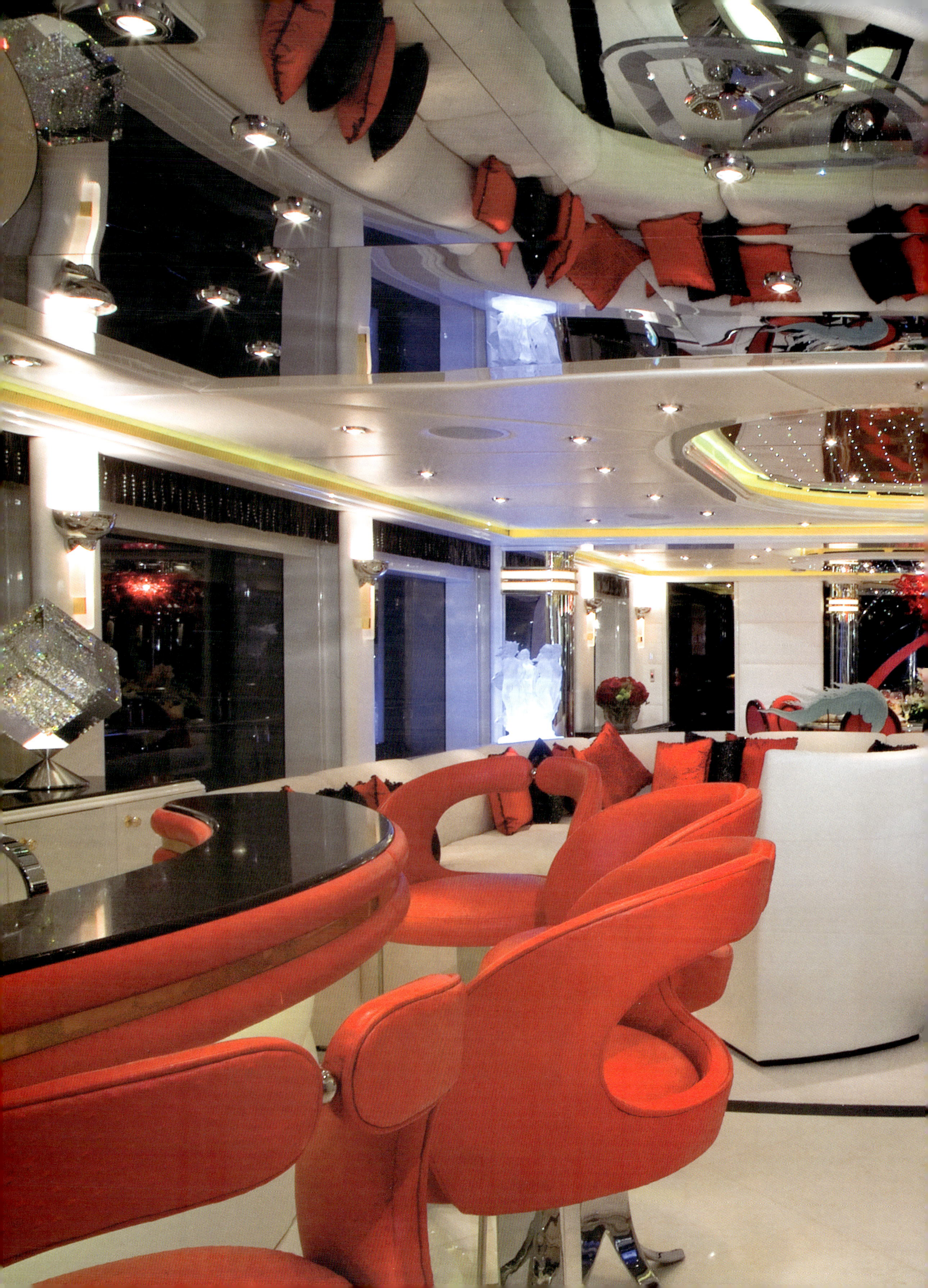

Norwegian Queen

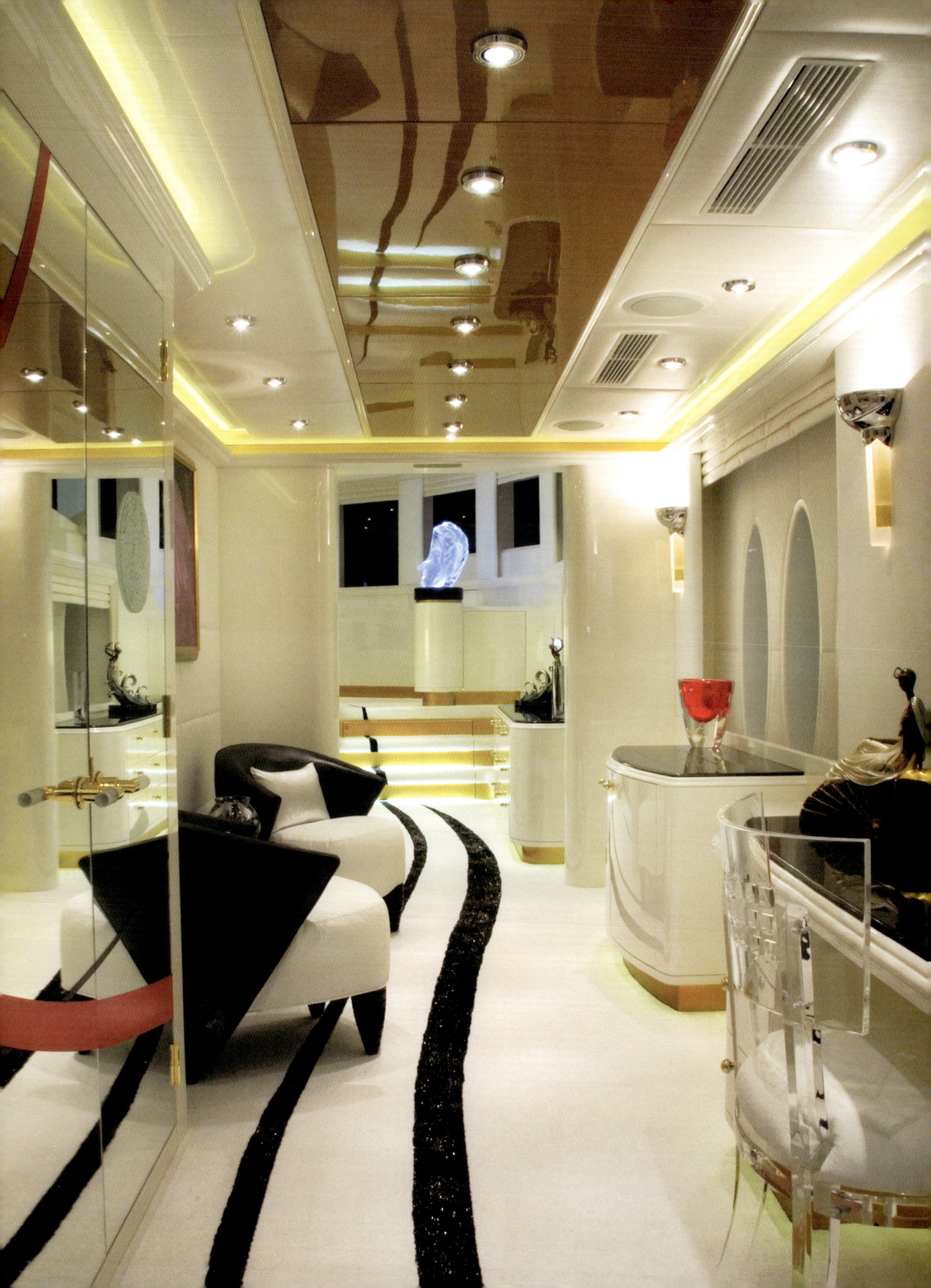

PRECEDING PAGES: Norwegian Queen's *main saloon is a study in red, white, black and silver. The mirrored ceiling reflects the beautiful marble and granite floor and handmade carpet.*

RIGHT: Black-stained ostrich-leather wall panels in the foyer on the yacht's starboard side set off a sparkling stainless-steel staircase.

A custom yacht is a creative collaboration involving the builder, the naval architect, the exterior stylist, and the interior designer, all of whose contributions are defined by the needs and desires of the owner. By far the most intimate of these collaborations is that between an owner and his or her interior designer.

When an experienced yachtswoman commissioned a custom yacht from Trinity Yachts, she hadn't yet decided on an interior designer and asked Trinity for recommendations. Among the names Trinity put forth was that of Evan K. Marshall, a versatile American designer whose firm, headquartered in London, designs custom and semi-custom interiors and exteriors for a wide variety of builders, including Trinity. Marshall initiated a dialogue with the client to establish the compatibility of their visions. The owner eventually hired his firm and the result of their collaboration is a stunningly original, utterly nontraditional yacht interior that blends the owner's vision and tastes, Marshall's creative sensibilities, and Trinity's skill as a builder.

Steel, aluminium and fibreglass long ago supplanted wood as the hull-building materials of choice in yachts, but joinery remains a staple of yacht interiors for all but a few modern vessels. Traditional teak, mahogany, cherry, and walnut, as well as exotic timbers with obscure names and psychedelic grains still adorn the vast majority of yachts built today. The owner of *Norwegian Queen*, however, eschewed the use of wood in favour of glass, metal, and other man-made materials. An observer would be hard pressed to find a single uncoated wood surface on board this yacht. The completed design is a study in white, red, black, and silver. Its undeniable feminine ambience is about as far as one can get from the traditional men's-club atmosphere of most yachts.

Before he and his team started designing, Marshall made several visits to the owner's home to discuss the project and assess her tastes. He found an open, light environment awash in colour, rich in glass, and filled with contemporary painting and dramatic sculpture. Armed with that knowledge, Marshall and company designed the layout of the yacht to make the most of the artwork. Before creating 3-D renderings of the layout, they sketched out original pieces of furniture. They found the owner receptive to many of their ideas and decisive in her choices. With visits to glass and furniture studios and fabric makers, the stylistic themes of the project began to take shape.

OPPOSITE: The dynamic black swoosh in the carpet in the outer part of the master suite is a design theme that runs throughout the yacht.

NORWEGIAN QUEEN / 67

LOA: 164' (49.9 m)
Beam: 28' (8.6 m)
Draft: 7' 6" (2.2 m)
Naval architect: Trinity Yachts
Exterior styling: Trinity Yachts
Interior design: Evan K. Marshall Yacht Design
Builder / year: Trinity Yachts, Gulfport, Mississippi / 2008
Top speed: 21 knots
Hull construction: Aluminium

One of the central thematic elements of the design is apparent upon entering the foyer on the yacht's starboard side. It is a subtle, black, sparkly stone swoosh that cuts through the foyer and dining area's white Naxos marble flooring, borders the black-stained ostrich-leather wall panels of the foyer, and sweeps through the custom-made white carpet from German manufacturer Olivier Treutlein in the main saloon. The theme carries through other horizontal and vertical spaces on the yacht as well.

Another central element of *Norwegian Queen*'s interior is glass. Marshall worked with Art Glass Environments, a Florida studio, to create custom doors, tabletops, shoji screens, and other pieces, notably an arresting 10-foot- (3-metre-) wide glass panel ornamented

ABOVE: Evan Marshall and Trinity Yachts collaborated on the yacht's exterior styling, which is sinuous and contemporary.

with swirling coloured-glass forms that separates the dining area from the foyer.

All of the yacht's free-standing furniture was designed by Marshall's office and built by Michael O of Miami. The dining table and sideboards feature backlit Murano glass disks from Campanello of Italy. All of the tabletops were made by Art Glass Environments of Florida. The chandelier over the dining table is a nest of swirled red-glass horns reminiscent of pieces by Dale Chihuly. It was created by the lighting company Wired.

Bathroom fixtures and door hardware are from the THG Paris Lalique collection. Even the yacht's drawer pulls are accented with bits of Lalique. The main saloon, dining room, and master stateroom boast a number of glass and crystal pieces, including sculptures by

ABOVE: *A glass panel ornamented with coloured-glass forms separates the dining area from the foyer forward. The chandelier over the dining table is a nest of swirled red-glass horns reminiscent of pieces by Dale Chihuly.*

70 / OUTRAGEOUS YACHTS

BELOW, FROM TOP TO BOTTOM: The soft furniture in the main saloon looking aft is upholstered in white baby-ostrich leather. The space is decorated with glass sculptures and a custom stainless-steel-and-glass coffee table. The galley's rich red-and-black-sparkle countertops echo the main themes of the interior design. The black, red, and white colour scheme extends to the pilothouse.

Frederick Hart, all secured to their surfaces to prevent them from crashing to the floor when the yacht rolls or plays host to large parties. The paintings throughout the main deck, except for the master bathroom, were specially commissioned for *Norwegian Queen* from Spanish artist Felix Mas.

Careful examination of many of the flat surfaces of the built-in furniture suggests that they are finished in stained burlwood, but in fact the veneer is pearlized lacquer—a difficult process that adds depth and underlying detail. The loose seating—bar stools and chairs—are covered in custom bright-white or red-stained dimpled baby ostrich leather.

The sky lounge shimmers from a combination of black high-gloss- and pearlized-lacquer finishes. Michael O, Art Glass Environments, Wired, and Oliver Treutlein contributed the various elements of the decor. Marshall designed the card and coffee tables.

Norwegian Queen's split-level master stateroom is thematically similar to the rest of the main deck, but is a space unto itself, with its grey palette and gold accents on the bedposts. The bed faces the stateroom's 10-foot- (3-metre-) high aft bulkhead and a large, vertical Mas painting that separates horizontally to reveal one of the three plasma TV screens in the stateroom.

The four guest staterooms are less ornate than the main-deck accommodations, but are bright and elegant nonetheless. Each is finished in high-gloss pearlized lacquer, and each bathroom features a different stonework palette on the floors and countertops. The galley adheres to the main themes of the interior design, but without the frills. It doesn't have any glass, but its rich red- and black-lacquered surfaces and black-sparkle countertops make the space more fun than industrial. A banquette allows guests a casual dining option and a front-row seat for watching the chef create meals.

Marshall and Trinity collaborated on the yacht's exterior styling, which is sinuous and contemporary. Her interior may be the major story, but her outdoor spaces are quite exceptional. Her sundeck features a hot tub, sunpads, lounge chairs, and a bar. Her swim platform is a waterfront destination in its own right, with recesses for umbrellas and pleasing underwater ambient lighting for sea-gazing after dark.

For all her femininity and frills, *Norwegian Queen* was designed by Trinity's naval architects as an oceangoing yacht. She has a pair of 2,250-horsepower Caterpillar diesels under the hood that propel her to a sprightly top speed of 21 knots. She may have been built tough as nails, but masculine she is not, as evidenced by her docklines—floating twelve-strand Plasma lines with a distinctly pinkish hue.

OPPOSITE, TOP: *The custom-designed bed is the centrepiece of the split-level master suite. The blue-lit crystal sculptures are by Frederick Hart.*

OPPOSITE, BOTTOM: *The mermaid-theme shower door in the master bathroom was commissioned from Casa Manolo of Miami, Florida.*

ABOVE: *A combination of black high-gloss and pearlized-lacquer finishes makes the sky lounge shimmer. Michael O, Art Glass Environments, Wired, Oliver Treutlein, and Marshall's design team contributed to the decor.*

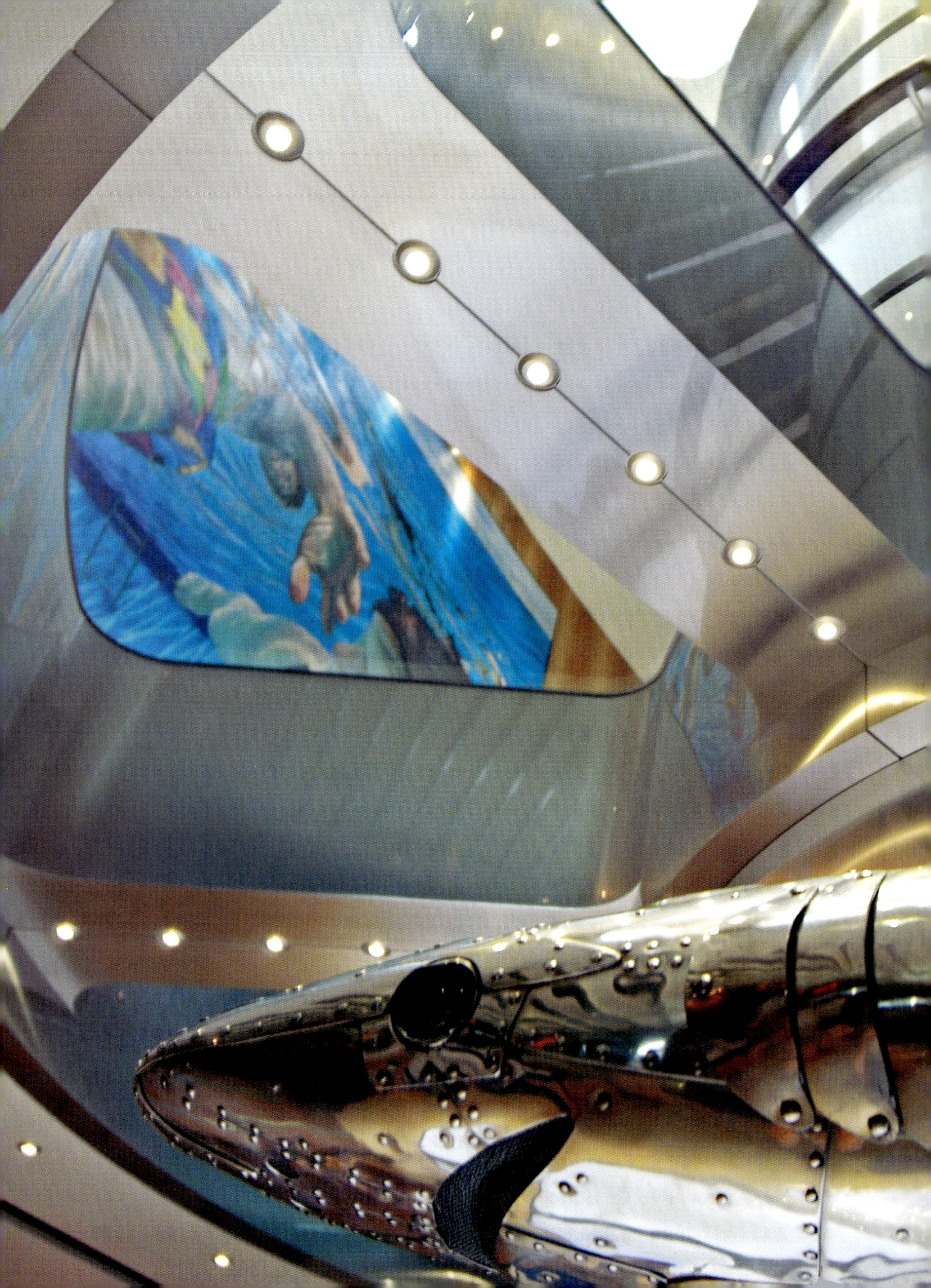

The Maltese Falcon

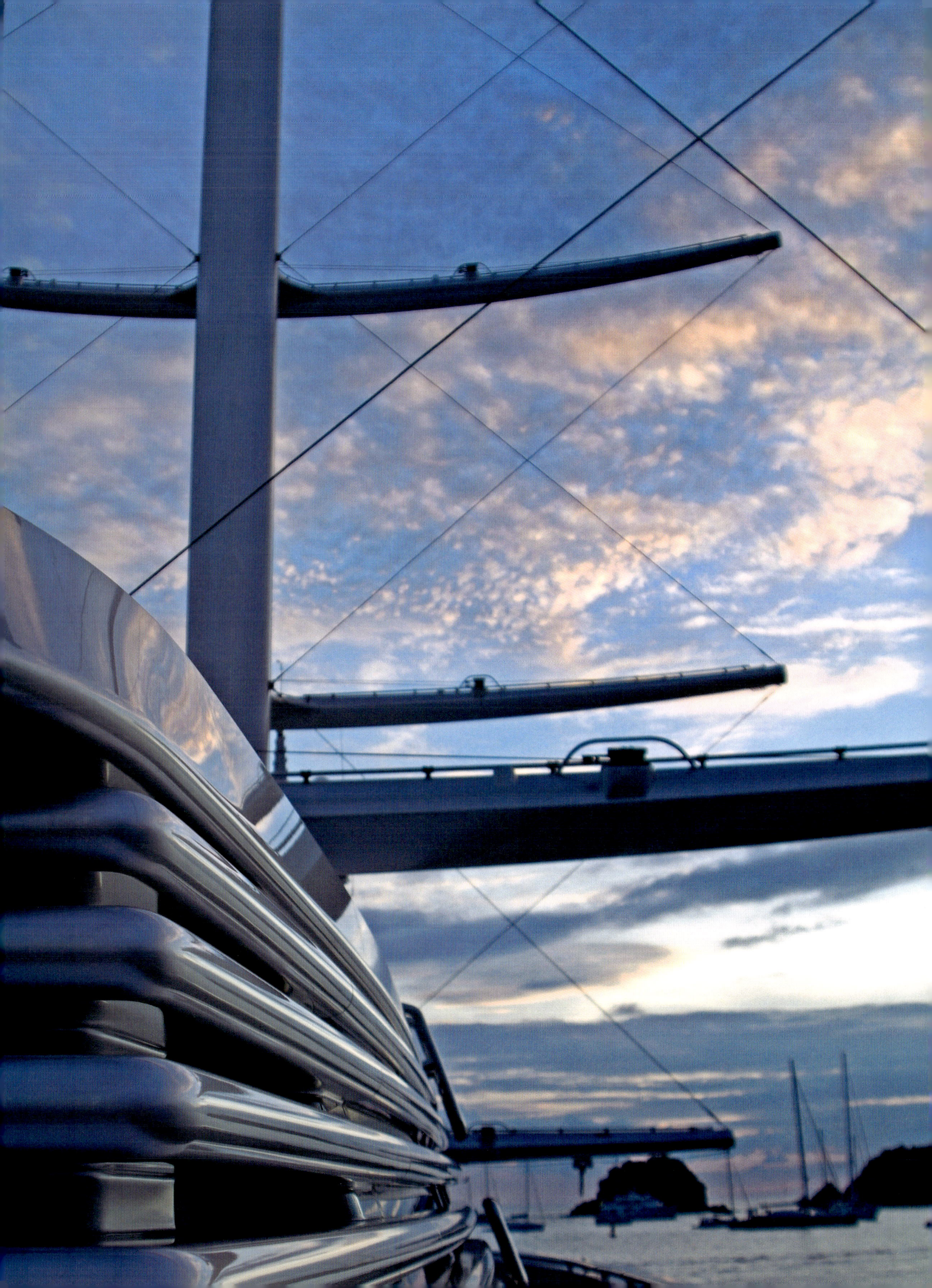

TOP: The Falcon *heeling hard while sailing at 17.9 knots.*

BOTTOM: *The sails and rig are controlled from a pedestal on the bridge.*

By any standards and by all accounts the *The Maltese Falcon* is the most extraordinary yacht of the new millennium. There are only two people in the world who could have conceived of such a project—visionaries Fabio Perini and Tom Perkins. Perini, an innovative boat builder based in Viareggio, Italy, launched his first mega–sailing yacht, the 128-foot (39-metre) *Felicita,* in the mid-1980s. Perini started out in the family paper business and by the age of seventeen had invented a machine for automatically feeding paper under tension (rolling paper towels, toilet paper, etc.). He also fashioned a high-speed device that converted paper into tissue and revolutionized that segment of the paper industry. Sailing was an avocation that he turned into a vocation when he built his first yacht with his own funds. His breakthrough invention was an automated captive winch that was based on the same principles as his automated paper machine, which, like winches on sailboats, involved drums and rollers. Perini's innovative trick was a "tensioning arm" that kept the sail's lines taut. Moreover, his winches were electric rather than hydraulic and could be hidden below deck, thus alleviating any tripping over deck gear and greatly improving the safety of the crew. He was one of the first to introduce mega–sailing yachts that were easy to handle. Perini was more of a designer than a boat builder, but he was a perfect match for American engineer and businessman Tom Perkins—a self-confessed MIT nerd.

PRECEDING PAGES: *Looking up from the base of the atrium's circular staircase through the glass floor above, guests encounter this stainless-steel shark, one of many artworks on the yacht.*

OPPOSITE: *The Falcon's exterior styling by designer Ken Freivokh is very sculptural.*

Perkins has a high profile in Silicon Valley; he is a former executive with Hewlett Packard, a co-founder of the venture capital firm of Kleiner, Perkins, Caulfield & Byers, and, among myriad other enterprises, a financier behind Genentech, Netscape, and Google.

In the mid-1980s Tom Perkins asked Fabio Perini to build the 142-foot (43.3-metre) *Andromeda,* a very large yacht at the time. Three years later he commissioned a stretch version—the 152-foot (46.3-metre) *Andromeda La Dea*—which he sailed around the world. After completing that challenge, Perkins amused himself with a thoroughly restored 1915 classic Nathaniel Herreshoff schooner, *Mariette,* winning regattas everywhere. He also created a mother ship for her, a 1940s motoryacht called *Atlantide,* completely refitted and redesigned by UK-based Ken Freivokh Design. Yet all of these escapades were but precursors to the amazing *Maltese Falcon.*

Fabio Perini has been very successful over the last twenty years or so in creating a fleet of vessels of varying lengths. To accommodate his ever-increasing production, he needed to expand beyond his Viareggio facilities, so he acquired a shipyard in Tuzla, Turkey. In 2000, while

LOA: 289' (88 m)
Beam: 42' (12.9 m)
Draft: 19' 8" (6 m)
Naval architect: Gerard Dijkstra & Partners / Perini Navi
Exterior styling: Ken Freivokh Design
Interior design: Ken Freivokh Design
Builder / year: Perini Navi, Viareggio, Italy / Yildiz, Tuzla, Turkey / 2006
Hull construction: Steel

visiting with Perini, Perkins saw a model of a large steel hull that had been built on speculation in Turkey. At 289 feet (88 metres), it was the length of a football field! Unlike other Perinis, this hull was sleek and designed to sit low in the water. Perkins knew it could be designed for speed—and Perkins likes to win. The project excited him, and after some soul searching he decided to take it on and create the largest, most innovative sailing yacht in the world. In time this yacht was given the name *The Maltese Falcon*. Malta would be her home port—he bought a permanent slip for her there—and he also was a fan of Dashiell Hammett's hard-boiled detective novel by the same name. Fabio Perini admits that he hasn't fully absorbed what *The Maltese Falcon* signifies for the future of Perini Navi's *barca che fa epoca*, a new class of yacht, as opposed to *barca d'epoca*, a classic yacht.

With an undertaking as huge as "The Falcon," as she is affectionately called, there were many challenges to be met, not least the rig. Dutch naval designer Gerard Dijkstra (who also designed Jim Clark's mega–sailing yacht *Athena*) came up with a modernized version of an intriguing German concept from the 1960s called a DynaRig. It was never implemented on sailing vessels back then because of its impractical weight, but Dijkstra, along with Perini and Perkins, found a way to make it work using twenty-first-century technology. The *Falcon's* rig consists of three freestanding masts, each with five sails in the shape of isosceles trapezoids. It bears a striking resemblance to the rig on the famous old clipper ship *Cutty Sark,* but modified and modernized—there are no hanging ropes, stays or shrouds. A mechanical furling system rolls up the sails, constructed by Doyle Sails, into the masts. Weighing twenty-five tons apiece and nearly twenty storeys high, the masts are made of carbon fibre. The material had to be strong enough not only to support the masts' weight and height but also to withstand moving parts. Perkins entrusted the creation of this complex carbon structure to Damon Roberts of Insensys, a British-based high-tech company. Perkins ordered carbon fibre in Japan, had it shipped to the UK to be woven into cloth, and then shipped it to Turkey, where he had leased a shed at the Yildiz yard to build the spars. The masts, their sails and the control systems represented an estimated 200,000 man-hours.

OPPOSITE: Cocktails are served in the lounge area on the aft deck.

ABOVE: The glass floor panels of the atrium provide views up into the rig. Artworks such as this painting of swimmers had to be adapted to hang on the curved bulkheads.

RIGHT: The yacht's main staircase spirals around a massive mast trunk.

OVERLEAF: The Maltese Falcon's rig, consisting of three freestanding masts, each with five sails in the shape of isosceles trapezoids, proved effective as she pressed along under full sail at the St. Barths Bucket Regatta.

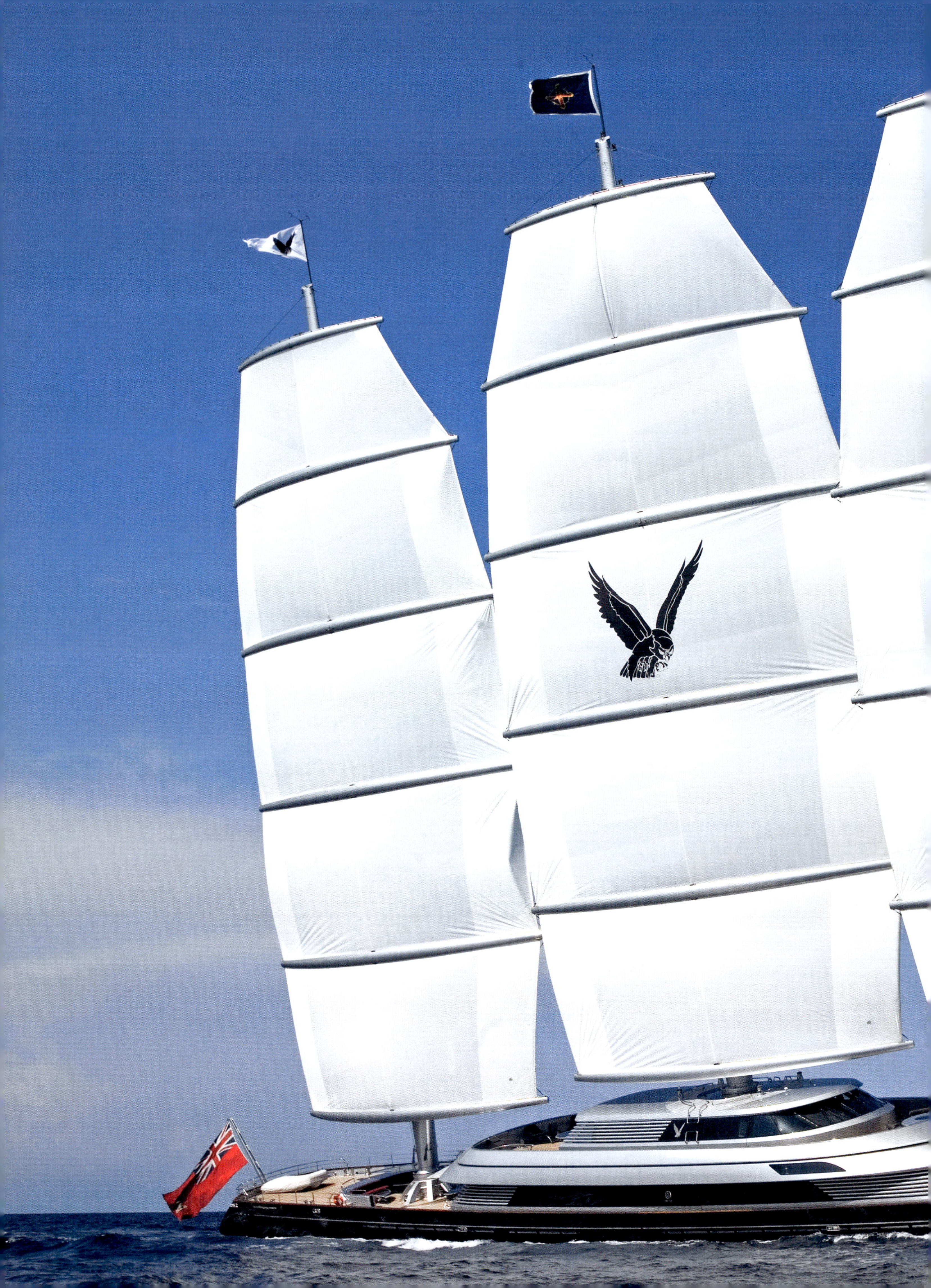

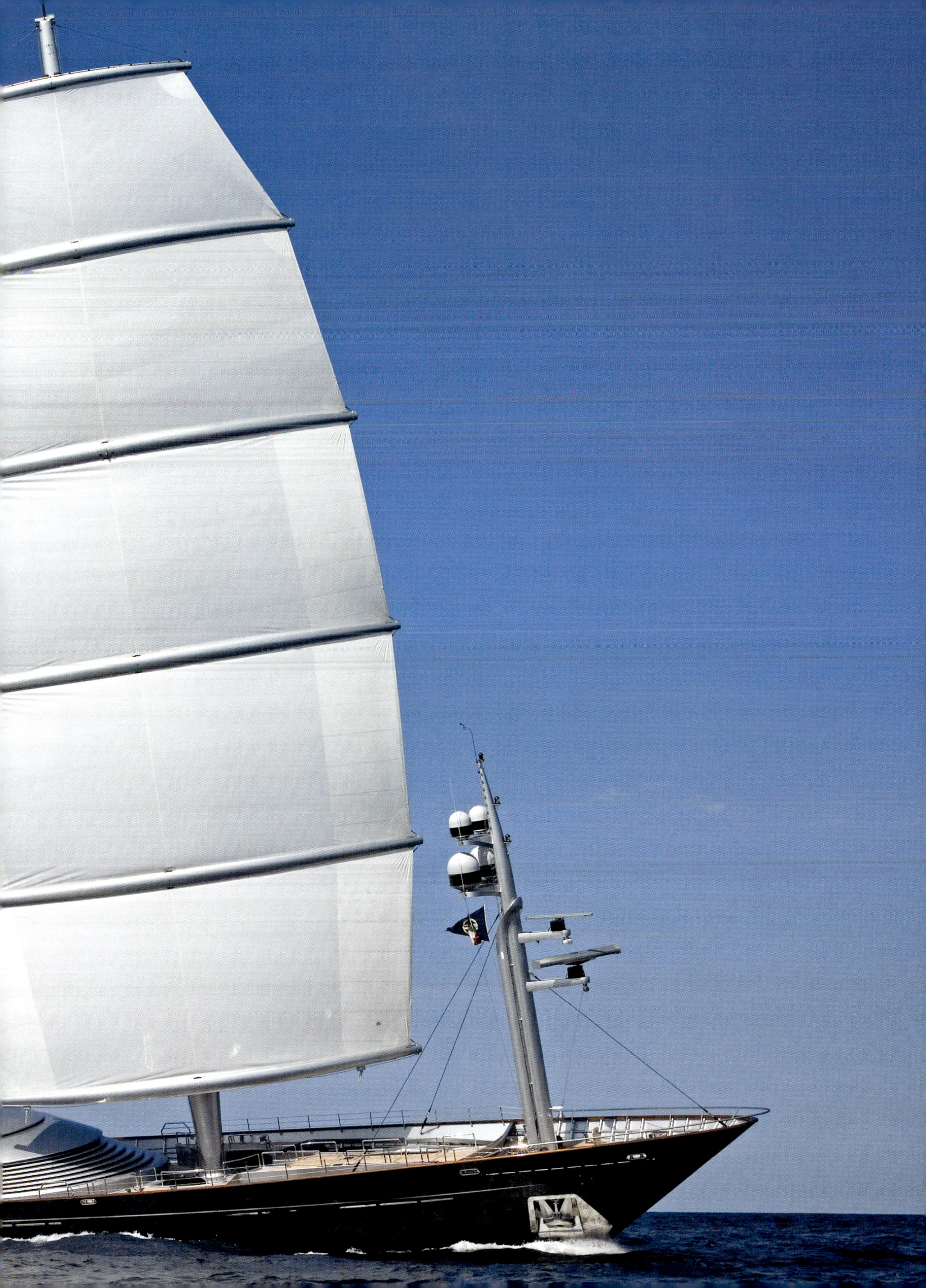

ABOVE: *The VIP cabin on the upper deck is the one preferred by owner Tom Perkins when he is aboard.*

LEFT: *The main saloon is appointed with built-in leather, wood, and stainless-steel furniture. As in the rest of the spaces aboard the boat, everything is designed to accentuate the curvilinear, even the overhead light.*

OPPOSITE, TOP: *Above the dining table is a skylight that provides a view of the rig. It opens and closes with an iris mechanism.*

OPPOSITE, BOTTOM: *The central sailing console and its surroundings would be equally at home on a starship.*

Ken Freivokh Design, the firm that had worked with Perkins on his little boat *Atlantide,* created both the exterior styling and the interior design. According to Perkins, Ken and his partner, Liz Windsor, "are the most talented design team around and have the ability to think outside of the box." Freivokh, himself a keen racing sailor, grasped the DynaRig concept at once. He understood that the *Falcon* would be a unique, groundbreaking machine, and he knew that the styling and the interior would have to be just as innovative. "In the same way a Bentley Continental or a Bugatti Veyron is more than a car," Freivokh says, "*The Maltese Falcon* is more than a sailing yacht." Some designers have a signature style, but in this case Perkins had his own ideas about the look of his yacht, and Freivokh honoured them. Freivokh is responsible for the seamless, sculptural exterior styling, the atrium's circular staircase, and the skylight glass floor, as well as the interior and deck decor. Perkins dislikes corridors on boats, so Freivokh created open spaces separated by sliding doors instead. He also worked with Perkins's extensive modern art collection, designing special spaces for his paintings and sculptures. In fact, many of Perkins' paintings had to be reframed before being mounted on curved bulkheads. A walk on the decks and through the interior accommodations extracts a gasp from every single person who has the privilege to visit the boat. Perkins takes pride in the fact that the sails can be set in five minutes right from controls in the pilothouse. With few crew in sight and not much fuss, you are off and sailing at twenty knots. Pure genius!

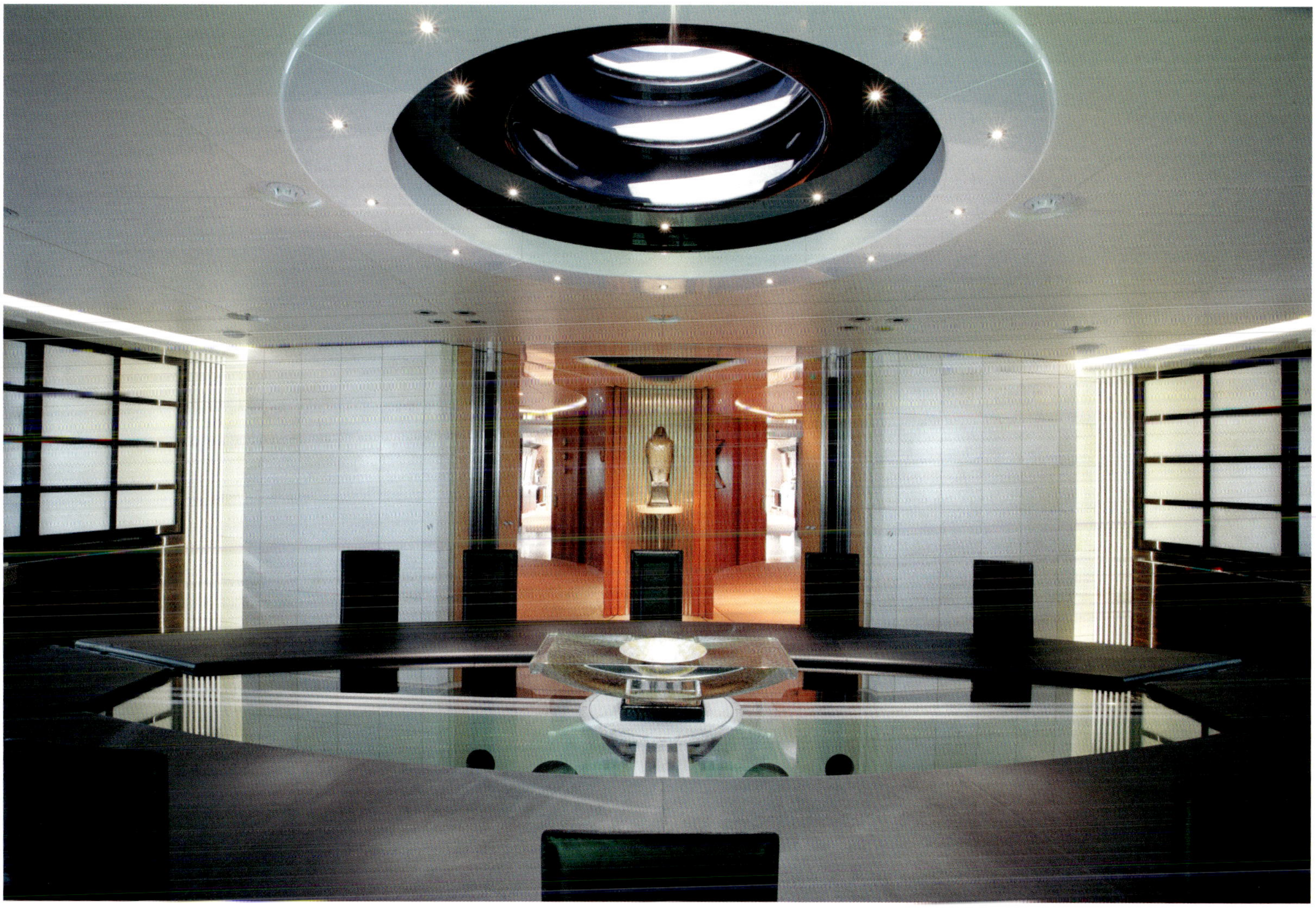

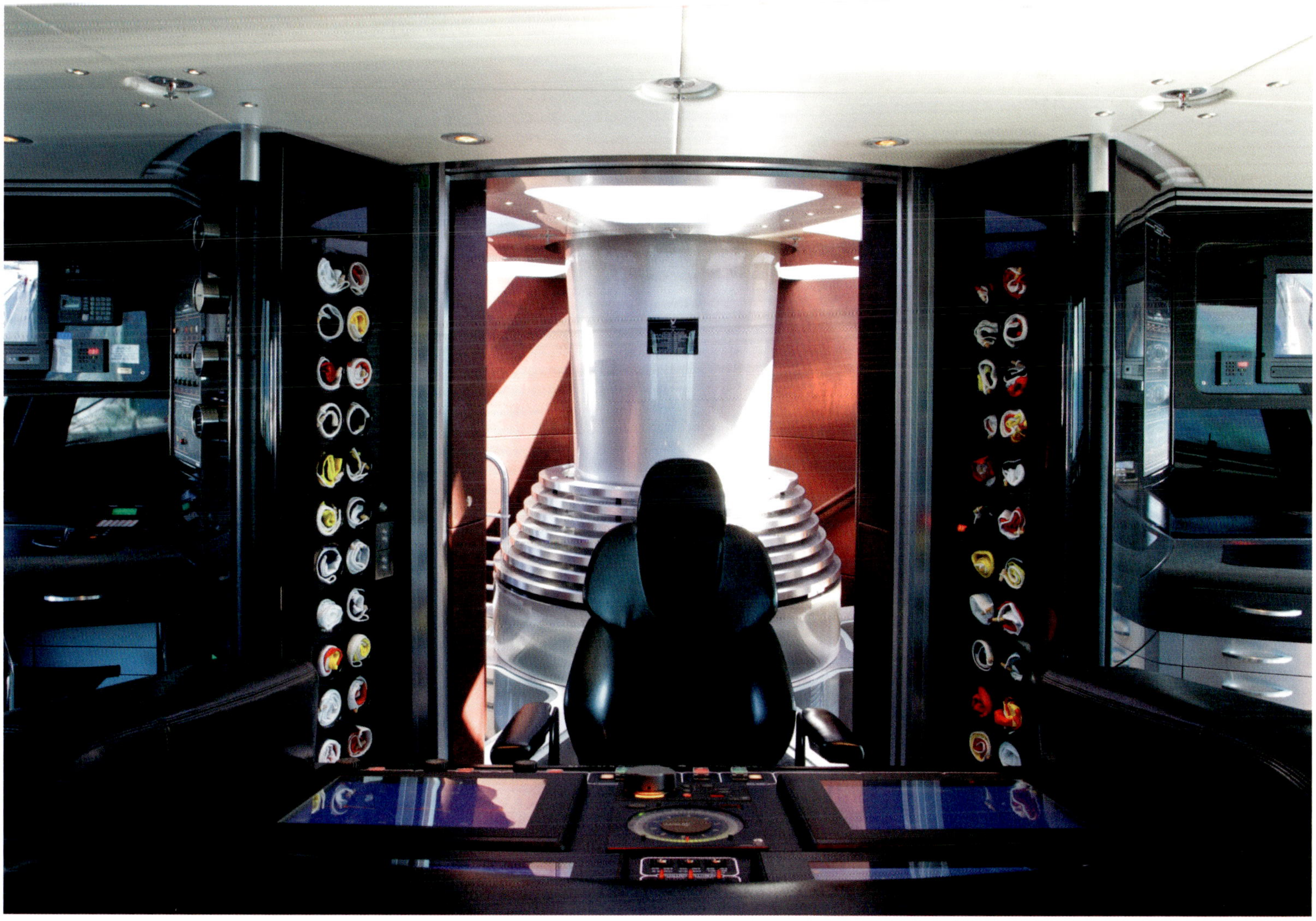

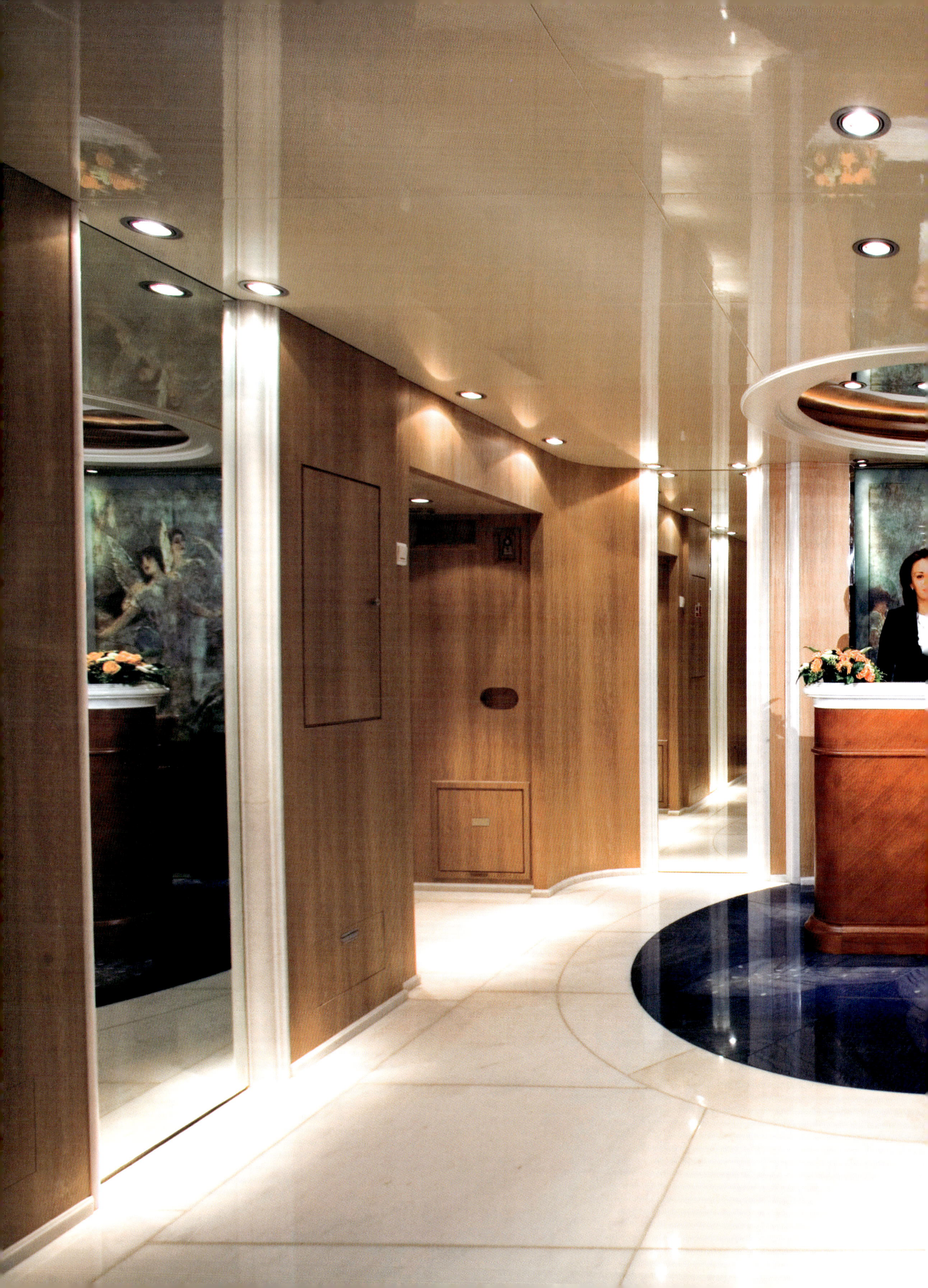

Alysia

LOA: 280' (85.3 m)
Beam: 47' 5" (14.44 m)
Draft: 13' 6" (4.15 m)
Naval architect: Alpha Marine
Exterior styling: Alpha Marine / Lally Poulias
Interior design: Alpha Marine / Lally Poulias / Sophia Dafnia
Builder / year: Neorion Shipyard, Greece / 2005
Top speed: 18 knots
Hull construction: Steel / Aluminium

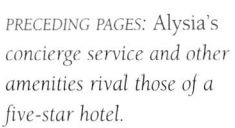

PRECEDING PAGES: Alysia's concierge service and other amenities rival those of a five-star hotel.

ABOVE LEFT: Entering service in 2005, Alysia is one of the two largest purpose-built charter yachts in the world. Her rate of 100,000 euros per day plus expenses and running costs is the highest of any charter yacht in the world.

ABOVE RIGHT: Her helicopter pad doubles as a sun lounge in the round.

Charging 100,000 euros a day, plus 25 percent more for running costs, *Alysia* and her sister ship, *Anneliesse*, are the two largest and most expensive yachts purpose-built for charter in the world. *Anneliesse* was the first of the two, coming into service in 2004, followed by *Alysia* in 2005. The yachts are structurally identical, but have some interior differences. As is often the case with the second in a series, small improvements were incorporated into *Alysia*. Both boats were designed and built within a two-and-a-half-year period at the cost of around $80 million each. Now of course, they would cost significantly more to build, well over $100 million. Both yachts were conceived by the late Greek Cypriot Andreas Liveras. In 2007 Liveras sold *Anneliesse* and retained *Alysia*.

To understand what makes *Alysia* a truly extraordinary charter yacht, one first has to know a little bit about the man who commissioned her. Andreas Liveras was an engaging, affable gentleman in his seventies who turned an avocation into a vocation. Yachting was a pleasure for him, but it also proved to be a viable business. Some yacht owners charter their yachts to defray a few of their maintenance costs or as a tax write-off—

ABOVE: The formal dining saloon accommodates all thirty-six guests in one sitting.

not Andreas Liveras. His company, Liveras Yachts, based in Monaco, is synonymous with successful big-boat charters. Of Greek origin, Liveras grew up on the island of Cyprus in a farming family. He proved to be quite the entrepreneur by his mid-twenties, when he put his house up as collateral and invested in a combine harvester—the first on the island—hiring himself and it out to neighbouring farms. His enormously expensive investment was beginning to pay off when one day he lost control of the machine and it plummeted off a cliff, falling three hundred feet into the sea. He escaped the same fate, but as he had not insured the machine, he lost his investment. He left Cyprus and headed for London to seek his fortune. He landed a modest job with Fleur de Lys Patisseries, earning about £8 a week selling cakes from the back of a van. Not wishing to work for someone else, he bought the company for £2,500, making weekly payments to pay off his investment. Over a period of nineteen years, he grew the company and sold it for $48 million. Frozen cakes were a novelty in those days and his frozen Black Forest gateaux were his ticket to success!

At fifty years old, Liveras retired and bought an 88-foot (26.8-metre) yacht, thinking he would sail around the world. The yacht wasn't big enough, however, and for that and other reasons the voyage did not materialize. A bit bored with all his leisure time, he invested in several more boats to fill up the hours and ended up refitting them and chartering them out. In the 1980s his first charter boat, a 138-footer (42.1-metre), went for US$4,000 a day. Liveras proceeded to buy, refit, charter and sell a series of well-known classic yachts, including *Haida G,* the former *Rosenkavalier*. He changed all of his boats' names to the names of his granddaughters: *Princess Tanya, Lauren, Annaliesse* and *Alysia*.

88 / OUTRAGEOUS YACHTS

His experience in the charter industry taught him to pay close attention to his clients' needs and desires. He determined that they wanted luxurious new boats that were fully equipped with all the latest bells and whistles, could sleep a lot of people, and were well run and safe. He saw that several of his clients were taking tandem charters because their parties could not be accommodated on one boat. Half of Liveras Yachts' clients are from the Middle East, and he has chartered to royal families who require luxe lodgings for their large extended families, as well as accommodations for nannies, security personnel, and perhaps a helicopter pilot or two. In the last ten years, Russian interest has burgeoned, and people in the Far East, including the Chinese, are now dipping into the charter market. Naturally, his clients also include a fair share of Americans and Europeans.

Liveras came to the conclusion that he needed a purpose-built charter boat to satisfy all of these demands. *Alysia* is a SOLAS-classed charter yacht, capable of taking thirty-six guests—in eighteen double cabins, all with en suite bathrooms—anywhere they want to go. SOLAS stands for Safety Of Life At Sea, and

TOP: *The sun lounge rivals the main saloons of many yachts smaller in size. Although open in plan, the furniture is arranged in a number of intimate groupings.*

ABOVE: *The commodious chairs in the sprawling media room are not likely to be found in any commercial cinema.*

OVERLEAF: *The spa is Alysia's crowning glory.*

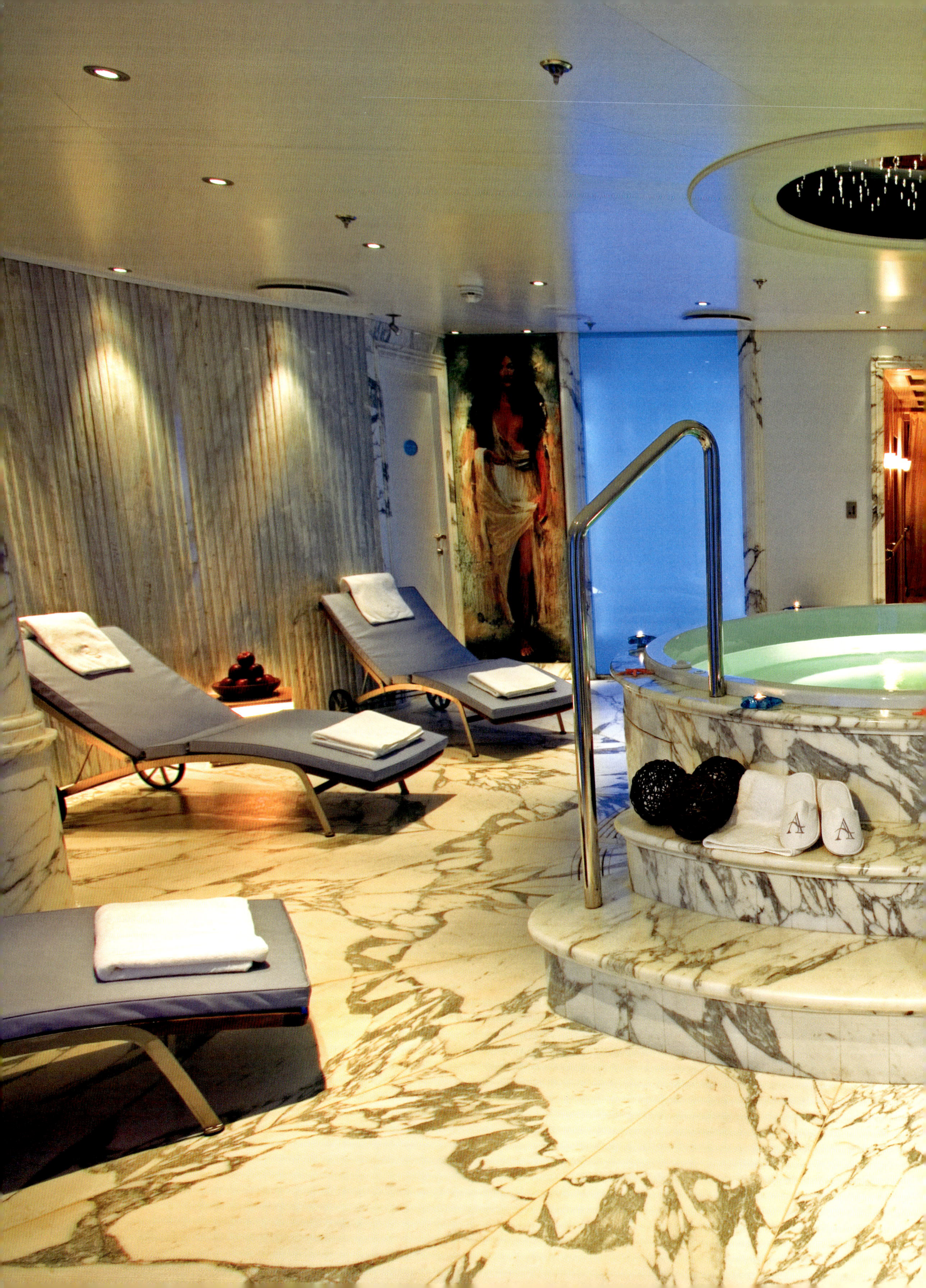

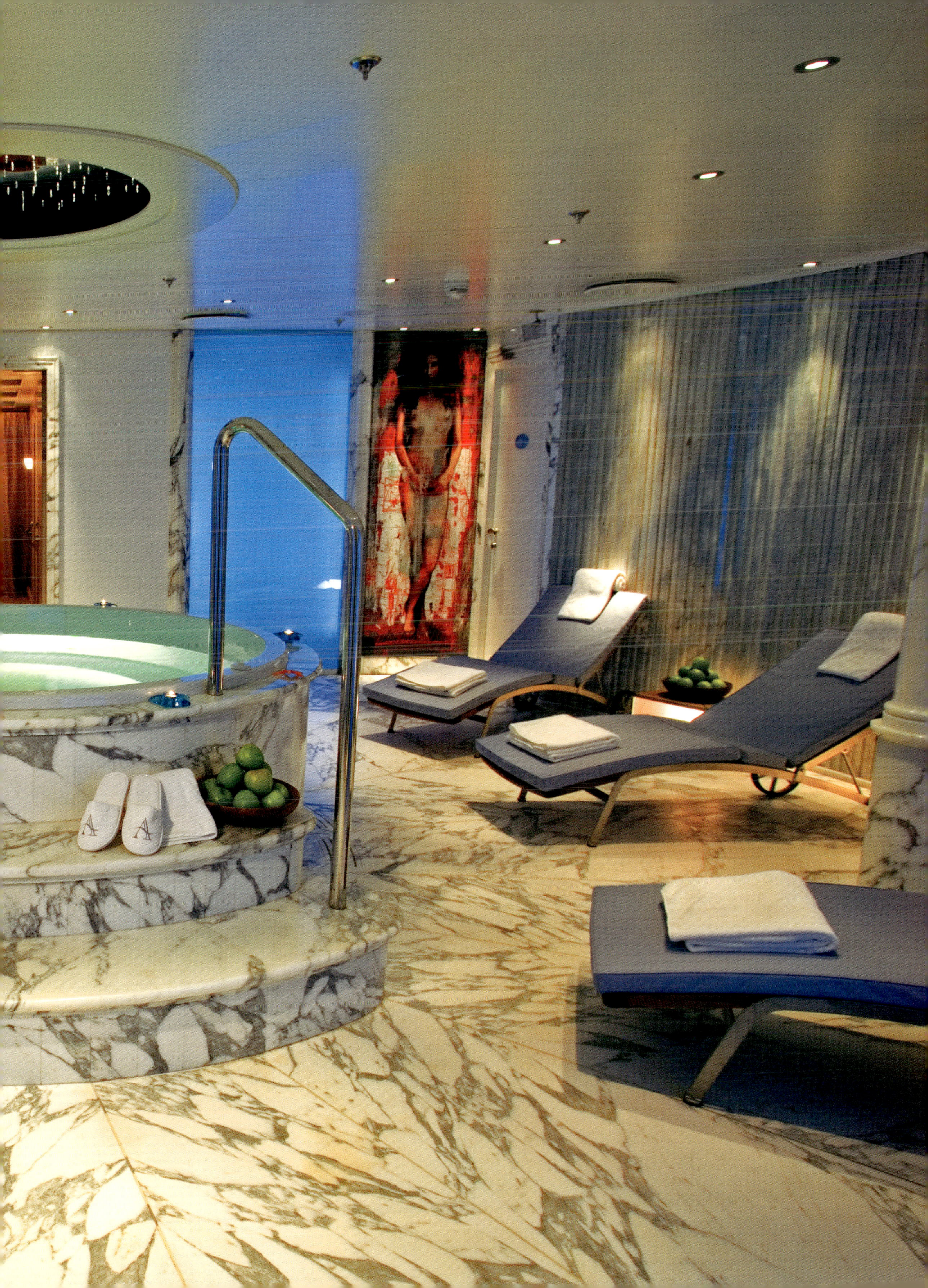

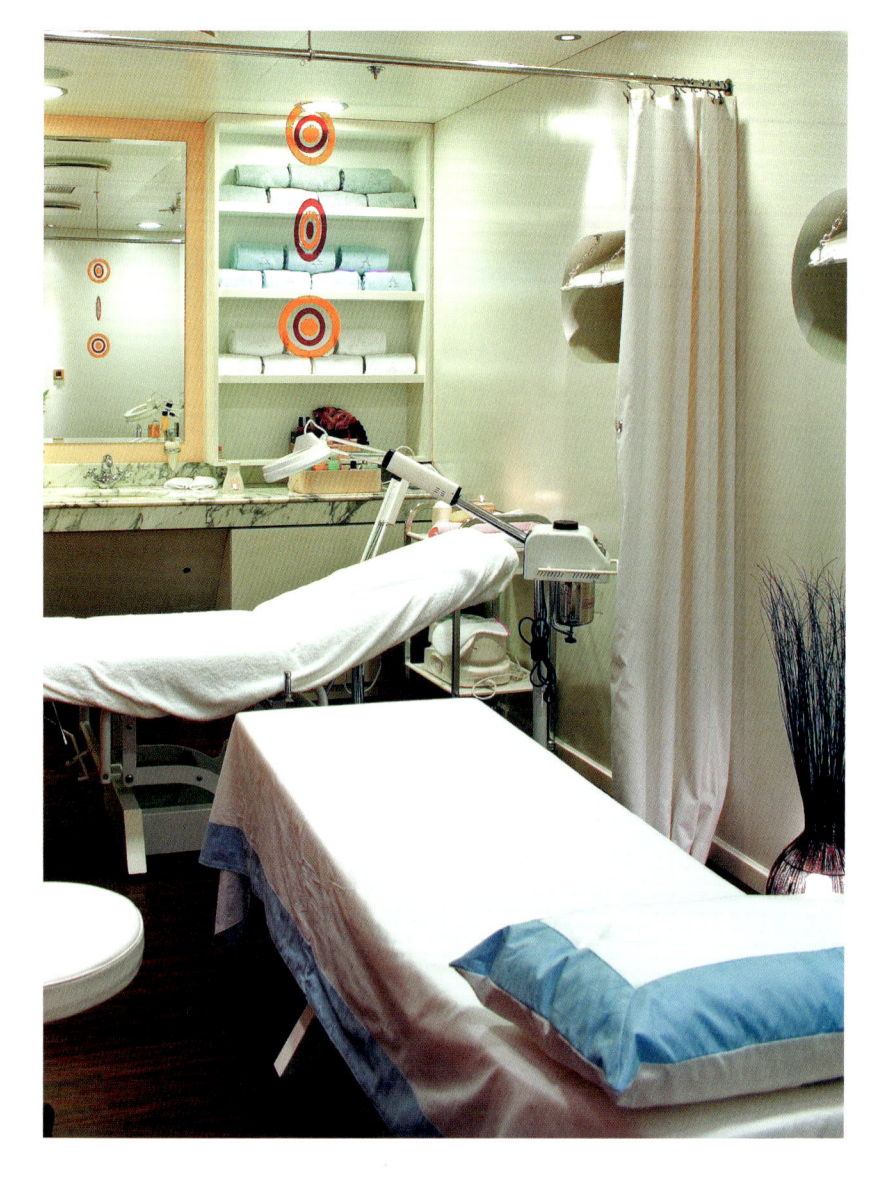

TOP: *The spa is equipped with treatment rooms for professional massage work and skin care.*

ABOVE: *The twin guest cabins can be converted into double bedrooms.*

SOLAS-classed boats are subject to many rules and regulations. For instance, there are strict guidelines about the necessity of fire-retardant and nonflammable materials. Perhaps that is why more marble than wood is used in the interior. This is not a cruise ship or a "head" boat; she can be rented only in her entirety, not by the cabin. The uninitiated may wonder about the benefits of chartering a yacht if one has the wherewithal to stay at the best hotels in the world. The short answer is that a yacht vacation is special. In addition to the prestige and the fun, a yacht offers the ultimate in privacy and luxury. Celebrities and other people in the public eye may worry about being hounded by fans or paparazzi in the public spaces of a hotel, whereas on a yacht like *Alysia,* not only is privacy assured but it is run almost like a hotel, complete with a concierge who sees to your every need. In addition to the well-appointed cabins, each with its own bathroom, there is a stunning master stateroom and a generous VIP cabin.

In the main saloon, large picture windows afford magnificent views. The room is decorated in neutral colours with custom-made carpets and sofas; the furniture is grouped in several conversation areas, making it equally comfortable for intimate tête-à-têtes and big parties. Off from the foyer, which is graced with impressive slabs of blue Brazilian marble, is an elevator that services all deck levels. The sky lounge features convivial seating and a bar; it leads out to the bridge-deck dining area, which has two tables that can seat forty people.

The sundeck has a large jacuzzi, a seating area forward, and a sun-lounging area aft, around the helipad. The yacht also features a cinema, beauty parlour, massage room, spa, and exercise room. With a crew of thirty-four, the ratio of staff to guests is nearly 1:1. The captain has his cadre of on-deck and engine-room support, the chef has his galley support, and there is a team of stewards and stewardesses. These people are the norm on any charter boat, but *Alysia* goes a step further; her on-board staff includes personal concierges, a sommelier, a beautician, a masseuse, a yoga instructor, a pianist, and a string quartet.

The pièce de résistance aboard *Alysia* is her spa, which resembles a Roman bath. The walls and soaking tub are covered in bright white marble with a hint of a grey vein. Four translucent panels placed at equidistant intervals around the room slowly shift though the colour spectrum, creating subtle changes of mood. Teak deck chairs with cushions and towels welcome de-stressing and lounging. Off the central room are men's and women's sauna and steam rooms, a cold plunge pool, locker rooms with showers, and Thai massage and beauty treatment rooms. The thalassotherapy bath is fitted out with massaging jets, and the Cleopatra bath offers seaweed wraps and aromatherapy. There is also a gym and a children's playroom.

More and more newly built yachts are incorporating all the luxury amenities that can be found in a five-star resort. Andreas Liveras's *Alysia* has set the trend. No doubt, there are even bigger yachts for charter on someone's drawing boards.

TOP: *Many of the guest rooms are arranged as a suite with their own lounge areas for a private morning coffee.*

ABOVE: *Alysia's bridge is on a scale similar to that of a small cruise ship.*

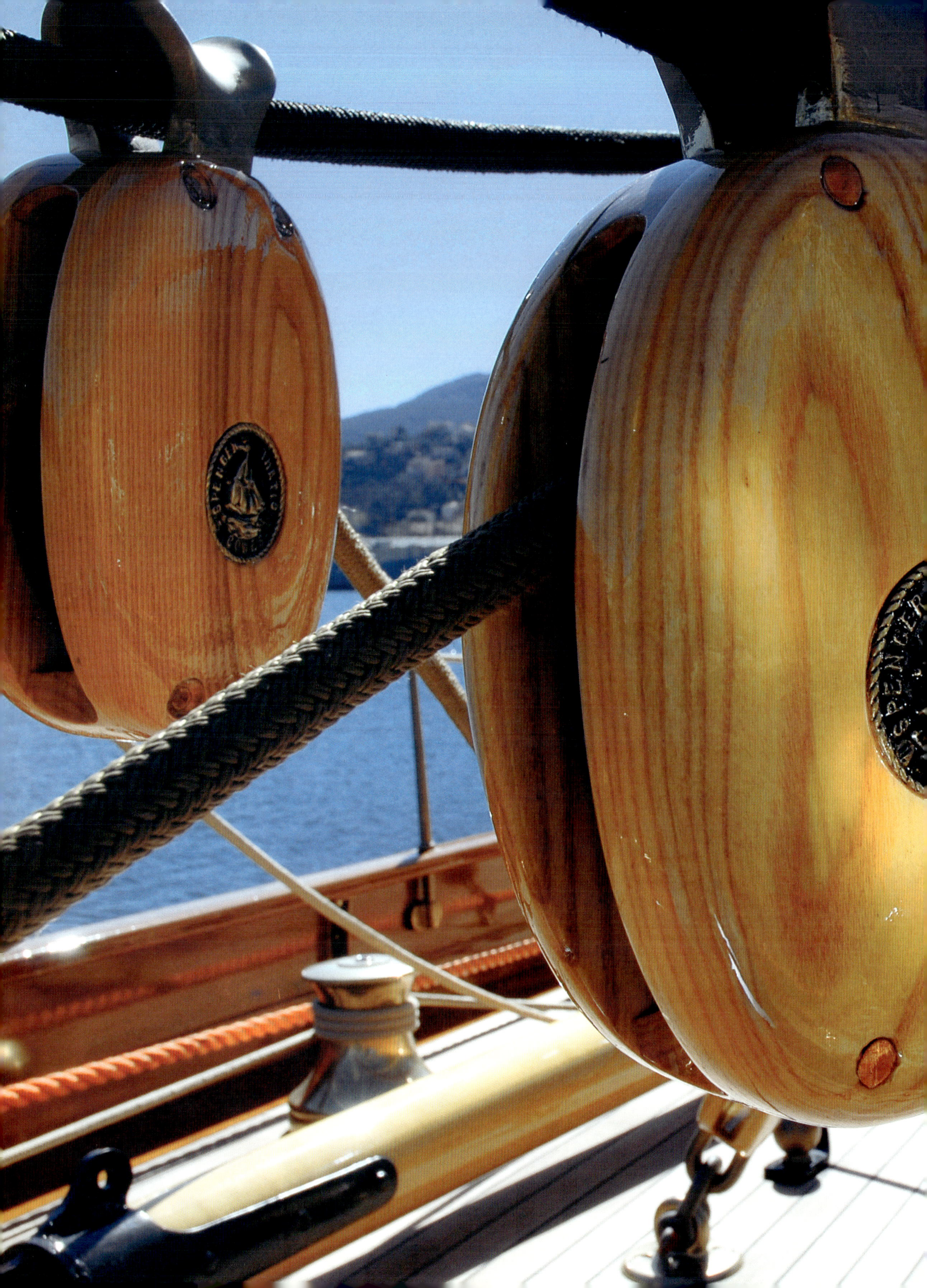

Lulworth

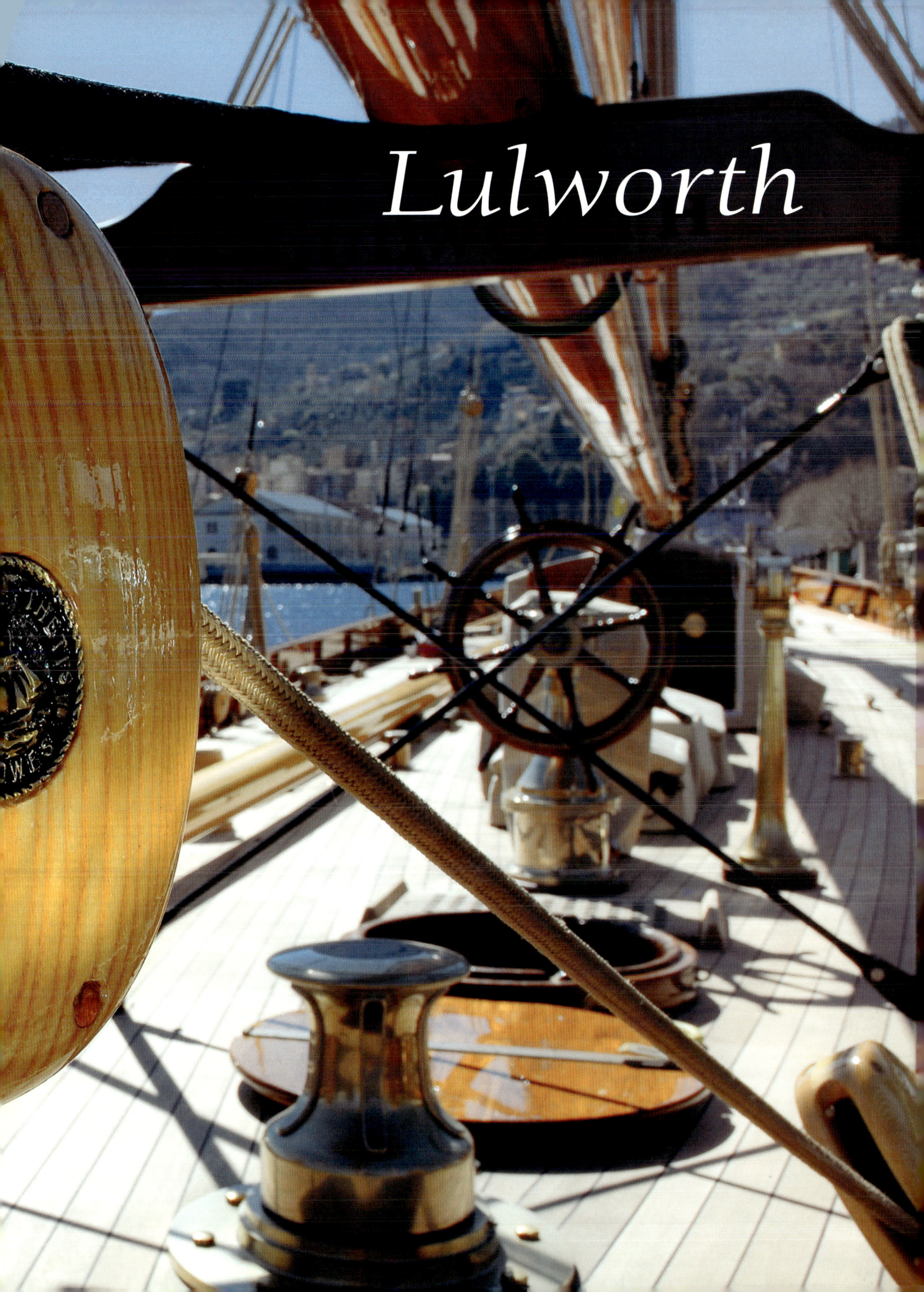

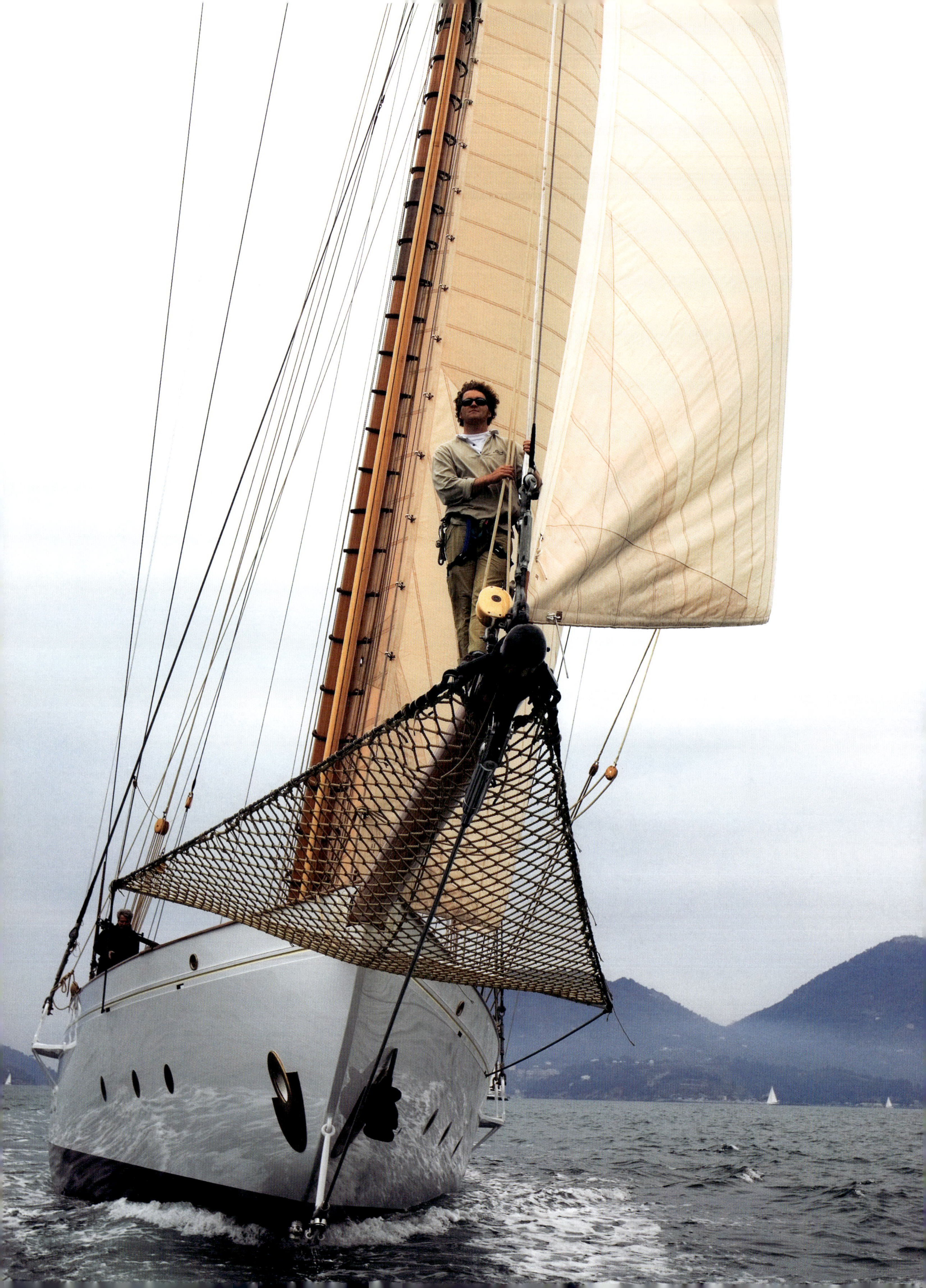

PRECEDING PAGES: *Lulworth's deck hardware has been painstakingly restored or re-created.*

OPPOSITE: *The bowsprit provides a great vantage point during sea trials.*

The saga of *Lulworth* and her resurrection as one of the world's most genuine restorations of a classic yacht is rich and complex. Originally built in 1920, her history speaks volumes. In fact, that history is meticulously recounted in Andrew Rogers's book *Lulworth, The Restoration of the Century*.

In 2006, after four-and-a-half years of courageous, painstaking effort, a dedicated owner and an extraordinary team of shipwrights, craftspeople, and artisans relaunched *Lulworth*. His Serene Highness Prince Albert II, who penned the introduction to Rogers's book, said, "In the case of *Lulworth*, an exceptional piece of maritime heritage has been brought back to life in an unprecedented manner. . . . She is one of the most authentic restorations ever undertaken."* In addition to being monarch of the Principality of Monaco, Prince Albert II is president of the Yacht Club de Monaco and himself an avid sailor who has often raced aboard the club's hundred-year-old classic yacht *Tuiga*.

At 152 feet (46.3 metres), *Lulworth* is the sole survivor of what was known as the "Big Five" from the so-called Big Class of the 1920s. The others were *Westward*, *White Heather II*, Sir Thomas Lipton's *Shamrock*, and the royal yacht *Britannia*. Between 1924 and 1930 *Lulworth* won 51 races and took 72 other flags. The advent of the J Class—based on the American Universal Rule—succeeded the Big Class and dominated the racing circuit of the 1930s, consigning the Big Five to reconfiguration, dismantling, or scuttling.

Lulworth was conceived by Richard H. Lee in 1919 and launched as *Terpsichore* in 1920. She was built at the White Brothers shipyard on the banks of the Itchen River east of Southampton. Lee's brief to the yard was to make her capable of beating *Britannia*. She was built in eight months, an absurdly short period of time by today's standards of superyacht construction. In her day, however, it was not uncommon for yachts to be completed in under a year; there were multitudes of master

ABOVE: *Original owner Richard Lee, left with Capt. Frederick Morse in the early 1920s.*

BELOW: *The yacht's hull was desperately in need of attention when she arrived at the Darsena Yard in 2001.*

---

* Andrew Rogers, *Lulworth, The Restoration of the Century: The World's Largest Gaff Cutter.* The Netherlands: Van den Bruele Holding BV, p. iii.

ABOVE LEFT: *After World War II, Lulworth was saved from destruction by Richard and Irene Lucas. They made the boat their full-time home.*

ABOVE: *Fully restored to her former glory in 2006, Lulworth competes in regattas once again.*

LEFT: *When the yacht was purchased by Herbert Weld in 1924, he painted the hull white.*

98 / OUTRAGEOUS YACHTS

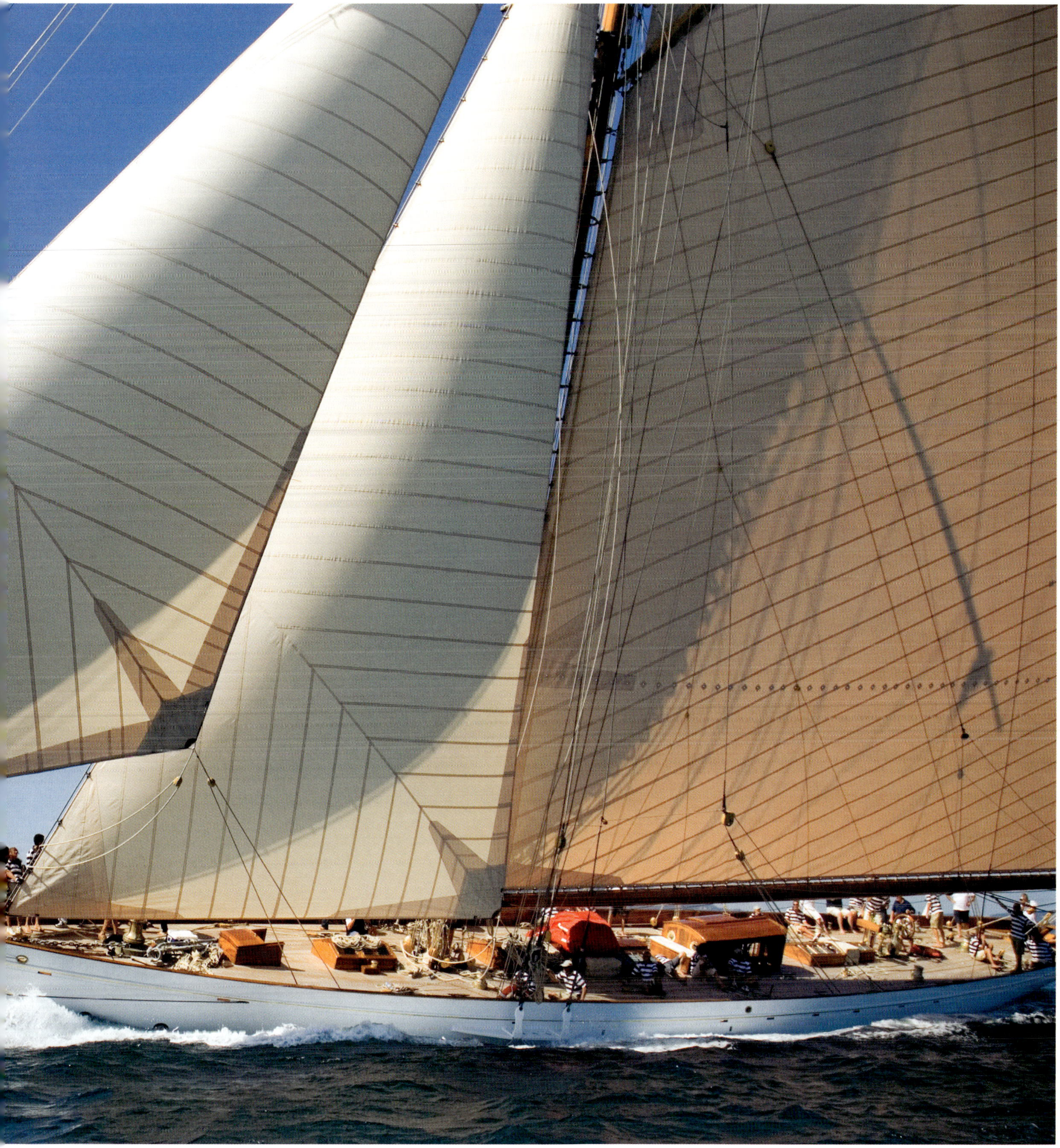

ABOVE: The main saloon is entirely original, from the skylights to the furniture.

LOA: 152' (46.3 m)
Beam: 22' (6.6 m)
Draft: 18' (5.5 m)
Naval architect: Herbert White
Exterior styling: N/A
Interior design: N/A
Builder / year: White Brothers, Southampton /1920
Restoration / year: Classic Yacht Darsena Yard, Viareggio, Italy / 2006
Hull construction: Honduran mahogany over steel frames

shipwrights and myriad platers, riveters, joiners, and other workers dedicated to the task. Large quantities of steel, timber, and other materials went into her build. Unfortunately, Lee died unexpectedly of a heart attack in 1924. His family sold the yacht to Herbert Weld of Lulworth Castle in Dorset, whereupon she was given the name she has carried ever since. Weld hailed from an illustrious yachting family. His grandfather Joseph and great-uncle James were founding members of The Yacht Club on the Isle of Wight, which became the famed Royal Yacht Squadron in 1833.

When Weld purchased the boat, he changed her hull colour from black to white. In 1925 he campaigned her successfully, placing in nearly every race he entered. The next year Sir Adam Mortimer Singer, a son of Isaac Merritt Singer, inventor of the home sewing machine, made Weld an offer he couldn't refuse. In 1928 Singer sold the yacht to Alexander Alan Paton, a member of an upwardly mobile cotton-marketing family in Liverpool. A bachelor, Paton sailed her with family and friends. (When *Lulworth*'s restoration was under way, anyone who had had anything to do with the boat was tracked down, including Paton's nieces, who remembered sailing with their uncle and were thrilled to board *Lulworth* some three-quarters of a century later.)

Paton decided not to convert her into a J Class, so she was retired from the racing circuit. In 1933, a year before his death, Paton sold her to Mary A. Beazley for about £8,000 sterling; for a brief time she was fitted out as a ketch and used for cruising instead of racing. In 1937 Carl Bendix bought her and installed her first propulsion engine, a 100-hp AEC six-cylinder diesel. Thwarted from a round-the-world voyage by World War II, she was consigned to a "mud berth" at the Camper & Nicholsons yard

ABOVE: The guest cabins look the same now as they did in the 1920s.

RIGHT: The companionway stairs provide elegant access to the accommodations.

in the south of England along with other pleasure yachts of distinction. In 1943 she was purchased sight unseen by Norman Hartly, but a German bombing raid hit her with debris and her mast was destroyed. The next owners, Richard and Irene Lucas, paid £3,000 for her in 1947, rescuing her from total demise, and brought her back to the White Brothers yard to be repaired. This adventurous couple decided to make her their full-time home. Richard died in 1968, but Irene continued to live aboard *Lulworth*, caring for her lovingly. After some forty years, however, she felt it was time to move ashore. Her pride and joy was in dire need of repair. The planking and deck woods had rotted and cement had been used to repair the gaps (this created a lot of problems during her restoration). Camper & Nicholsons' brokers purchased her for the Colombo-Vink family in 1990, and the boat was hauled to the famed

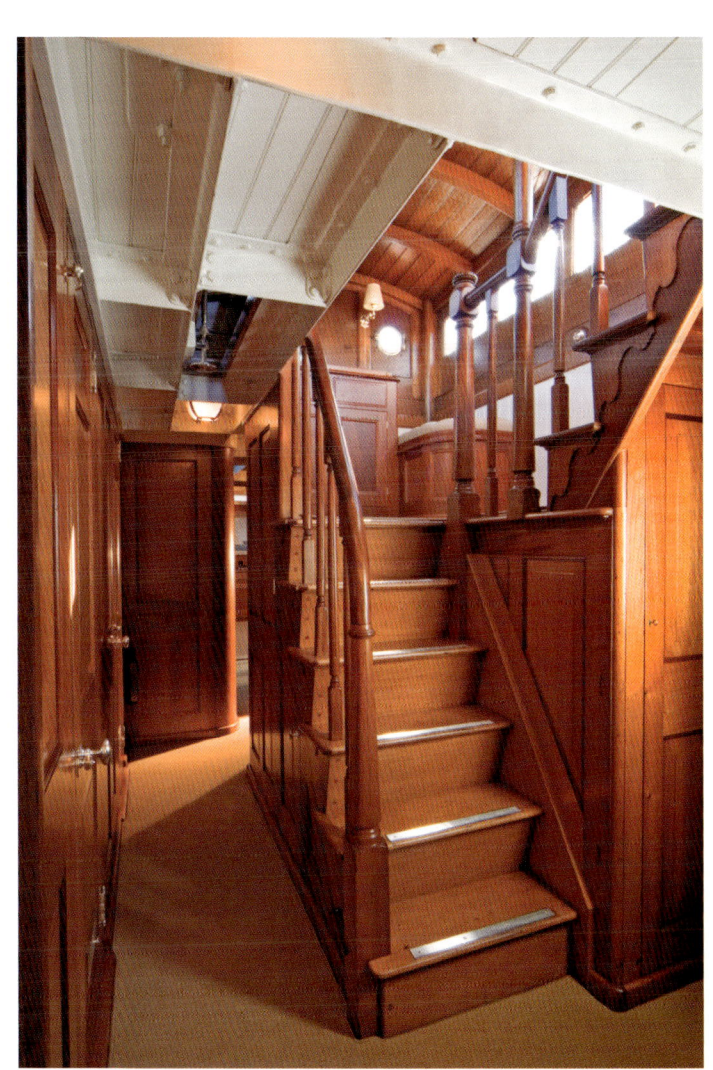

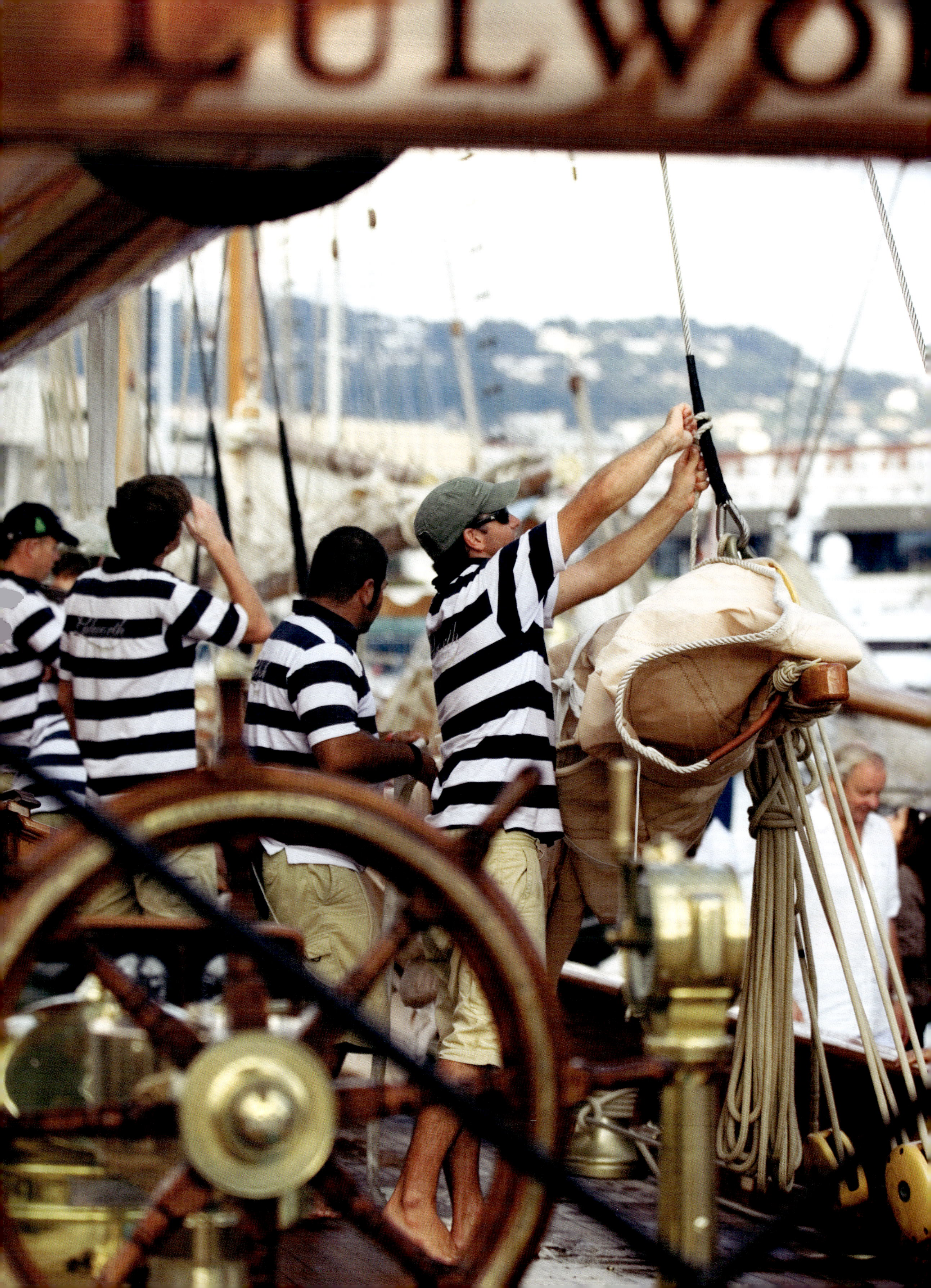

Beconcini Shipyard in Italy for the refit/rebuild. She had been all but dismantled when disputes arose among the owners, naval architects and shipyard. Apparently the costs for rebuilding her had become prohibitive. Lawyers became involved and all work ground to a halt.

In 2001 Giuseppe Longo discovered the remains of *Lulworth* by accident. Longo was the manager of the Classic Yacht Darsena Yard in Viareggio, Italy, which had been established to restore the 1939 *Iduna*—a ketch built by the De Vries Yard, which later joined forces with the Royal Van Lent Yard and became known as Feadship— for a Dutch gentleman, Johan J.M. van den Bruele. Having completed the restoration of *Iduna*, Longo was seeking another project. He went to the Beconcini yard to see a 72-foot (22-metre) cutter, but espied *Lulworth* in her skeletal state. She had been reduced to a "rib cage of symmetrical steel clad with acres of Honduran mahogany."** Based on his gut reaction to the sheer aesthetics of her hull shape, Longo brought van den Bruele to see the yacht. The two researched her pedigree, discovered her historic significance, and spent months negotiating her purchase with the many feuding parties.

Van den Bruele was the ideal owner to take on this monumental project. He had the perspicacity, tenacity and resources to restore her to her original state. A perfectionist, he had found the perfect manager in Longo, who shared his vision that the resurrection of *Lulworth* was not to be a mere *rebuild* but a bona fide *restoration*. They moved the boat to the Darsena yard and began their labour of love by hiring the best craftsmen from all over the world. The four-and-a-half year process was tantamount to a major archaeological dig. There were six containers at the yard filled with boat parts, furniture, cabinets, skylights, deck boxes, hardware, and bits and pieces. A worldwide search began for information and artifacts. Decisions were made as to what was salvageable and what was not. The results of this labour-intensive project can be seen on the pages of this book.

The classic *Lulworth* is the antithesis of the modern innovative sailing yacht *The Maltese Falcon* (see pages 74–83), also completed in 2006, yet both yachts possess a wow factor that is unsurpassed. And they have other key factors in common: dedicated owners, a team of extraordinary builders and craftspeople, and the power of passion and dedication.

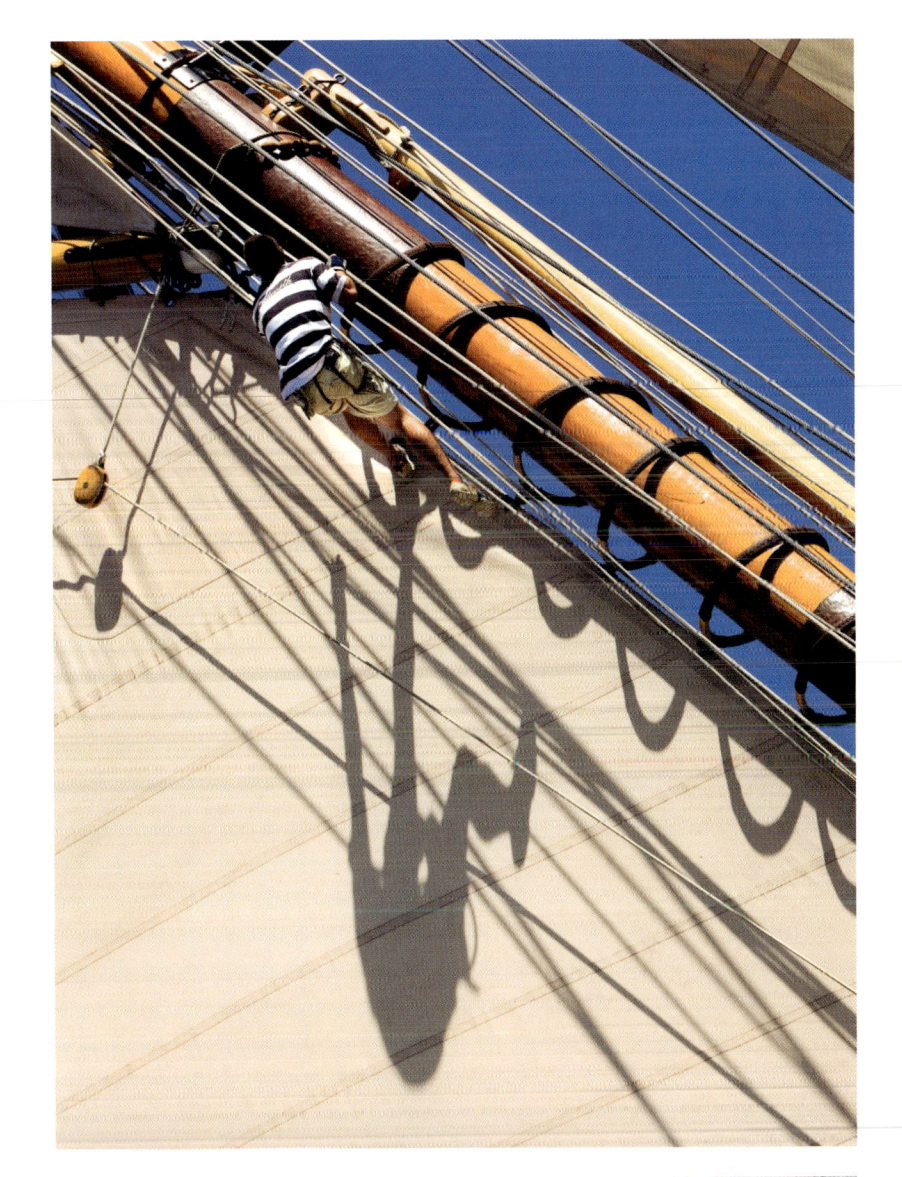

** Ibid., p. 179.

OPPOSITE: *The crew prepares for a day of racing at the Cannes Régate Royale.*

TOP: *A crewman tends to an issue up the rig in Le Grazie, Italy.*

ABOVE: *The crew quarters are typical of those on all racing yachts, both classic and modern.*

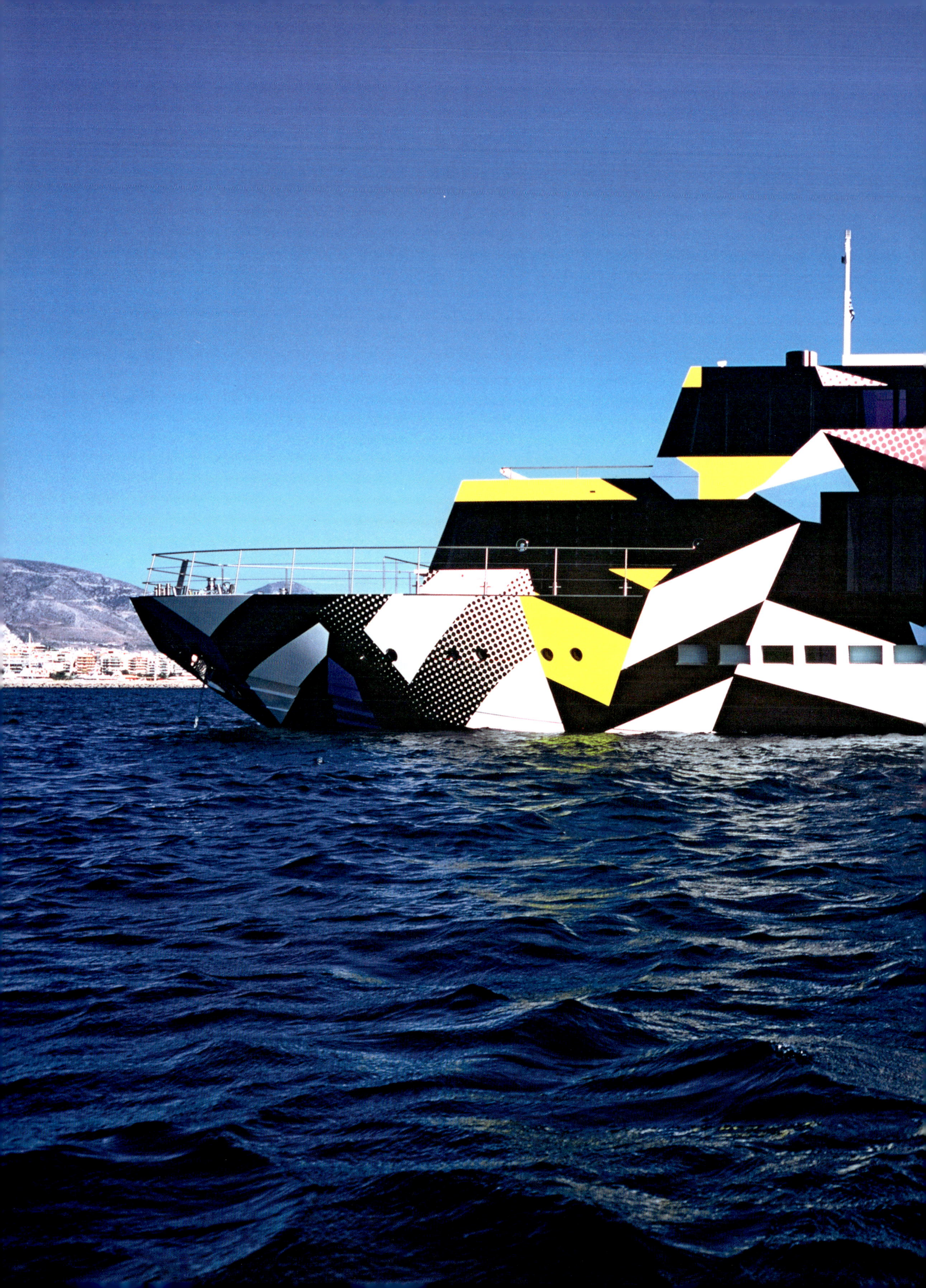

Guilty

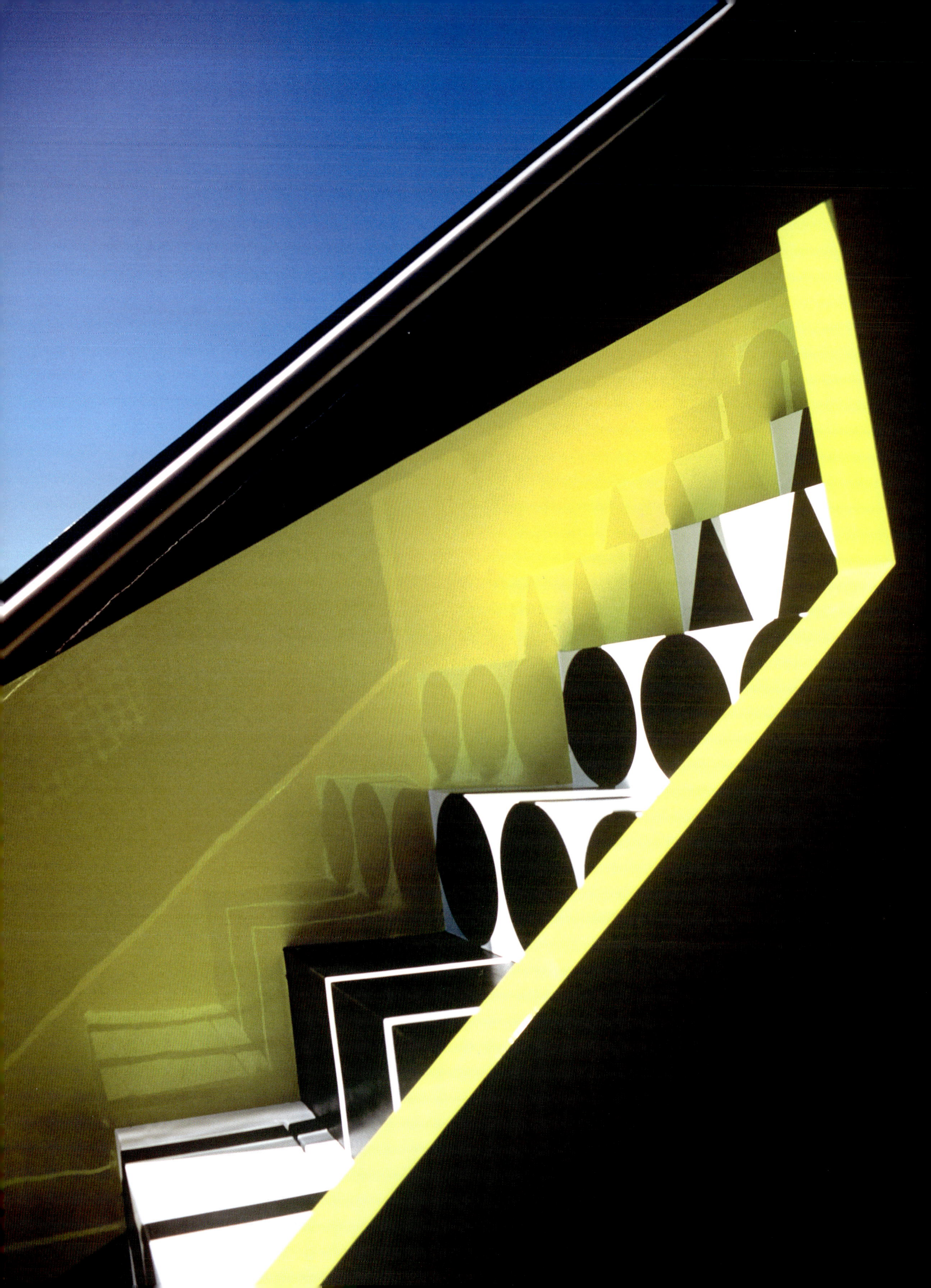

PRECEDING PAGES: *Artist Jeff Koons painted Guilty's exterior to resemble a 3-D Roy Lichtenstein painting, but it also harks back to early-twentieth-century warship camouflage.*

OPPOSITE: *The Ben-day Dot pattern taken from Lichtenstein is evident on the staircase.*

TOP: *The protected exterior aft deck offers both lounging and dining options.*

ABOVE: *The dining table in the main saloon, designed by Fernando Campana and manufactured by Edra, is made from Colorflex glass and reflects the water.*

What do you get when you cross a contentious, playful, pop contemporary artist such as Jeff Koons with Zen contemplative Italian designer Ivana Porfiri? Well, it's not a 43-foot (13-metre) topiary sculpture of a West Highland Terrier comprised of varietal flowers;* nor is it a yoga meditation retreat. What you get is *Guilty*, one of the wildest looking yachts of all time. In fact, she looks more like a floating 3-D Roy Lichtenstein painting than a yacht.

Dakis Joannou, one of Europe's leading collectors of contemporary art, is the forward thinking yacht owner who commissioned *Guilty*. A Greek Cypriot industrialist based in Greece, Joannou collects works by a wide range of international artists, including Jeff Koons, Liza Lou, Joseph Kosuth and Takashi Murakami. Purportedly, nothing in Joannou's collection predates 1985—the year he first viewed Koons's *Three Ball Total Equilibrium Tank*—three basketballs semisubmerged in a tank half full of distilled water.

A true art enthusiast, Joannou enjoys living with his artwork as much as, if not more than, exhibiting it to the public. His new 116-foot (35.3-metre) tri-deck yacht, *Guilty*, provides the perfect opportunity for him to live with—and in—art catered specifically to his taste. Joannou must have had a lot of fun conceiving *Guilty*. She is completely unconventional, from her eye-catching exterior paint job to her unusual external styling and unboat-like interior. This yacht was built in Italy at Cantieri Navali Rizzardi, a yard that builds a wide range of pleasure yachts, but never one quite like *Guilty*. Both the hull and the superstructures are made of the composite material GRP. Her two engines (MTU 16V 4000M90) allow her to reach a maximum speed of 29 knots.

Ivana Porfiri, who has designed fourteen yachts in addition to numerous private and commercial spaces, was responsible for both the exterior and interior styling. Porfiri specializes in "sensorial and perceptive aspects of spaces and objects." She says of *Guilty*, "The boat architecture is generated by an overlap of blocks, organized vertically and horizontally around a path, guiding the boat life and the travel experience. [In keeping with the overall look] . . . the external lines are squared, sharp, instead of rounded." Talk about thinking outside the box—well here, boxes figure heavily in the master scheme. White boxes to be precise—the traditional showcase for exhibiting art. Throughout the boat the floors are white Corian and the walls and ceilings are painted white. Porfiri incorporated works in Dakis Joannou's collection into every corner of these white boxes, from Anish Kapoor's sculpture to the

---

* On view outside of the Guggenheim Museum in Bilbao since 1997.

LOA: 115' 10" (35.3 m)
Beam: 24' 4" (7.4 m)
Draft: 7'2" (2.2 m) max
Naval architect: Arrabito Naval Architects
Exterior styling: Ivana Porfiri, Porfiristudio
 (assistant Paola Gorla) / Jeff Koons
Interior design: Ivana Porfiri, Porfiristudio
 (assistant Paola Gorla)
Builder / year: Cantieri Navali Rizzardi, Sabaudia, Italy / 2008
Top speed: 29 knots
Hull construction: composite material GRP

ABOVE LEFT: An internal staircase with large windows provides glimpses of the water.

ABOVE RIGHT: The state-of-the-art pilothouse is the one no-nonsense area of the boat.

OPPOSITE, TOP AND BOTTOM: The inner walls of the office in the master suite are lined with mirrored stainless-steel panels that reflect external images day and night.

Campana brothers' and Karim Rashid's furnishings to video art by Nathalie Djurberg. *Guilty* is a virtual gallery on the high seas.

Jeff Koons was brought in to paint the exterior. The painting is a type of camouflage. Although it looks modern, this technique was invented in World War I to impede the enemy from determining a ship's type, size, distance, speed, and direction. It was called the Razzle Dazzle effect and remained efficacious until the advent of sonar and radar. The exterior painting additionally owes its inspiration to two specific icons of pop culture. Art aficionados will recognize that Koons is paying homage to the late great pop artist Roy Lichtenstein. Known for his Ben-day Dots style, Lichtenstein himself had painted *Young America,* a 1995 entry in the America's Cup. When you view *Guilty* from above, you will notice a silhouette of another one of Koons's idols, singer Iggy Pop. Porfiri says, "The exterior colours and design chosen by [Koons] have succeeded in their mission; they provoke both positive and negative comments, but either way it's a great conversation piece and opens a new page in yacht design."

Guilty has three decks. The lowest accommodates four guest cabins: one VIP cabin, two twin cabins, and a smaller single cabin near the staircase. In one of the guest cabins, artist David Shrigley covered the walls with some of his darkly witty drawings in black acrylic paint while the boat was under construction. In another is a work entitled *Eclipse,* which artist Ricci Albenda created specifically for the space. In the VIP cabin Sarah Morris's painting *Guilty,* purchased after Jouannou had named the boat, has pride of place over the bed.

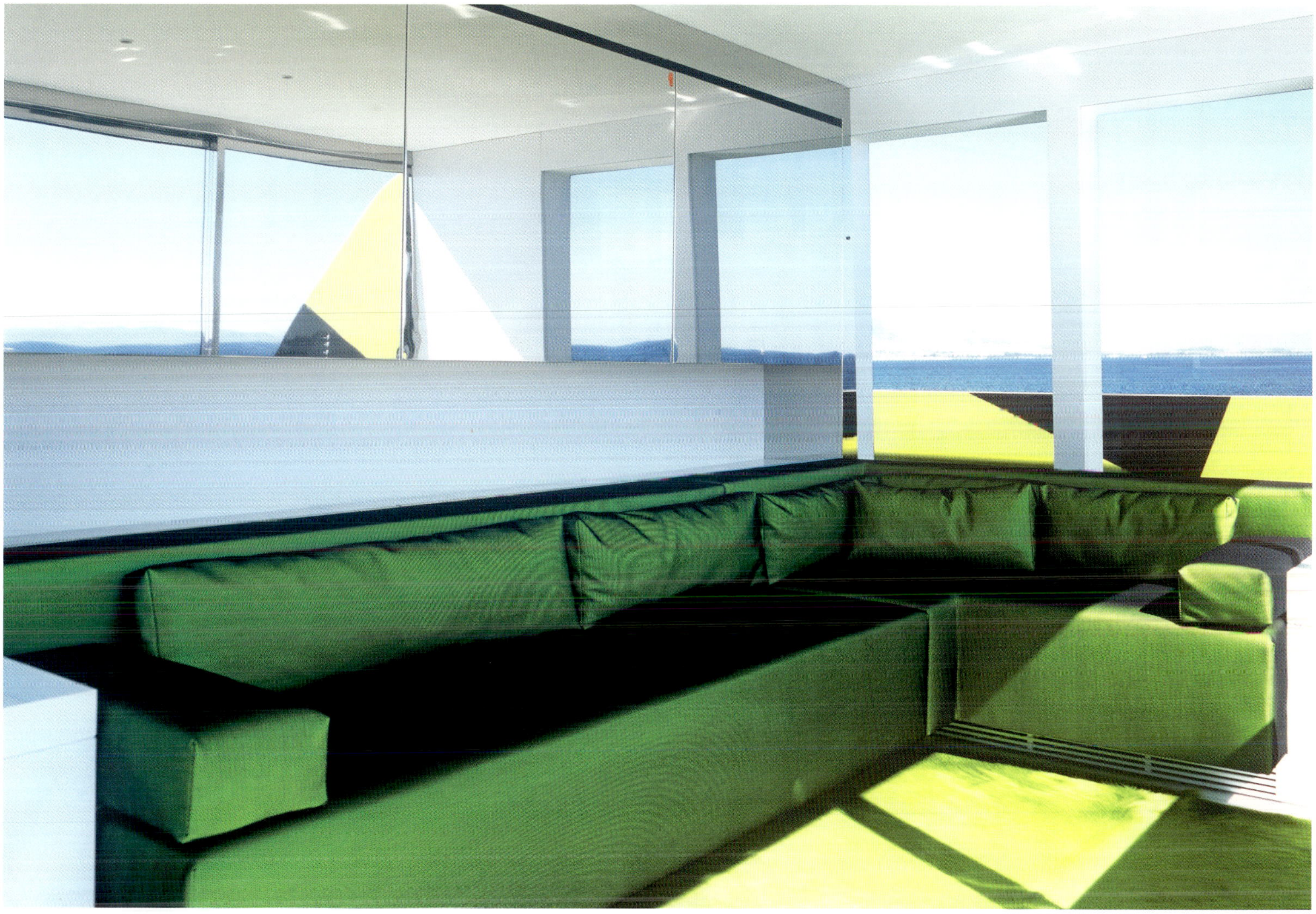

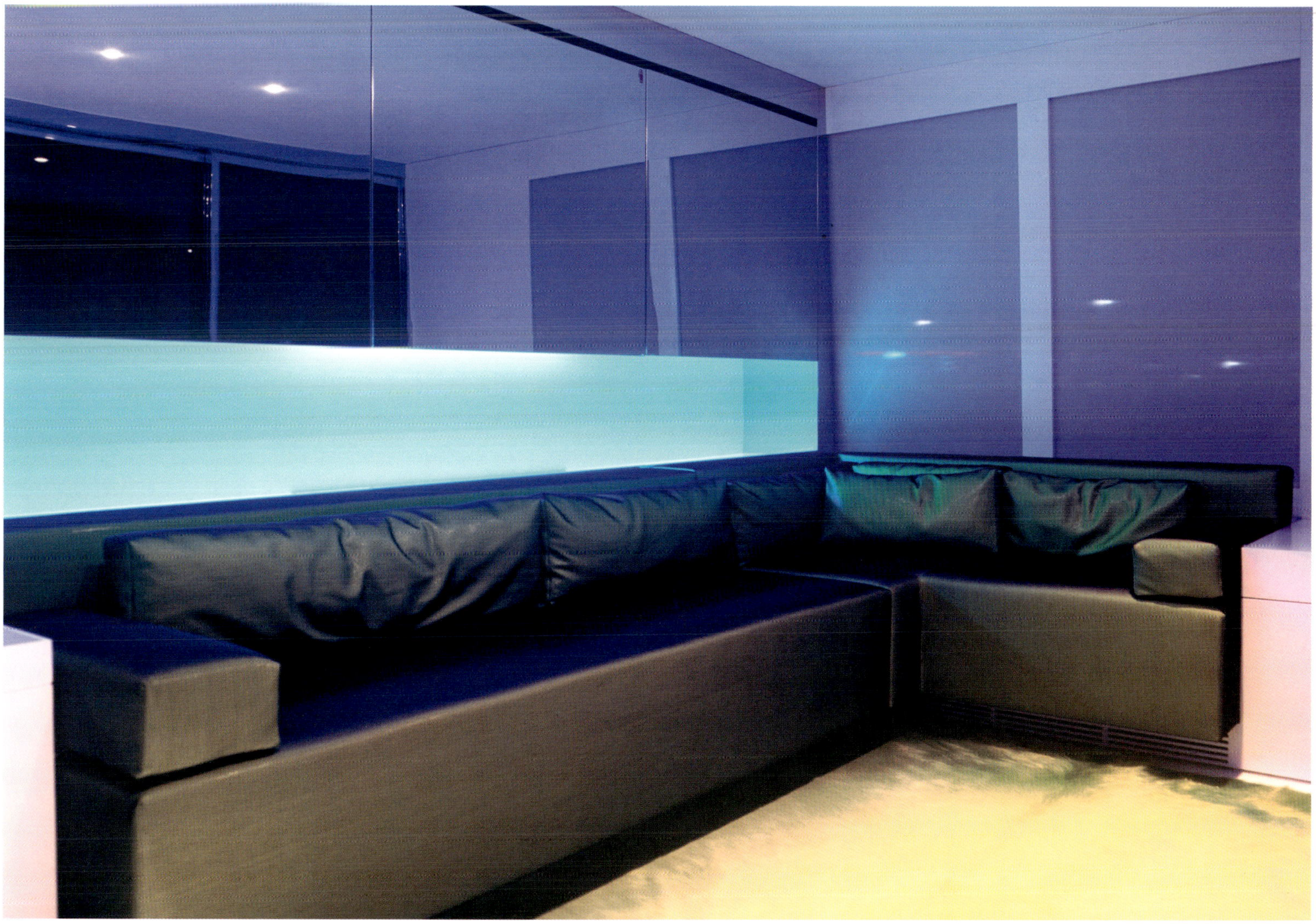

ABOVE: *The focal point of the main saloon is Anish Kapoor's Crate, a circular concave dish composed of hexagonal mirror tiles.*

RIGHT: *The design aesthetic carries through the entire yacht, including the crew mess.*

ABOVE: Like the mirrored wall panels in the owner's suite, the bathroom also has a shimmery reflective surface.

In the main saloon, or lounge, on the main deck, floor-to-ceiling windows provide sweeping views of the surroundings whether the boat is under way or at anchor. And the lack of side decks makes the panorama all the more expansive. The focal point of the room is Anish Kapoor's *Crate*, a circular concave dish composed of hexagonal mirror tiles that reflect the surrounding space and views in reverse. Forward of the saloon is the service zone: galley, pantry, day toilet, and wheelhouse. The owner's master suite occupies the entire upper deck. His cabin has a king-size bed, a 180-degree view and an office. The inner walls of this area are lined with mirrored stainless-steel panels so that the external images are continuously reflected inside. The featured artwork here is Martin Creed's *Feelings,* a neon tube that pulses and flickers, changing colour and rhythm day and night. The aft office opens onto the upper aft deck through large sliding doors. The upper aft deck offers dining and lounging options. With all the visual stimulus, it is hard to imagine just kicking back on this yacht, but to each his own. Owner Joannou has made a huge statement in the yachting world and there is no reason whatsoever for him to feel guilty about it.

112 / OUTRAGEOUS YACHTS

OPPOSITE, TOP AND BOTTOM LEFT: *The guest cabins reflect designer Porfiri's "white boxes" theme. The drawings on the wall and window shade are by artist David Shrigley.*

OPPOSITE, BOTTOM RIGHT: *Like some of the bedrooms, this guest bathroom is white with splashes of intense colour.*

ABOVE: *Martin Creed's* Feelings, *a neon tube that constantly changes colour and rhythm, has pride of place in the master suite.*

RIGHT: *Sarah Morris's painting* Guilty *hangs in the VIP cabin. It was purchased after the name of the boat had already been chosen.*

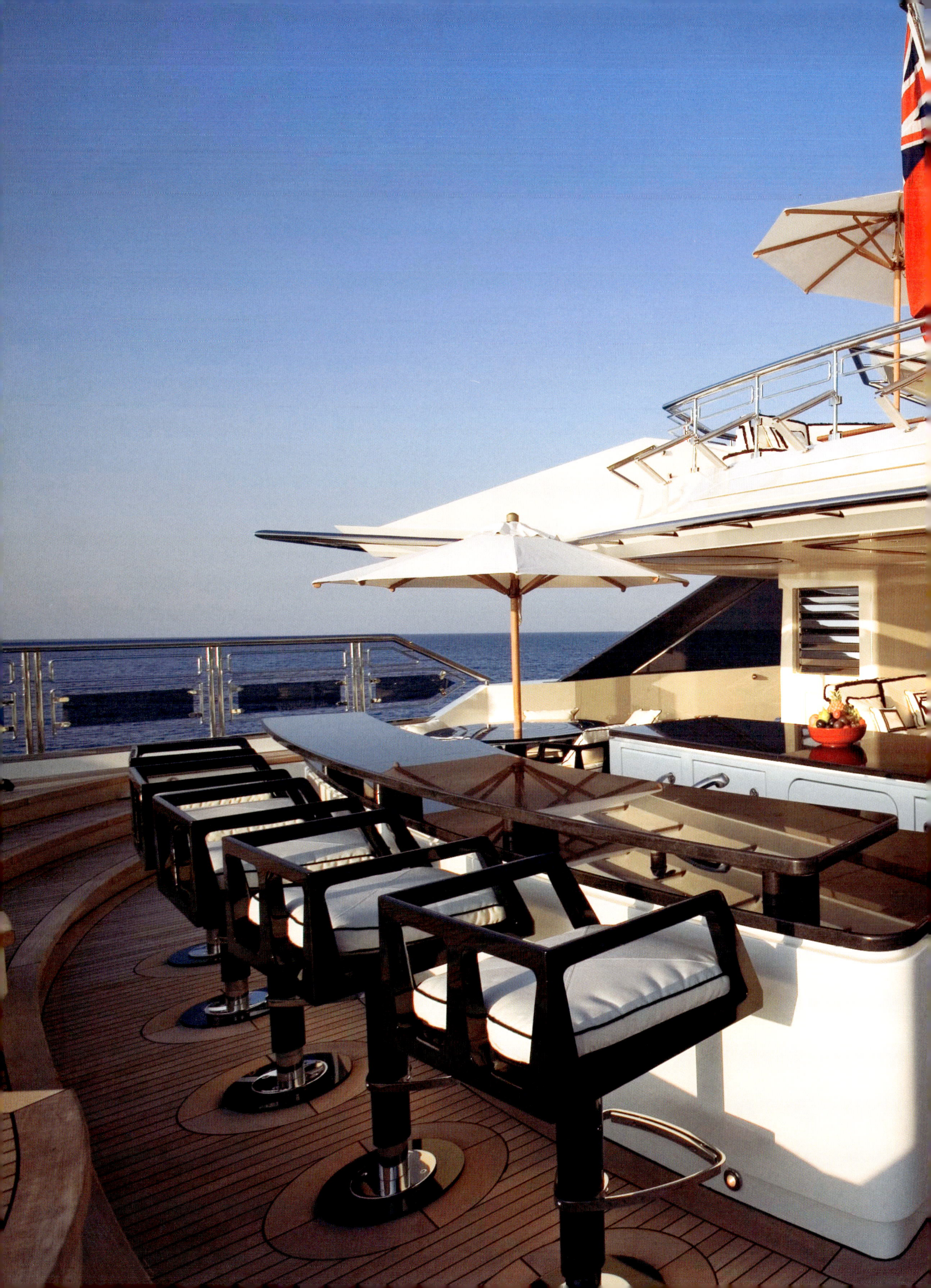

Alfa Nero

ALFA NERO
GEORGE TOWN

RIGHT: *Retractable balconies over the water have become de rigueur on yachts. They open otherwise closed spaces to the fresh salt air and natural light.*

Alpha is the first letter in the Greek alphabet, the equivalent of "A." It also designates the brightest and main star in a constellation. From Alpha we can extrapolate Alfa, and the motoryacht *Alfa Nero* is certainly a star wherever she journeys. The whole package is striking, but it is the yacht's infinity swimming pool that generates the immediate wow factor.

Following her launch in May 2007, the buzz on the world yachting circuit was that she was the "yacht of the year" in much the same way as the *Maltese Falcon* was the breakthrough yacht of the previous year. The owner, a Greek shipping magnate and businessman, also happens to own the yard that built her—Oceanco in Alblasserdam, Holland. He conceived *Alfa Nero* after owning a long succession of yachts. He worked closely with Nuvolari and Lenard, an innovative design team based in Venice, Italy. Their goal was to achieve a low-volume superstructure and at the same time incorporate two major requirements: a helicopter pad and a sizable, state-of-the-art "swim-in-place" pool. These are not unusual requests in the realm of mega-yachts; what makes this yacht unique, however, is the remarkable execution of the two items.

PRECEDING PAGES AND OPPOSITE: *Alfa Nero was designed to make the most of the sun-drenched Mediterranean lifestyle. In many ways, the expansive outdoor aft main deck is the heart and soul of the yacht.*

The 23' x 11' 5" (7 x 3.5 m) pool is located aft on the main deck, offering a transparent view through a waterfall transom. The effect, according to designer Dan Lenard, is "to connect life onboard to the sea." Most motoryachts have multiple, tiered deck levels that form a high profile resembling a wedding cake. But *Alfa Nero*'s swimming pool is situated on the main deck, where one would ordinarily find a U-shaped settee surrounded by raised coaming and protected by the overhang of an upper deck. The lack of an overhead deck creates a stunningly sleek, low profile.

The swimming pool can be filled with salt water, if thallasotherapy is desired, or (stored) fresh water, if the guests prefer, in only thirty minutes. The water that spills over the pool's edges is drained to a balance tank and then routed back to the pool. When the water is completely drained, the pool serves its second purpose. The teak floor, emblazoned with a large "H," rises up flush with the main deck and turns into a helicopter pad. A rim seal closes off the 8,321 gallons (31,500 litres) of water. An engineering marvel, the movement of the platform is operated not by levers or hydraulic cylinders but by electrically powered spindles that prevent it from collapsing under the weight of a helicopter.

Forward on the main deck is an expansive entertainment area with chaise longues, a complete bar, and a seating area for alfresco dining. Similar to restaurants such as Club 55 in St. Tropez and Eden Roc in St Barth's, the outside decks on Alfa Nero are equipped with an ingenious misting system that is cleverly incorporated into the stainless-steel railings that line the overhangs from the upper deck.

Alfa Nero boasts more than 4,000 square feet (371.6 square metres) of living and entertaining space. You enter the full-beam saloon from the pool/main deck, and when the glass doors are fully open you have a fabulous sensation of indoor/outdoor living. The decor is both Art Deco and contemporary. For lounging there are vanilla-coloured sofa and armchairs upholstered in Edelman leather and goatskin, their frames inlaid with mother-of-pearl and dark wood. The custom-made, coffee-and-cream-coloured carpet features a delicate geometric pattern. Handcrafted, highly polished stainless-steel lamps add an artful accent. In fact, art plays a big part in Italian designer Alberto Pinto's scheme. The jet-black grand piano in a corner of the saloon is decorated with a white, wavelike design; Picasso-like figures grace its legs. It is one of only eight ever produced.

The guest accommodations for twelve include one master suite, two double VIP cabins, two double guest cabins, and one twin stateroom. The upper deck is given over entirely to the master residence, which includes a study, a king-size sleep room, a bathroom with steam shower and Jacuzzi, walk-in wardrobes, a sky lounge with plasma TV and surround sound, a dining room, and even a private patio with a hot tub that is not visible or accessible from any other point on the yacht.

The two VIP suites are lavishly decorated and furnished. The "red" suite, on the main deck, offers a fully carpeted bedroom and lounge. At the starboard beam is a seating area with two couches and a coffee table. In the centre is a desk and computer workspace, while on the opposite beam is the king-size berth and doublewide walk-in closet. The "green" suite, of equal size and amenities, is located on the lower deck, as are the regular guest staterooms. Every book in the library of the green suite sports a green cover. The colour schemes in the other rooms are carried through just as meticulously.

Alfa Nero has three separate dining areas, a glass-enclosed elevator, a theatre lounge, a dance floor, a gym, a beauty salon, and a master-suite veranda. The materials used in the interior include Italian marble for the bathrooms, goatskin for wall panels, Edelman leather

OPPOSITE, TOP: *The Macassar ebony walls of this lounge are inlaid with circles of zebrano wood.*

OPPOSITE, BOTTOM: *The whimsically decorated Pleyel grand piano in the main saloon is one of only eight ever produced.*

TOP: *The galley is as well equipped as some hotel kitchens.*

BOTTOM: *Retractable walls open the intimate upper-deck dining saloon to the elements.*

OVERLEAF: *The 269-foot (82-metre) Alfa Nero forsakes the stacked, wedding-cake profile of many modern motoryachts in favour of a sleeker, more aggressive look.*

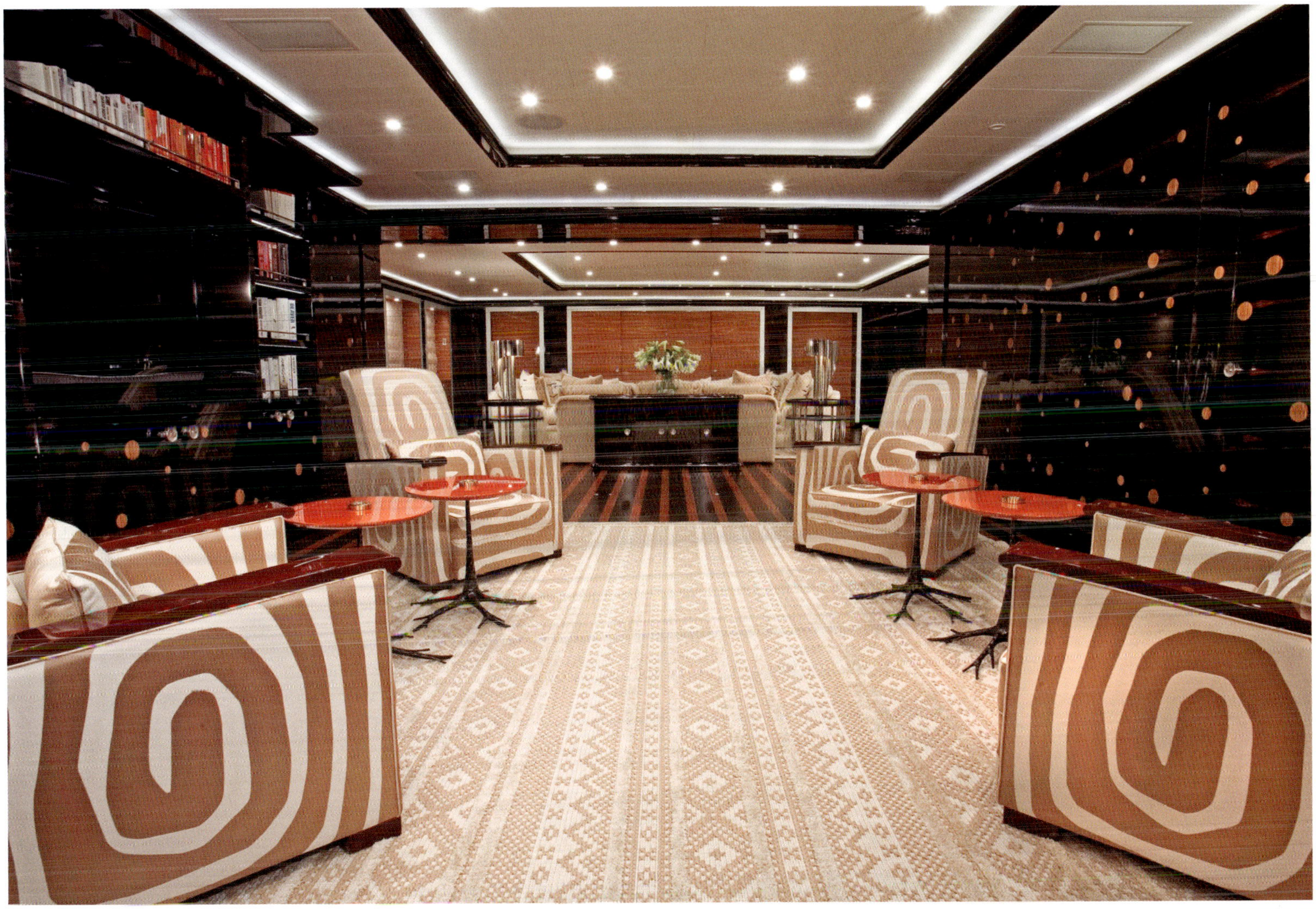

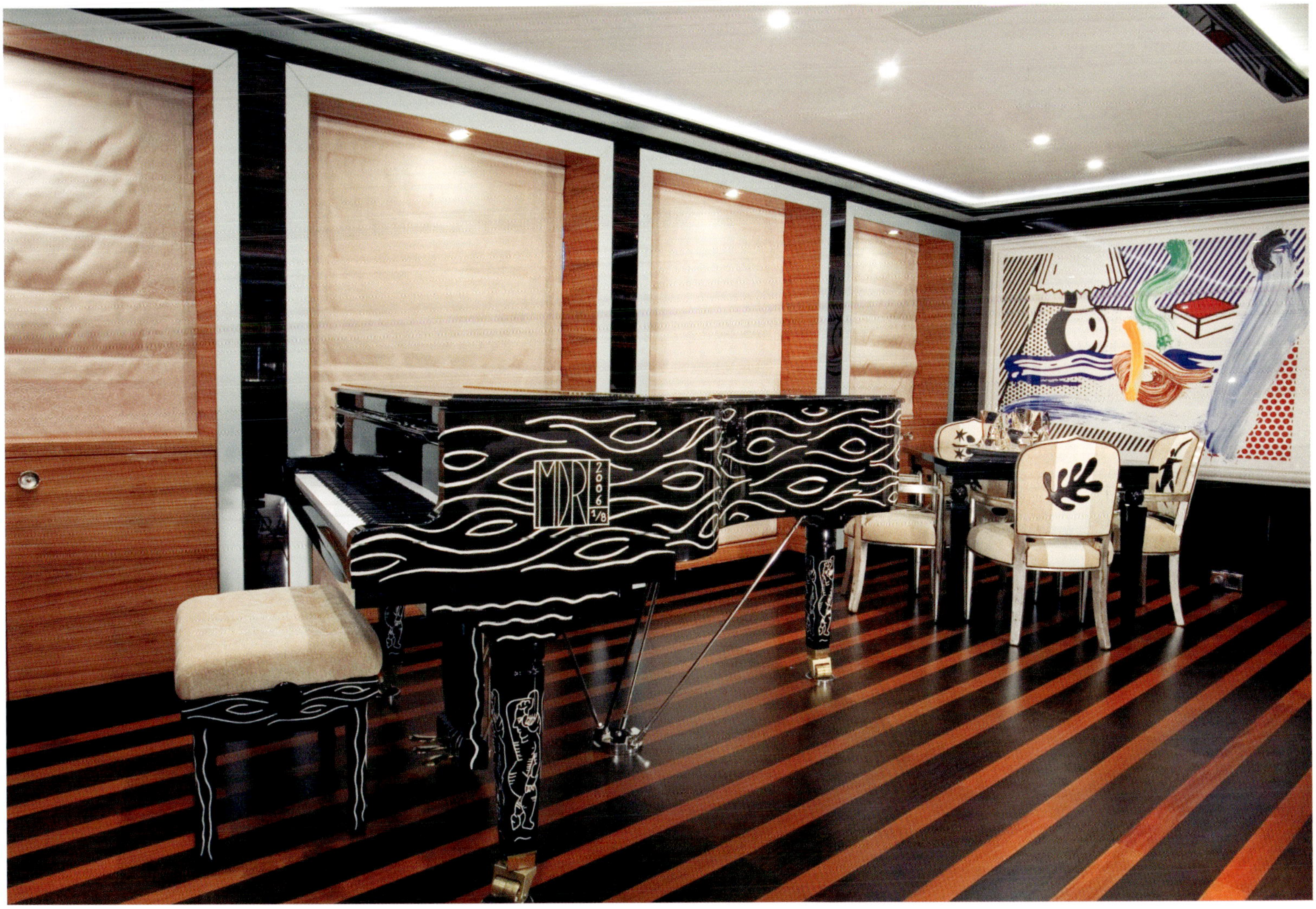

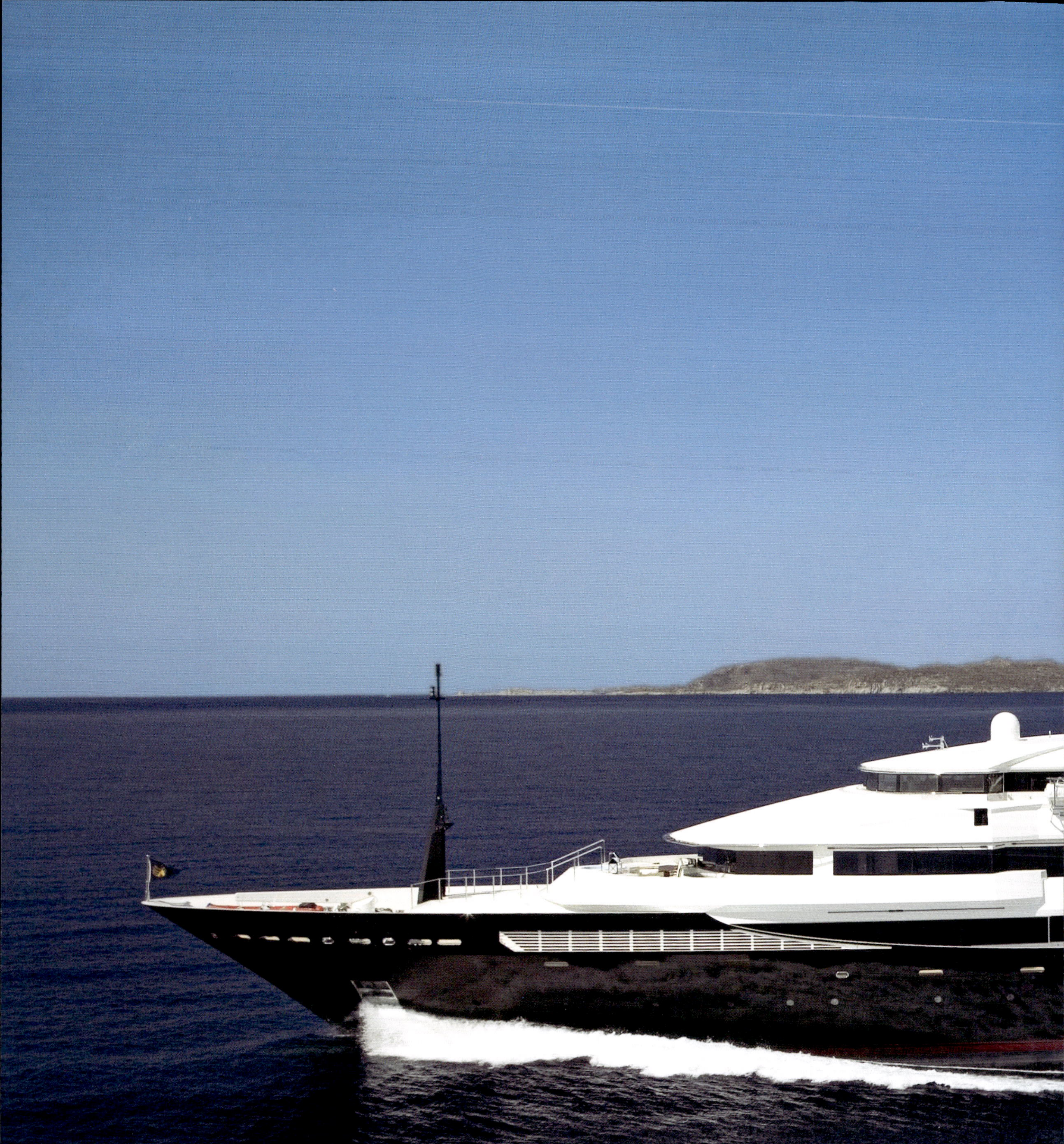

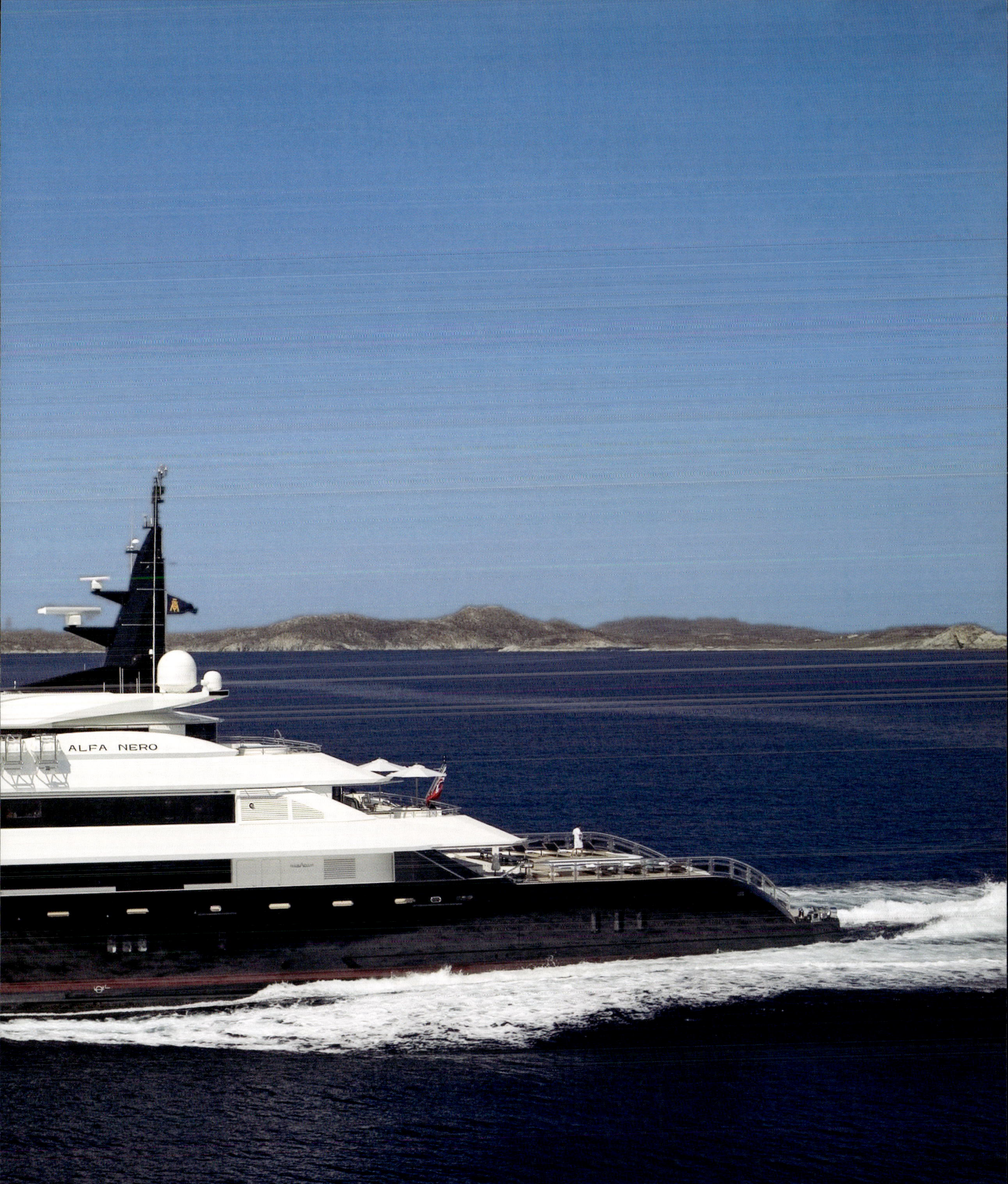
ALFA NERO

ABOVE: *The gym, on the bridge deck, offers a spectacular view wherever the yacht is anchored.*

LOA: 269' (82 m)
Beam: 47' 7" (14.2 m)
Draft: 12' 9" (3.9 m)
Naval architect: Oceanco
Exterior styling: Nuvolari-Lenard, S.r.l.
Interior design: Alberto Pinto / Nuvolari-Lenard, S.r.l.
Builder/year: Oceanco, The Netherlands / 2007
Top speed: 20 knots
Hull construction: Steel / Aluminium

for the stair treads of the central staircase, sycamore and brushed-stainless-steel flooring, Macassar flooring, and wenge wood cabinetry. A glass-enclosed elevator, surrounded by a spiral staircase, services each level of the yacht. LED illumination lights each passageway, day and night. There is also a Van Berge Henegouwen Crestron entertainment system, which, through Sea Tel, offers more than a thousand CDs and DVDs. Surround sound is accessible throughout the yacht.

One of several intimate dining areas on *Alfa Nero*, and possibly the most enchanting, is the "Tea Room." Its walls are covered with goatskin panels, and an off-white woven carpet sets off the polished Macassar parquet floor and wengé wood cabinetry.

Alfa Nero's ultramodern galley is up to the task of five-star service. A large stainless-steel food prep area occupies the centre of the room, with its composite blue stone floor. The chef enjoys first-class Moeleker appliances and double-door Koeling refrigerator/freezers for meals or banquets of any size. Microwaves, convection ovens, and cook tops are grouped for easy traffic flow. Crew movement and service is routed separately, away from passenger traffic.

Due to *Alfa Nero*'s size, the bulwarks are daunting. An actual shelf had to be fitted into the bow peak and steps port and starboard to enable the crew to provide guidance to the captain during anchoring. *Alfa Nero* also boasts two auxiliary wing stations at bridge level to assist docking and manoeuvering in close quarters. At the heart of the yacht is the command centre, which is outfitted with state-of-the-art navigation and communications equipment. Tunnel thrusters and joystick steering aid manoeuvering in tight spaces. Large, vertical, shaded windows allow superior views from the bridge. The open rear view also permits observation directly aft, which is not often the case on a private yacht. Seven screens display integrated NACOS and DEBEG nautical systems, long and short vector radar, Inmarsat satellite communications, SSB and weather information, while a CCTV monitoring system continually scans the entire yacht with a total of eighteen cameras. These keep watch over the engine room as well as each deck, plus surrounding territories with a night-vision view from the top mast.

Alfa Nero is truly a star among motoryachts.

ABOVE: *The "red" VIP suite on the main deck offers a luxuriously appointed bedroom, lounge, and computer workspace.*

RIGHT: *The treads of the spiral staircase are covered in Edelman leather.*

BELOW: *All the comforts of a five-star hotel, even a beauty saloon.*

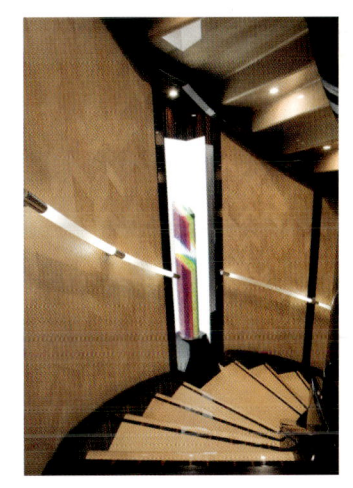

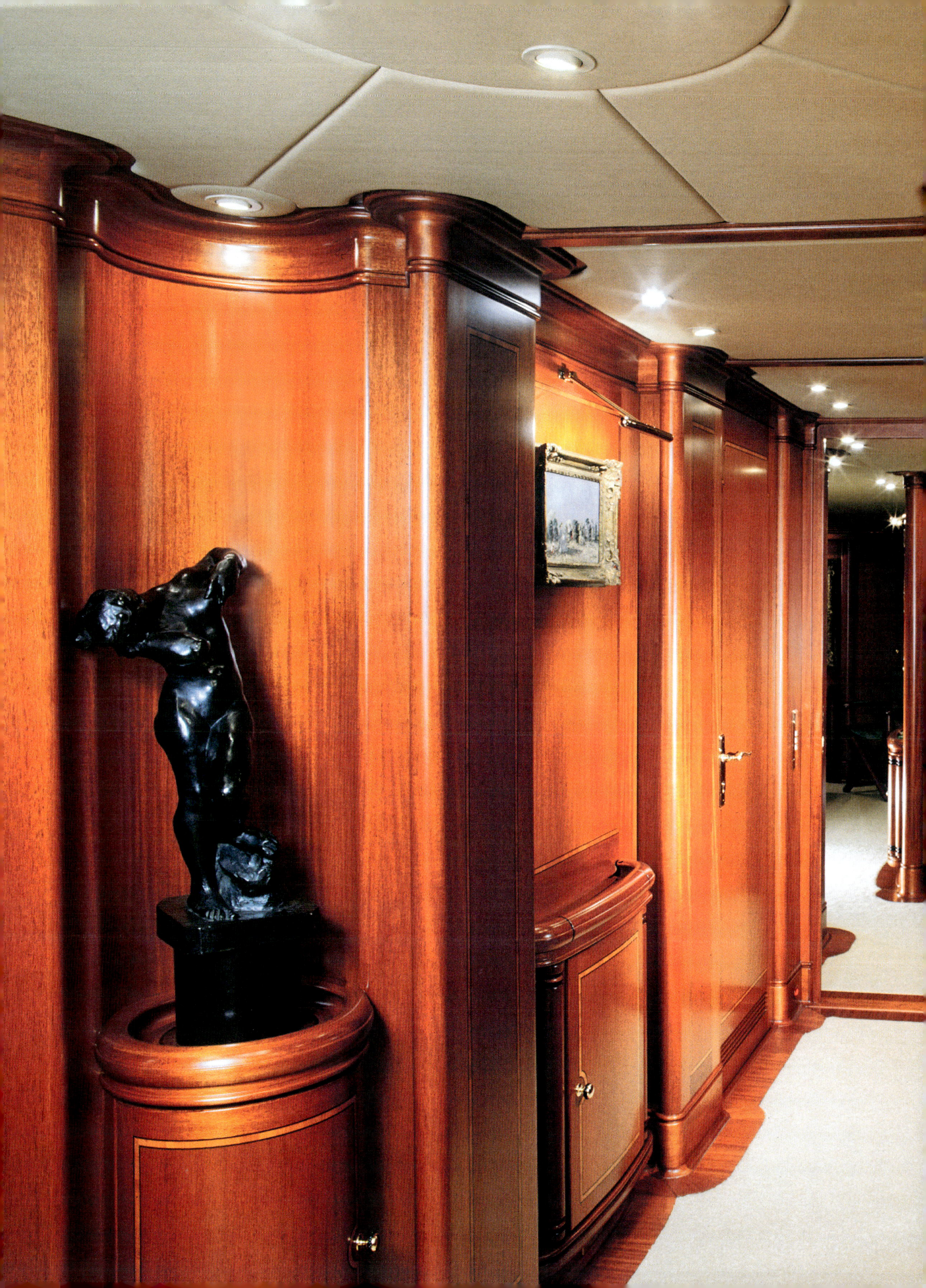

Hyperion

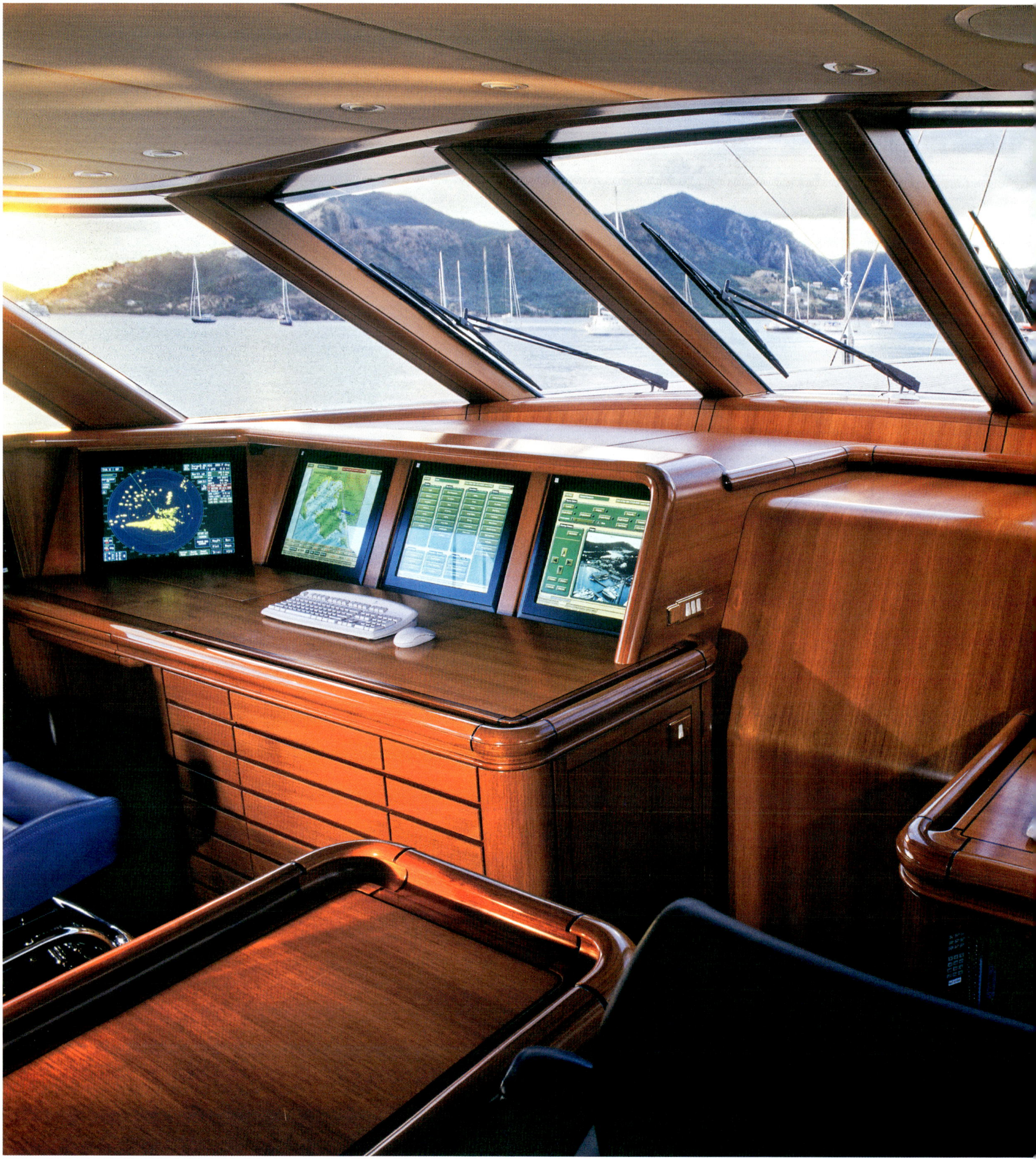

One would expect nothing less of pioneering Silicon Valley entrepreneur Jim Clark than a yacht that pushes the technology envelope. After all, through his companies Silicon Graphics and Netscape, Clark was instrumental in bringing the internet to the masses.

As Clark's success in business advanced, so did his interest in sailing. After owning several yachts of increasing size, Clark turned to Royal Huisman shipyard in the Netherlands to create a sailing superyacht that would merge luxury and technology on an unprecedented scale.

In 1998 Royal Huisman launched Clark's 155.5-foot (47.2-metre) *Hyperion* to intense interest around the world. On the surface, the yacht broke no significant ground in styling—save her scale. But her heart and soul clearly were out of this world. In the years prior to her launch, Clark and a team of engineers in California designed the most elaborate computerized monitoring and control system ever installed on a yacht. Clark wanted everything on the boat that could be controlled to be controllable via flat-panel touch-screen displays—functionality that long predated the iPhone. More than seven thousand elements were to be measured and displayed in real time, from engine performance to rig loads to on-board media.

The system included an astonishing array of technology: twenty-four screens, twenty-four computers and two servers. The yacht carried a dedicated crewmember to manage and maintain it all in a separate command centre. The yacht's data vascular system comprised some forty miles of wiring. All the information the system provided could be beamed by satellite in real time to Clark's desk in California when he was not aboard, prompting some to presume that he could actually sail the yacht from his office—the ultimate remote-control toy. Others speculated that the yacht could sail herself. Neither supposition was true.

PRECEDING PAGES: *The hallway to the master cabin doubles as an art gallery.*

ABOVE LEFT: *The pilothouse is home to a good part of* Hyperion's *astonishing array of technology, including no fewer than twenty-four computers and two servers.*

ABOVE RIGHT: *Hyperion makes way under full sail in light air in the St. Barths Bucket Regatta.*

HYPERION / 127

ABOVE: *The main saloon, located amidships, is panelled in Honduras mahogany with yew trim, bordered by narrow strips of wenge. It provides a luxurious setting for Clark's impressive collection of paintings.*

Still, at the end of the day, *Hyperion* is a sailing yacht powered the old-fashioned way—by the wind. Her carbon-fibre mast—at the time, the largest ever built—rises some 194 feet (59.1 metres) above the water and supports nearly 12,000 square feet (1,115 square metres) of sail, including a mainsail that weighs more than 1,300 pounds (589.7 kilograms). Her rig produces more than 200 tons of compressive force at the base of her mast in a strong breeze. Forces on her halyards, sheets, and stays can exceed an astonishing 20 tons. Her mast height was limited by the clearance under the Balboa Bridge, which spans the Panama Canal. The mast clears the bridge by a scant few feet.

As one would expect, the yacht is brimming with amenities and creature comforts. A movable two-person crow's nest can lift guests from the deck to as high as 120 feet (36.6 metres) above the water—still only three-quarters up her mast. In charter trim today, she is loaded with the latest water toys, including a diesel tender, water skis and related equipment, a kiteboard and fishing and snorkelling gear. The yacht is capable of sailing speeds as fast as 19 knots.

Her aluminium hull was designed by Argentine designer German Frers. Its shape was optimized for performance sailing. Her keel contains 80 tons of lead in its bulb. She draws 16 feet (4.9 metres), which allows her to enter most major yacht harbors. A carbon-fibre daggerboard extends eight feet below the bulb for better performance sailing to windward. She is fitted with a 1,100-horsepower MTU diesel engine and an automatic variable-pitch propeller that provide 10 knots of cruising speed when the wind isn't quite up to the task.

Hyperion's exterior and interior styling was done by Pieter Beeldsnijder Yacht Design of the Netherlands. The furnishings of her "new classic" interior are made

ABOVE: *The galley is as richly appointed as the rest of the yacht.*

primarily of Honduras mahogany with yew trim bordered by narrow strips of wenge. Her owner's stateroom, located aft, spans the yacht's entire 29-foot (9-metre) beam. The master bathroom features Italian marble that beautifully offsets the mahogany furniture and moldings. The two elegant guest suites are similarly appointed. Her luxurious saloon and formal dining area are found amidships; her crew areas, forward.

Royal Huisman is widely recognized as one of the finest sailing-yacht builders in the world. *Hyperion's* execution is a testament to the yard's skill and versatility. Her custom-built furniture is exquisite and the yard handily accommodated Clark's innovative and unique computer control and monitoring systems.

Clark has moved on to other yacht projects. A popular 2000 book by Michael Lewis, *The New New Thing*, begins with Clark attending sea trials of the cyberyacht while making notes on what would become his next yacht, the spectacular 295-foot (89.9-metre), three-masted schooner *Athena*. *Hyperion* has a new owner and is available for charter to technophiles and Luddites alike.

LOA: 155' 6" (47.2 m)
Beam: 28' 9" (8.78 m)
Draft: 6' 7" (1.85 m)
Naval architect: German Frers Naval Architecture & Engineering
Exterior styling: Pieter Beeldsnijder Yacht Design & Naval Architecture
Interior design: Pieter Beeldsnijder Yacht Design & Naval Architecture
Builder / year: Royal Huisman Shipyard, Vollenhove, Holland /1998
Hull construction: Aluminium

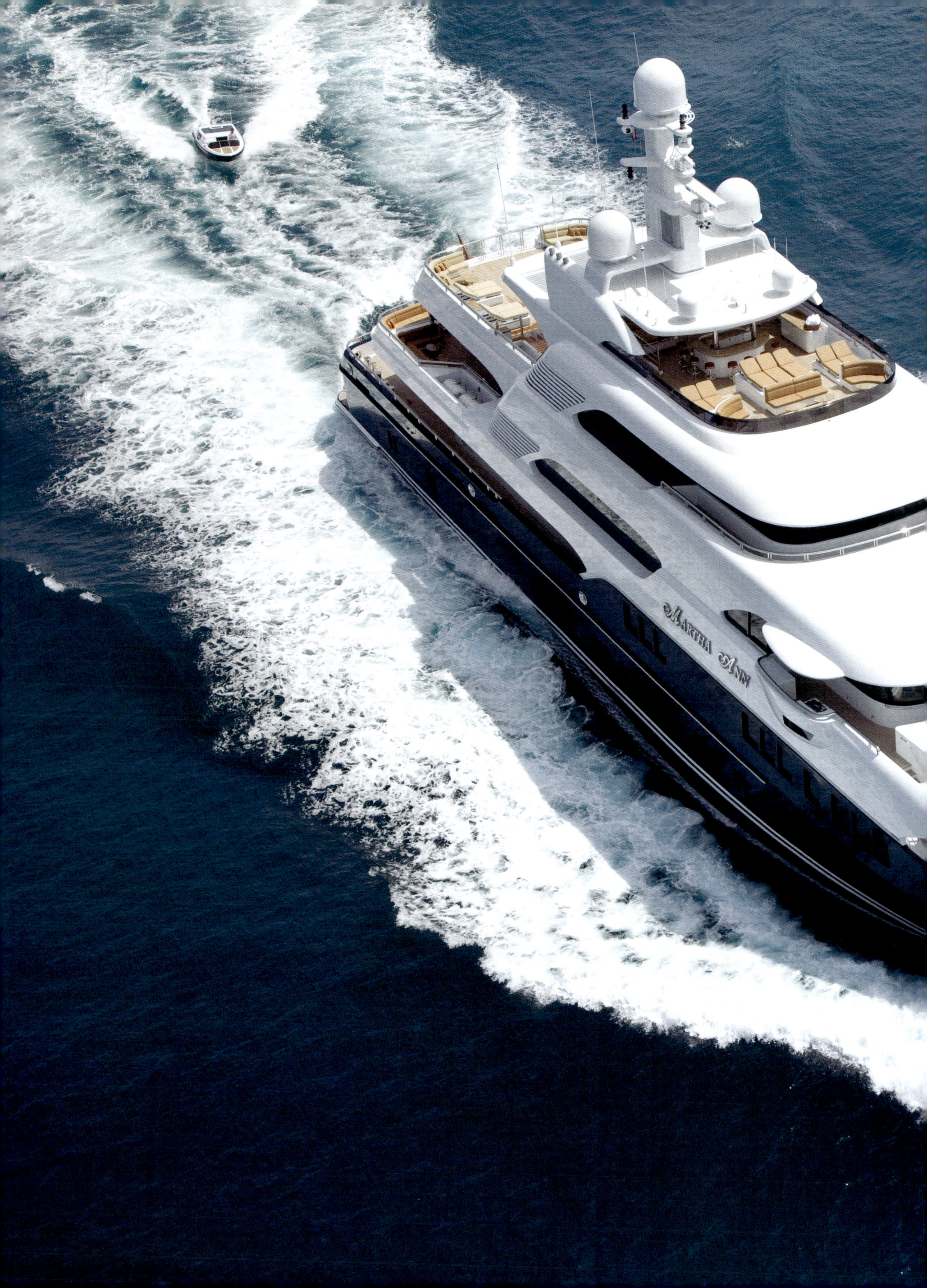
MARTHA ANN

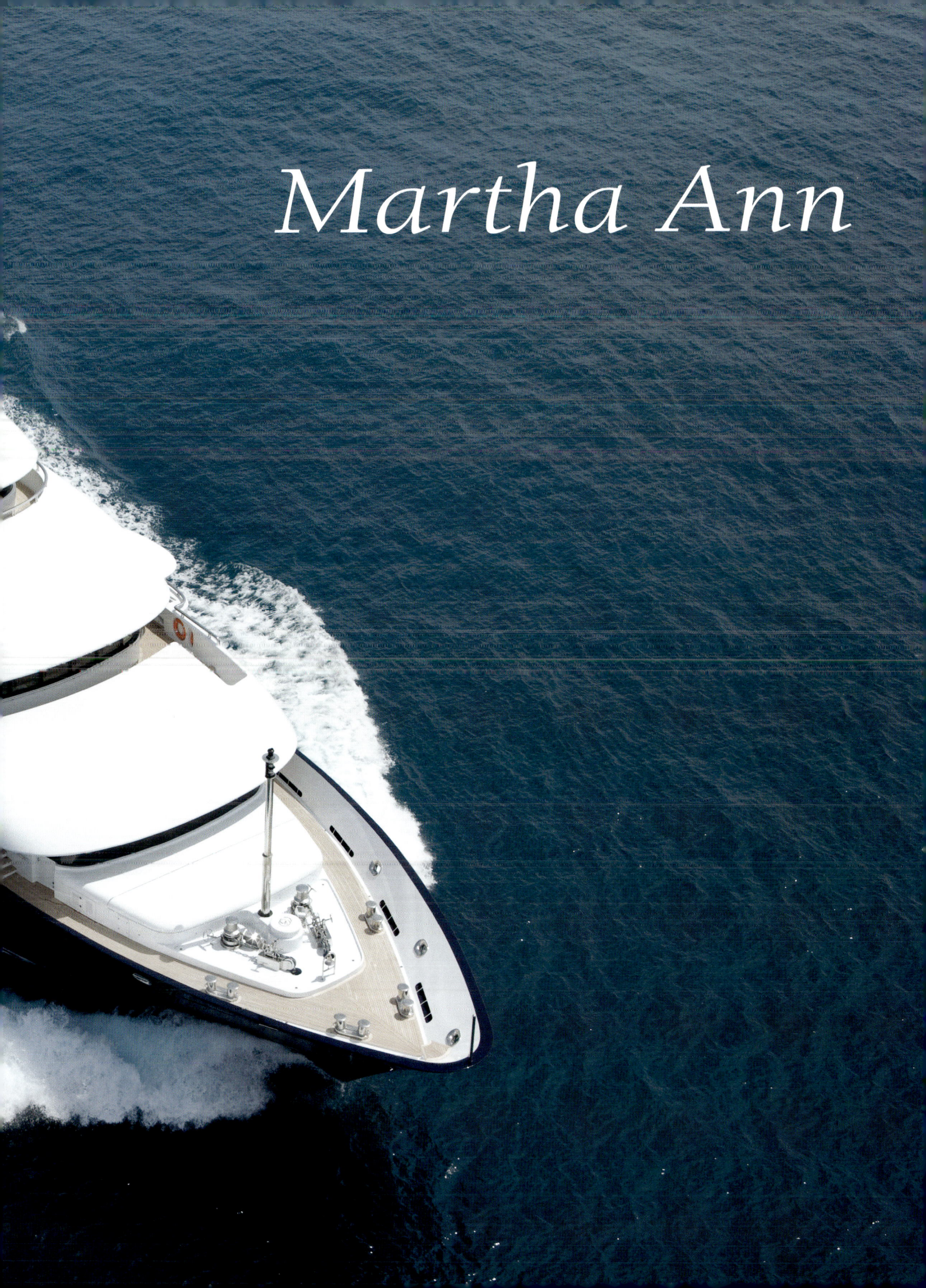

Martha Ann

132 / OUTRAGEOUS YACHTS

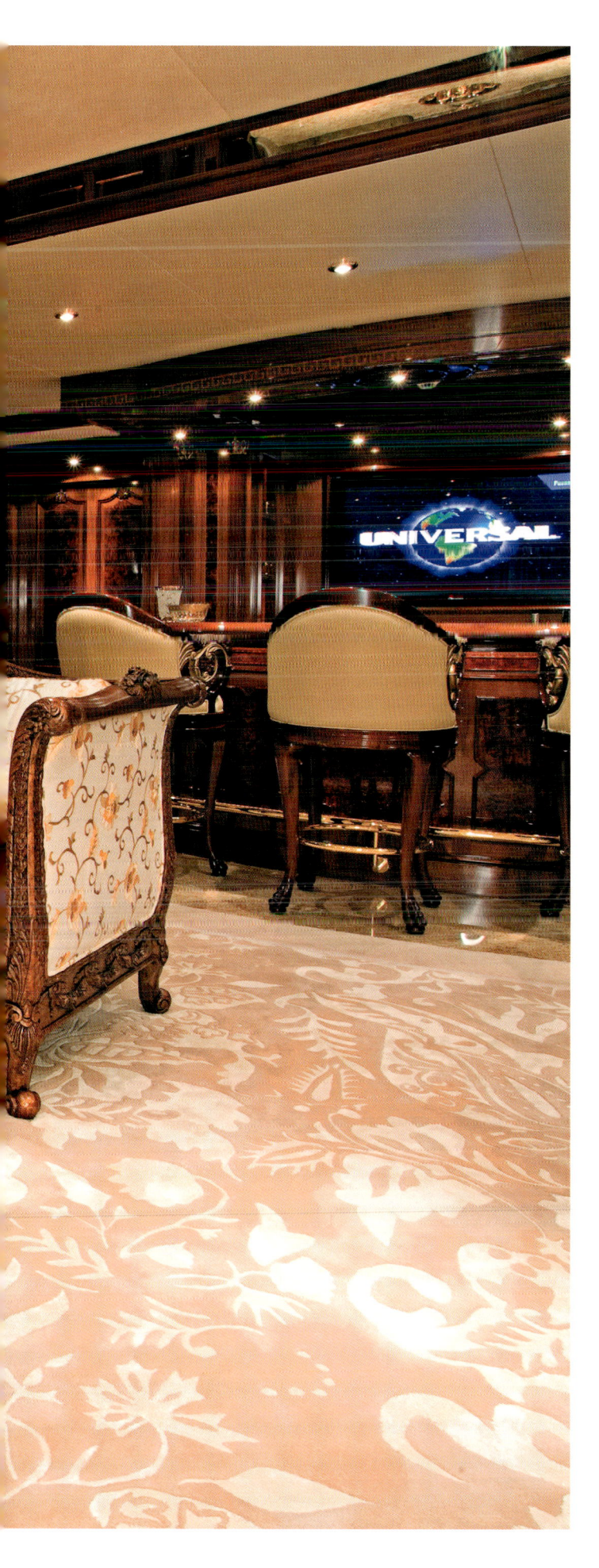

PRECEDING PAGES: *The massive interior volume (13,000 square feet, 1,207.7 square metres) of the 230-foot (70-metre)* Martha Ann *is evident from above as she steams along, powered by twin 2,010-horsepower diesels.*

In her use of interior space, the 230-foot (70-metre) *Martha Ann* from Germany's Lürssen shipyard is a colossal whole that is the sum of many small parts. Carefully and purposefully arranged throughout the yacht's six massive decks are dozens of intimate conversation areas intended to prevent her twelve guests and eighteen crew from feeling dwarfed by her 13,000 square feet (1,207.7 square metres) of air-conditioned interior space and her sprawling outdoor areas.

Many yachts that have an interior volume of comparable size do not feel "full" unless there is a party going on. When only a few guests are cruising and sleeping aboard, they can sometimes imagine they're hearing echoes as they converse in cavernous saloons and lounges. *Martha Ann*'s design team of Espen Øino, François Zuretti, and the yacht's owner conspired successfully to minimize the drafty-mansion effect while maintaining the opulent feel of a royal residence. They accomplished the feat by breaking the larger spaces into smaller, more intimate areas that make even groups of two or three feel comfortable, whether they are alone on the deck or in the midst of a party of a hundred. The effect is achieved less through the use of walls or bulkheads than through the layout of the spaces and the arrangement of furniture, both built-in and loose. Even

ABOVE: *One of* Martha Ann's *seven wet bars is in the main saloon.*

RIGHT: *The expansive bridge-deck lounge has its own bar.*

LOA: 230' (70.2 m)
Beam: 42' (13.1 m)
Draft: 12' 1" (3.7 m)
Naval Architect: Espen Øino
Interior Design: François Zuretti / Greenline
Builder / year: Lürssen / 2008
Hull construction: Steel

the expansive crew lounge—as big as the main saloons on some smaller yachts—is divided into several zones.

Martha Ann's amenities are legion. She has seven wet bars scattered about her indoor and outdoor areas, any of which could be the focal point of a party. One bar abuts the lap pool on the sports deck. It has four swim-up stools in the water and seats eleven on the opposite side. In the centre of the pool is a removable fountain for use during parties. The pool and bar are outdoors, but covered by a hard top with louvers that can be opened to let sunlight in.

The sports deck is designed for all-around physical and spiritual renewal. In addition to the pool, it includes a gym equipped with a wide assortment of commercial-

LEFT: *Martha Ann's ornately decorated formal dining room creates a luxury-liner ambience for twelve to fourteen guests. Some guests, however, prefer to have their meals in the more casual dining room on the bridge deck.*

BELOW: *The master suite takes full advantage of the yacht's 12-foot (13.1-metre) beam. Situated on the main deck, it is the size of an average city apartment. Its amenities include a library, walk-in closets, a sitting room, and a split-level private lounge.*

grade exercise machines; a second small bar; large flat-screen monitors; and a cinema lounge forward with a 110-inch (280-centimetre) projection screen and surround sound.

Several decks below is the massive tender garage that houses the yacht's watercraft and recreation equipment. The boats, which include a Royal Denship limo tender that seats twelve in climate-controlled comfort and a landing craft-style Nautica rigid inflatable, deploy through the sides of the yacht.

Martha Ann's seven guest cabins are dispersed among three decks. Her accommodation deck houses four staterooms with king-size beds and a cabin for children, nannies, or other staff. The bridge deck is home to a large VIP stateroom with a queen-size bed and a walk-in closet. All staterooms have luxuriously appointed bathrooms.

The full-beam (42 feet, 12.8 metres) master stateroom is located on the main deck forward and occupies the space of a respectable city apartment. It has a private library/study, three separate closets, a sitting area with a sofa, cocktail table, and wet bar next to the bed, and his-and-hers bathrooms joined by a central spa tub and trimmed in warm, honey-coloured onyx. A split-level forward lounge is furnished with a substantial sofa, occasional tables, and a large TV.

Five of the yacht's decks are served by a circular glass elevator. The woodwork in all guest living areas and all the built-in furniture was crafted by Dubai-based Greenline in a combination of satin and high-gloss finishes. The lustrous panelling throughout is walnut with elm burl.

If measured by her television-to-guest-and-crew ratio, Martha Ann likely rates near the top among yachts in service. Distributed throughout the guest areas and crew quarters are more than forty flat-screen monitors, each connected to the yacht's Kaleidescape movie and music libraries and controlled by Crestron touch-screen remote controls.

The ornately decorated main saloon and formal dining room are truly breathtaking, imbued with an ambience reminiscent of the luxury liners of the steam age. The theme carries through to the entrance foyer, which, with its wide staircase and elevator access, creates a lasting first impression. As in most areas on the yacht, the saloon's furniture is configured in several intimate groupings. But when the baby grand player piano is in use, it becomes a unified family or party space.

The dining room is one of the rare spaces on board that is not broken up. Its twelve-to-fourteen-person formal table and lavish accoutrements are stunning. Nevertheless, the majority of charter guests prefer the circular dining room on the bridge deck with its curved glass doors that open to the elements.

ABOVE: *The sports deck was designed for complete physical and spiritual renewal. It has a gym with commercial-grade equipment, a bar, intimate seating areas, and a cinema lounge with a 110-inch (280-centimetre) projection screen.*

The crew spaces—the bridge and the crew living quarters—are the only interior areas on the yacht that are not dressed to impress, but they are still very stylish and tasteful. They may be finished in business attire, but as everywhere else on the boat, they are arranged to be conducive to conversation. Even the engine room has an unusually large central area that could easily accommodate a small cocktail reception (although for obvious reasons it is not equipped with a bar). The captain's cabin and the separate ship's office, situated behind the bridge, possess the same quality of finish and decor as the guest areas.

Her twin 2,010-horsepower Caterpillar diesels provide her with a top speed of 16.5 knots and a 14.5-knot cruise.

Martha Ann is the last of three similar yachts that the owner commissioned from Lürssen in quick succession. The other two, which eventually were named *Apoise* and *Saint Nicolas*, were started on spec and sold before completion. The owner kept *Martha Ann* for himself. Although the owner enjoys his time aboard with family and friends, he makes her available for select charter to those who want it all—in tasty bits and pieces.

The pool has multiple features. It has a counter-current option and a jacuzzi, and also functions as the ultimate wet bar with four swim-up stools. When the pool is not in use for fitness, a decorative fountain can be installed.

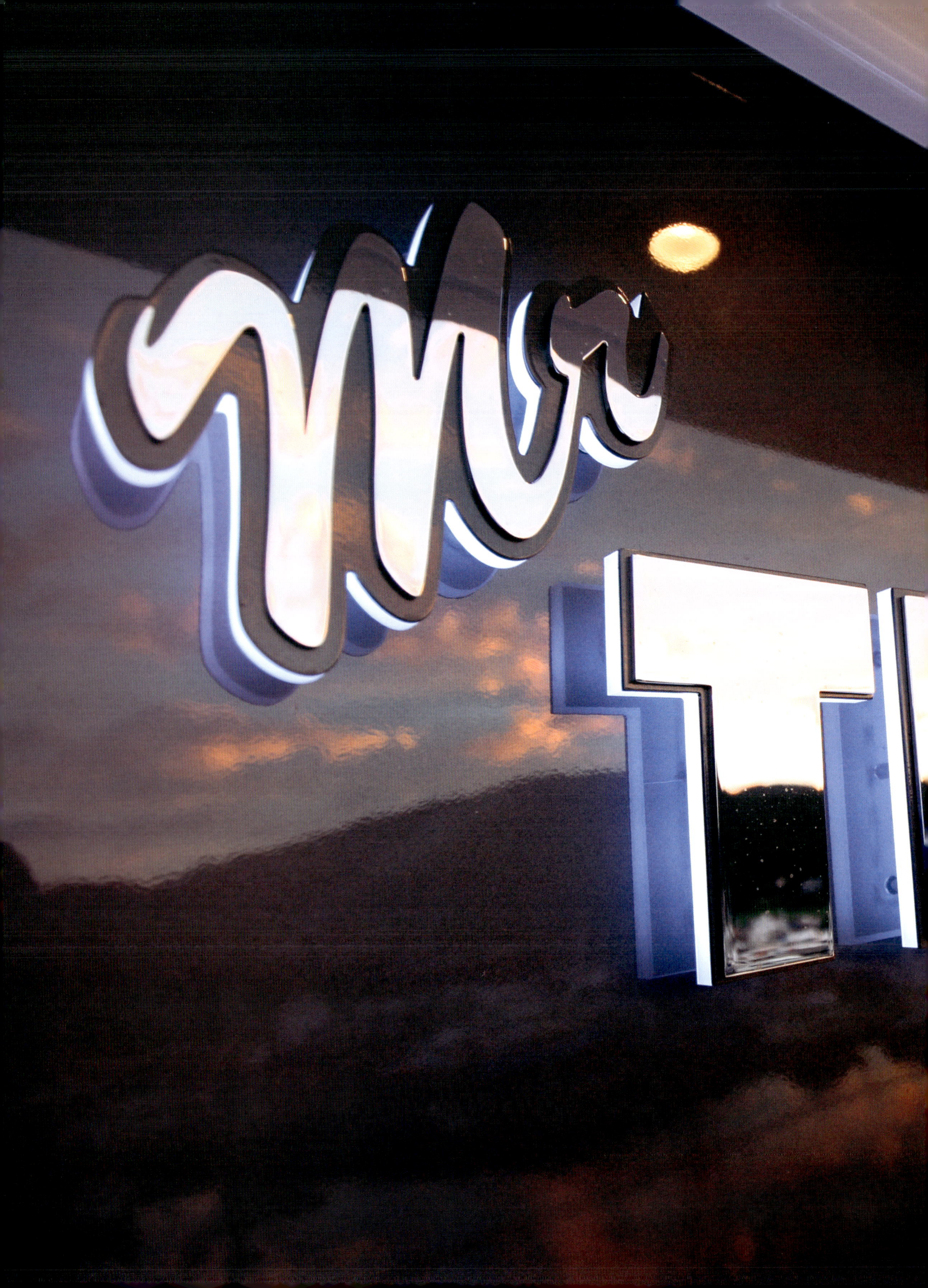
Mr

Mr. Terrible

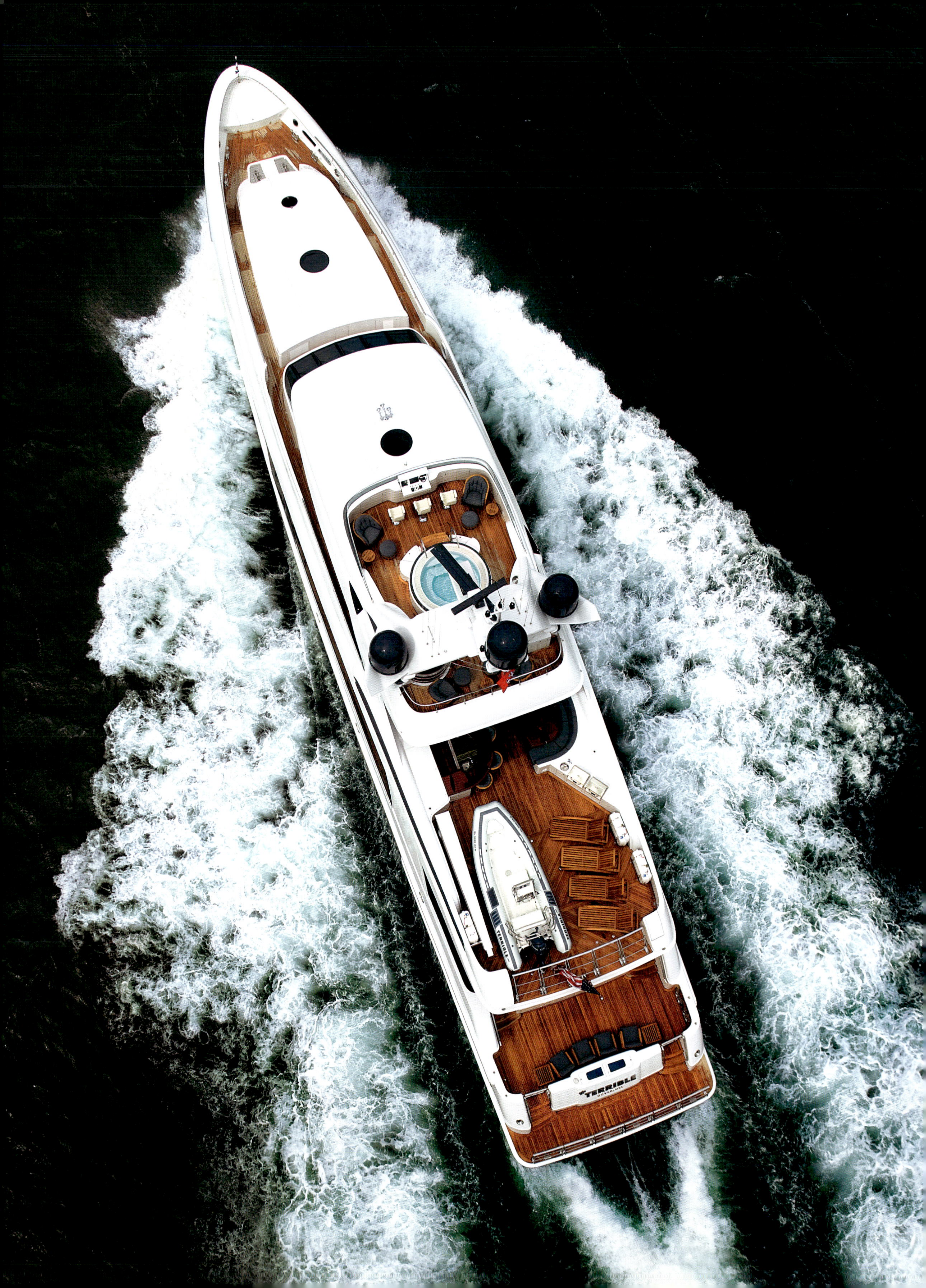
TERRIBLE

TOP: *Mr. Terrible was made to move and cuts a sleek figure.*

BOTTOM: *The yacht's exceptional joinery is in evidence even on the bridge. A settee affords guests a skipper's-eye view of the yacht and her surroundings.*

Mr. *Terrible*, what kind of name is that? In colloquial French, to say something is *terrible* (pronounced ter-EE-bluh) means that it is really good. The owner of this 154-foot (46.9-metre) semi-displacement yacht built at Delta Shipyard in Seattle, Washington, is not French, but he obviously has a sense of humour. He could have done what so many yachtsmen do; he could have named his boat after his wife. Instead he named it after his company's trademarked logo, Mr. Terrible, a mustachioed cartoon bandito in a ten-gallon hat who wears a star and brandishes a gas-pump nozzle instead of a six-gun. The business is the Terrible Herbst Oil Company, a privately held gas station and gaming company in the western United States. Among other businesses under the Herbst Company umbrella are motor sports events with crews known as "The Best Bad Guys in the West."

The interior design of the yacht could not be further from this rootin'-tootin' Wild West sensibility. Elegant and exotic, the decor, by interior designer Adriel Rollins, has two major themes: Polynesian, in the selection of materials and patterns; and aerodynamic, in the sleekness of shapes and forms. As rich as the interior design is, the floor plan itself is conventional: main saloon aft, then the dining area, pilothouse, and master stateroom forward; the sky lounge up a deck; and five double staterooms below decks. The design scheme of all the guest staterooms is the same, but each has a different palette. The guest accommodations are equipped with Pullman berths for children and include two VIP suites.

PRECEDING PAGES AND OPPOSITE: *The oddly named* Mr. Terrible *is owned by the founder of the western U.S. service station and gaming company Terrible Herbst Oil. The yacht's MTU diesels carry her to a speedy 24 knots.*

The Polynesian flavour is particularly noticeable in the use of a great variety of exotic woods. Koa, indigenous to Hawaii, is the featured veneer. The ornamental facing on the credenzas, the dining room hutch and the bathroom vanities is bamboo. The floors are African walnut; the console in the pilothouse is finished with a bloodwood veneer and quartered-and-figured makoré. Bubinga forms the main structural joinery of the cabinets, staircase, and overheads; cerejeira is used on the vanity tops and in inlays elsewhere. The credenza and game table in the sky lounge are finished in European pearwood. Honduran mahogany in a starburst weave adorns the entrance foyer, lacewood veneer has been used to create a gradation effect along with the pearwood inlay and ebonized wenge is used for the baseboards.

If the wood isn't enough to make you put on a grass skirt and wear a lei, there is more. The carpets are boldly patterned with lush tropical flora. A woven leather panel above the dining room table creates the illusion of a thatch roof. A snakeskin pattern on the drawers of the dining room buffet and on the leather top of the game table adds to the jungle flavor. The dining saloon, with

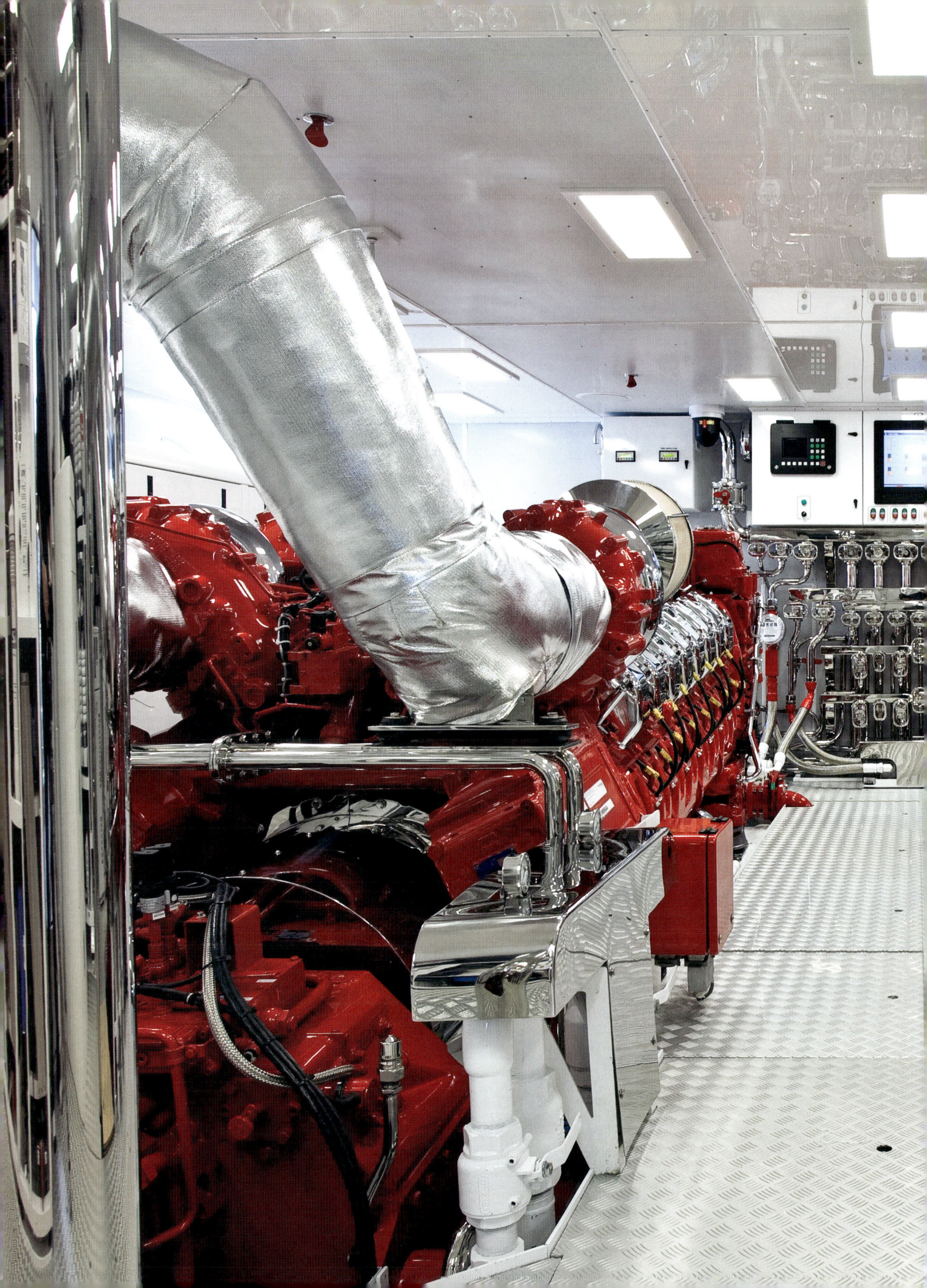

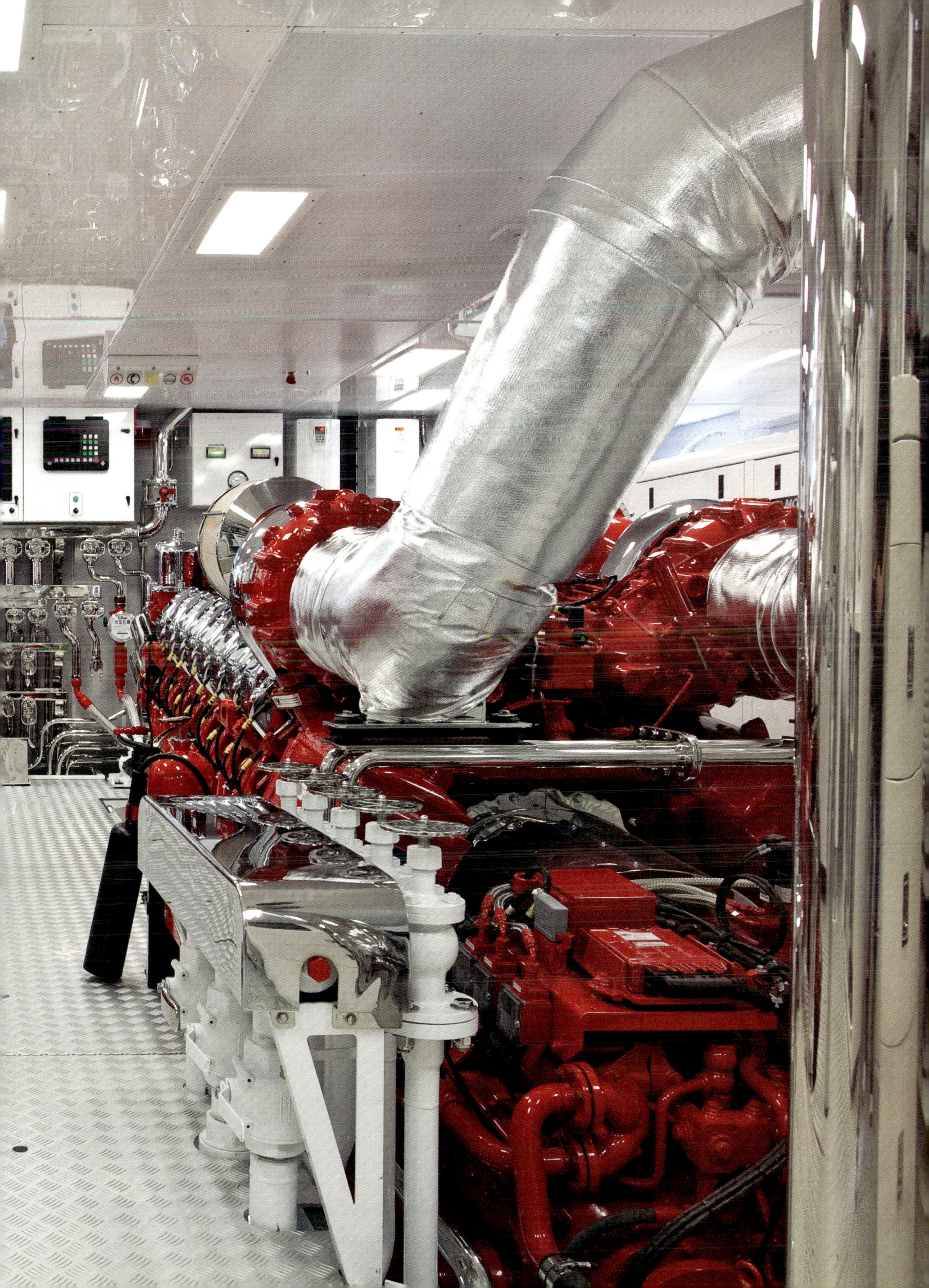

PRECEDING PAGES: *Delta Marine is renowned for its spacious, superbly finished engine rooms. Mr. Terrible's houses a pair of powerful MTU 16V4000's.*

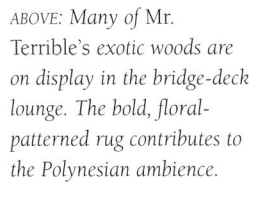

ABOVE: Many of Mr. Terrible's *exotic woods are on display in the bridge-deck lounge. The bold, floral-patterned rug contributes to the Polynesian ambience.*

RIGHT, FROM TOP TO BOTTOM: *The main dining saloon, with its tripartite blown-glass chandelier; the spiral staircase that connects all three decks; the richly textured, beautifully appointed main saloon.*

OPPOSITE: *The master suite is brightened by a stained-glass skylight in the shape of a nautilus shell. The coral-patterned carpet continues the marine theme.*

TOP: *In the master head, bronze and black glass mosaic tiles create a dramatic backdrop for twin, hand-turned wood sinks.*

ABOVE: *Each of the five guest staterooms is finished in a wide variety of exotic woods, and each has a different colour scheme.*

LOA: 154' (46.9 m)
Beam: 28' 8" (8.74 m)
Draft: 7' 6" (2.2 m)
Naval architect: Delta Design Group
Exterior styling: Espinosa Yacht Design Inc. / Delta Design
Interior design: Adriel Rollins / Delta Design Group
Builder / year: Delta Marine, Seattle, Washington / 2007
Top speed: 22 knots
Hull construction: Composite

a table that seats fourteen, is graced by a unique tripartite chandelier of blown-glass botanical forms and brushed-aluminium palm fronds. Each part is suspended from a dome of solid bubinga. On the bulkhead are colourful jellyfish objets d'art made from diachronic fused glass. This treatment can render glass both reflective and opaque, creating a kaleidoscope of colour. The wall sconces throughout the boat are computer-machined, conceived from sketch to installation to be safe in generating heat, but also to throw a patterned light. High above the king-size bed in the owner's bedroom, a glorious seashell-inspired stained-glass oculus lets in resplendent natural light, which can also be screened out at the touch of a button. In the master head, bronze and black glass mosaic tiles create a dramatic backdrop for twin hand-turned wood basin sinks and an opulent copper soaking tub.

Rollins is a proponent of "seeing is believing." He wanted the yacht to look as though she actually were from a tropical setting, instead of just bearing a resemblance to one. Whatever the intentions of this talented designer, *Mr. Terrible* was sturdily built not in the South Pacific but in the Pacific Northwest at Delta, one of America's premier shipyards. Rollins purposely designed details such as handrails and crown mouldings in an aerodynamic way, to reflect and enhance the sense of movement that is inherent to life aboard a yacht.

Mr. Terrible was indeed built to move. Her J. C. Espinosa/Delta–designed exterior is sleek with a low profile. She is a high-performance yacht and can reach a maximum speed of 24 knots. Powered by twin MTU 16V4000's and carrying 14,786 US gallons of fuel, she has a cruising range of 3,500 nautical miles.

In addition to cruising long distances, *Mr. Terrible* is thoroughly equipped for deep-sea fishing. The fishing cockpit on the main deck features a live-bait tank and rod locker. Guests can also take advantage of the nitrox dive compressor and six full sets of dive gear on board. Underwater cameras installed under the transom capture deep-sea curiosities in real time and broadcast the action live. Other toys include two tenders for water-skiing or ferrying to and fro and sea kayaks. Well built and well appointed, *Mr. Terrible* is, well, not so terrible.

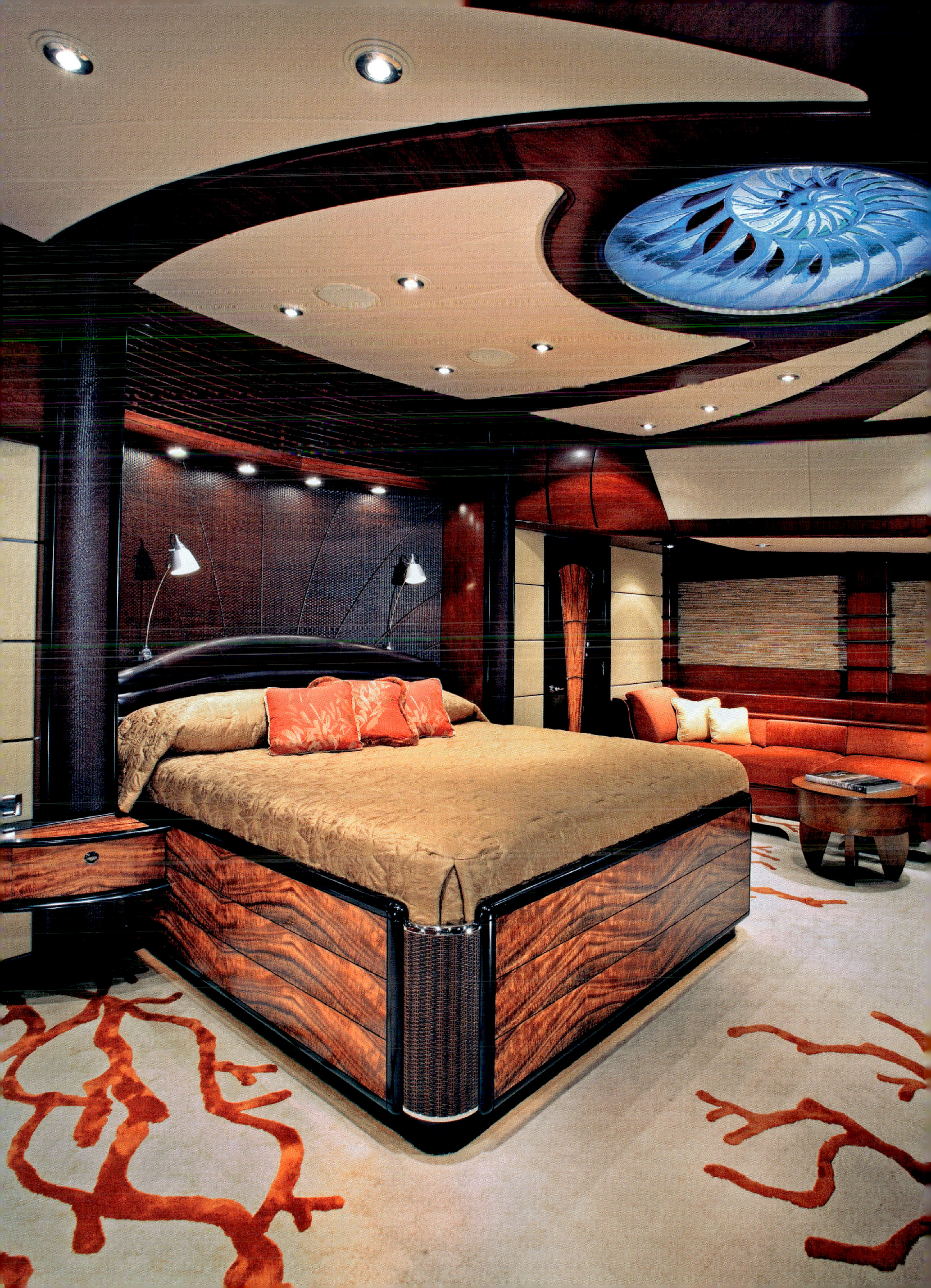

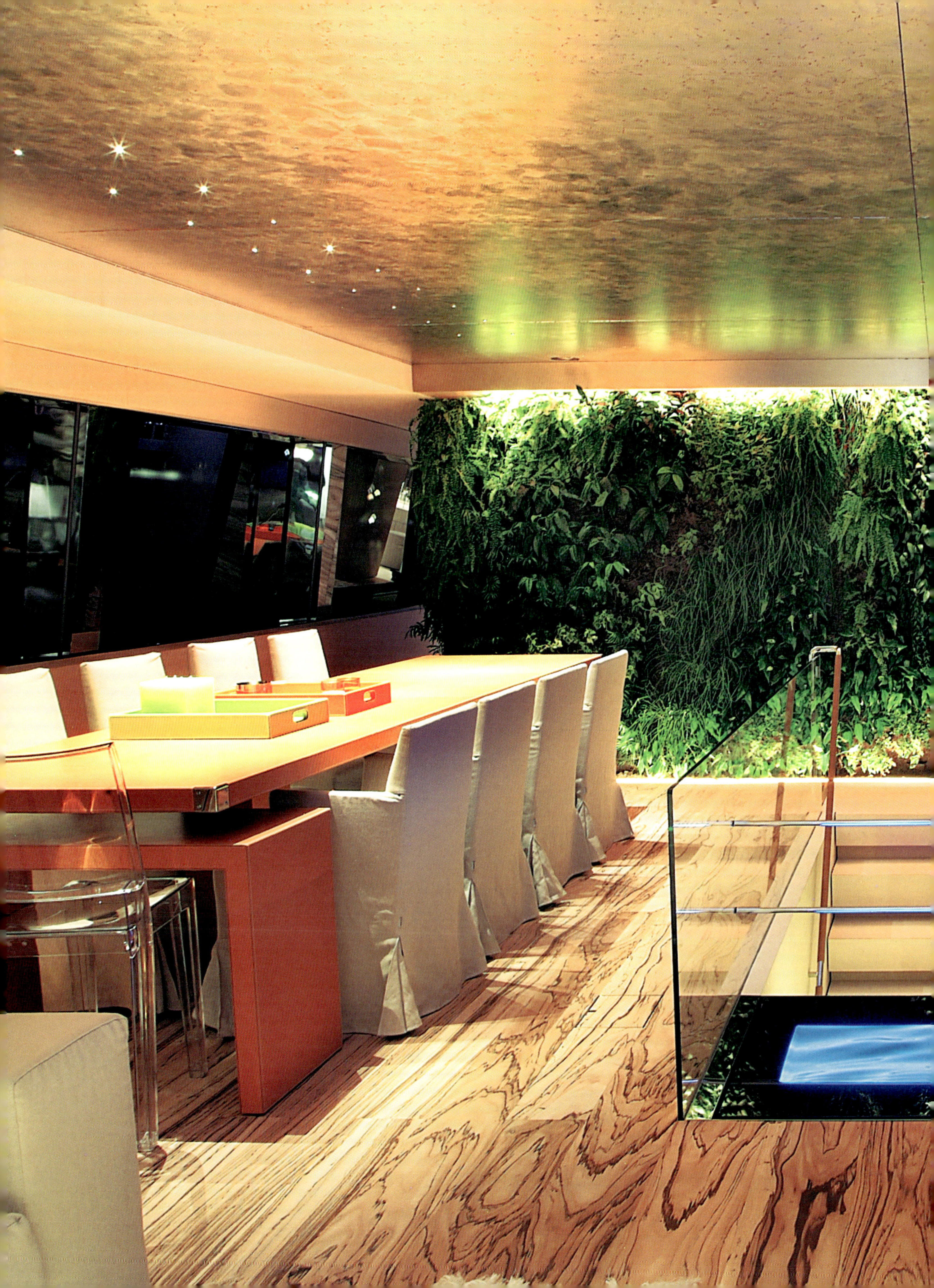

Nina J

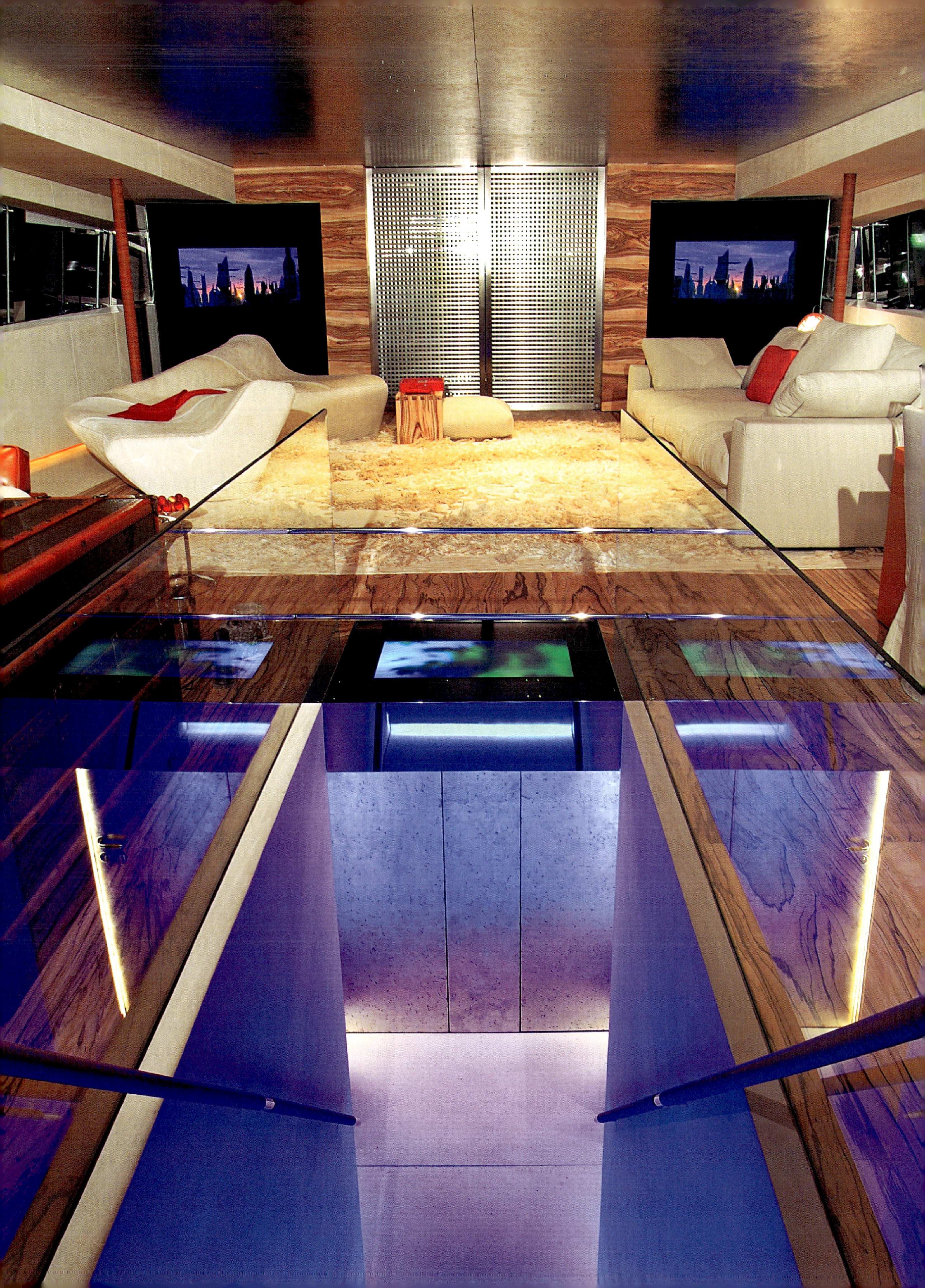

PRECEDING PAGES: *As guests enter* Nina J's *main saloon, they are greeted by the spectacular vertical garden on the forward bulkhead.*

*N*ina J is all about breaking the mould and defying the norm. She is snazzy from the outside, but it's the interior that takes your breath away. She has, arguably, the most original interior of any yacht afloat. This 140-foot (42.2-metre) aluminium yacht was built at the Baglietto Shipyard in Italy. Known for its lightweight-alloy motoryachts, the yard once produced wartime torpedo boats as well as race boats. Prior to launching *Nina J*, such Baglietto yachts as *Blue Ice* and *Thunderball* and *Tatiana per Sempre* turned heads in every harbour. Tommaso Spadolini, designer of the *Nina J's* exterior, follows in the footsteps of his naval architect father, Pierluigi, who created the modern Akhir series for Cantieri di Pisa. Everything about Tommaso's design is sleek and streamlined, from the clean, simple lines of the planing hull to the flush black windows, gunmetal grey paint, and red boot stripe. The wide-body, full-beam hull without side decks allows for greater interior volume.

Architect and interior designer Ivana Porfiri worked very closely with the owner to make sure that the boat conformed to his lifestyle. "Life onboard should reflect the owner's life on land," Porfiri says. "For one thing, you have to take advantage of the panorama and natural light, which are constantly changing. My challenge as a designer is to capture the changing environment so you always feel in contact with the world outside." Photographs cannot fully capture the extraordinary feeling you have when you are on board.

Entering from the main deck aft, you walk through a graphite-black bar area with Artesian stone flooring and iridescent blue LED lighting that reflects off a silver-coloured, grated screen. The stunning difference between the natural light of the outside and this otherworldly space is intentional, according to Porfiri. It acts as a transition to the inner world of *Nina J*. The bar leads into the main saloon. Large picture windows flank the length of the saloon and in fact the entire main deck. Light floods in through the windows, dappling the living area in patches of sun and shadow. An LED monitor recessed into the floor displays a continuous loop of undersea images. Similarly, video monitors on the walls serve as a constantly changing art gallery.

As innovative and unusual as these electronic elements are, the pièce de résistance in the main saloon is the vertical garden on the forward bulkhead, which separates the saloon from the master stateroom. French botanist Patrick Blanc, known for covering entire

OPPOSITE: *The guest accommodations are accessed by a staircase leading down from the main saloon. An LED monitor recessed into the floor displays a continuous loop of undersea images.*

RIGHT: *A graphite-black bar area with iridescent blue LED lighting that reflects off of a silver-coloured, grated screen leads into the main saloon from the main deck aft.*

LOA: 140' (42.2 m)
Beam: 26' (8 m)
Draft: 5' (1.5 m)
Naval architect: Rodriquez Engineering
Exterior styling: Tommaso Spadolini / Design Studio Spadolini S.r.l.
Interior design: Ivana Porfiri / Porfiristudio
Builder / year: Baglietto, Italy / 2005
Top speed: 35 knots
Hull construction: Aluminium

ABOVE: The master suite is filled with sumptuous textures, including linen, cashmere, fur, and suede, and the room is flooded with natural light.

BELOW: The exposed curve of the hull adds a maritime feel to the interior of one of the two identical double guest cabins.

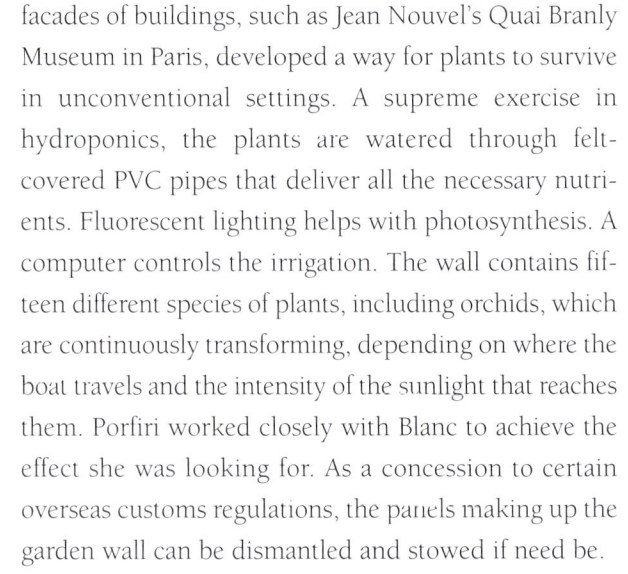

facades of buildings, such as Jean Nouvel's Quai Branly Museum in Paris, developed a way for plants to survive in unconventional settings. A supreme exercise in hydroponics, the plants are watered through felt-covered PVC pipes that deliver all the necessary nutrients. Fluorescent lighting helps with photosynthesis. A computer controls the irrigation. The wall contains fifteen different species of plants, including orchids, which are continuously transforming, depending on where the boat travels and the intensity of the sunlight that reaches them. Porfiri worked closely with Blanc to achieve the effect she was looking for. As a concession to certain overseas customs regulations, the panels making up the garden wall can be dismantled and stowed if need be.

In the saloon, the striking African zebrawood floor is partially covered by a hand-woven cotton, silk, and jute rug. Running the length of the boat along the port and starboard edges is a strip of white plaster mounted on marine plywood. For the barefooted passengers, a vari-

OPPOSITE: The curve of the yacht's hull in a guest bathroom plays off the squareness of the slab of stone housing the sink.

OVERLEAF: Nina J rests at anchor off Monaco.

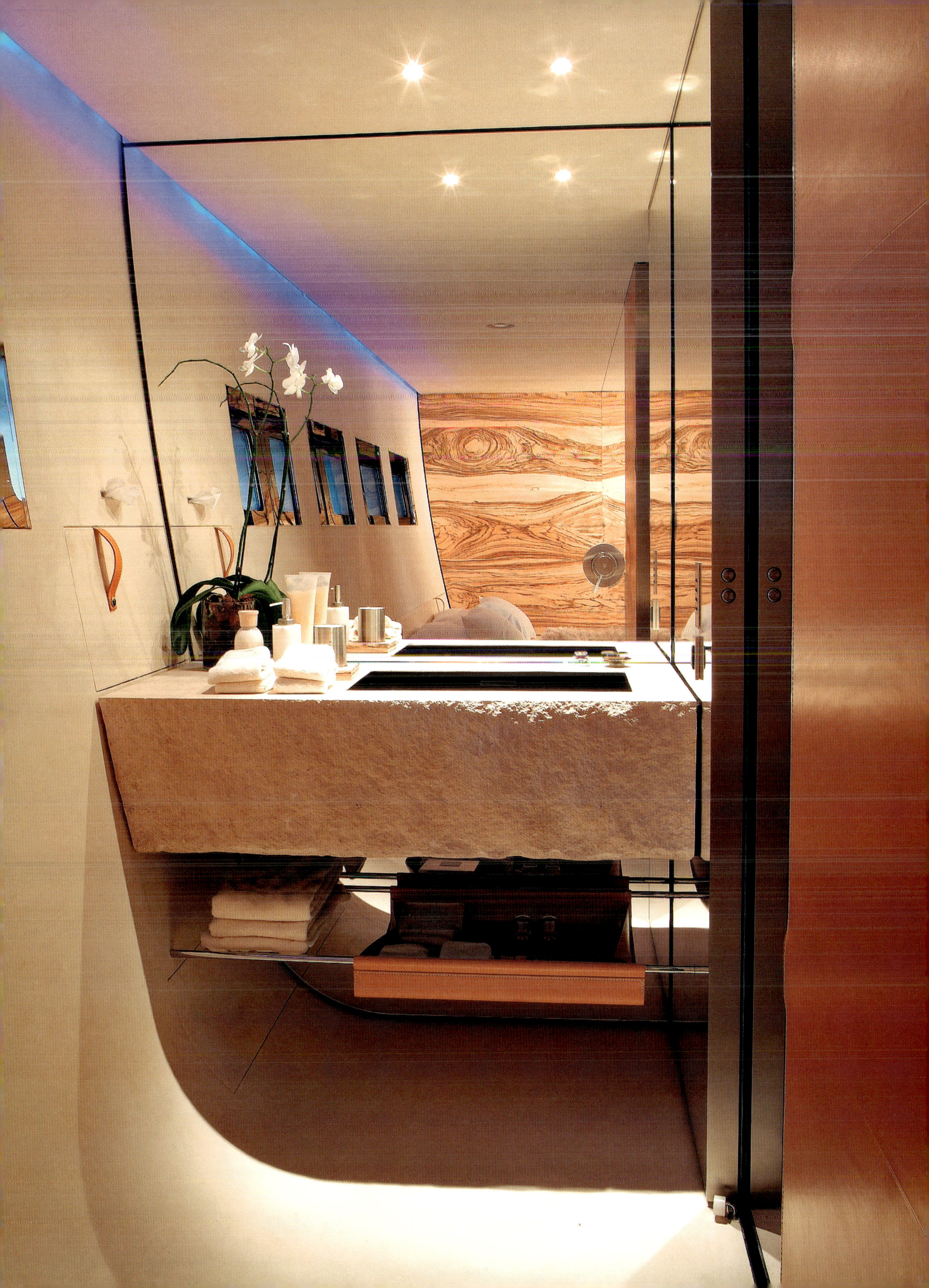

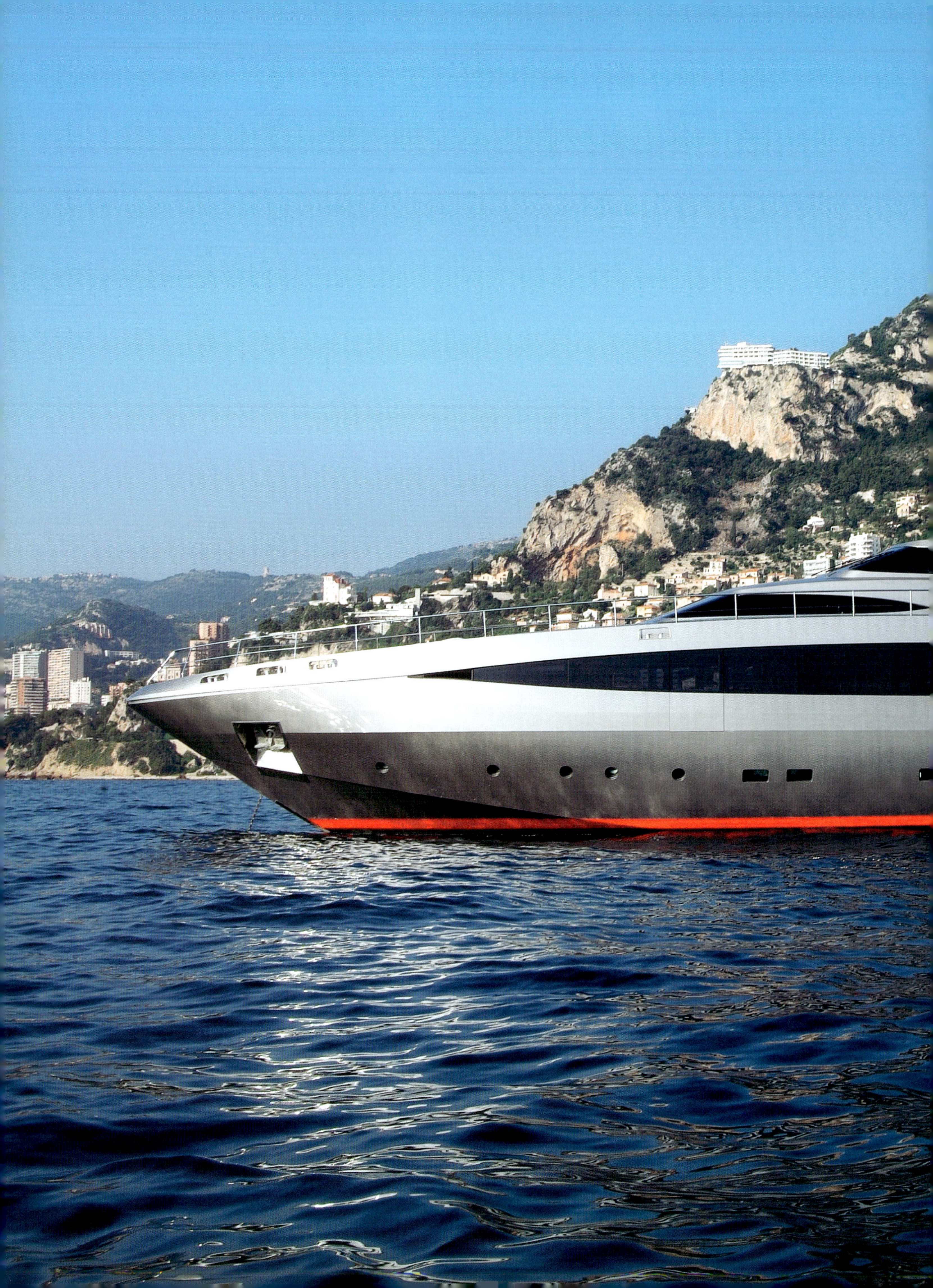

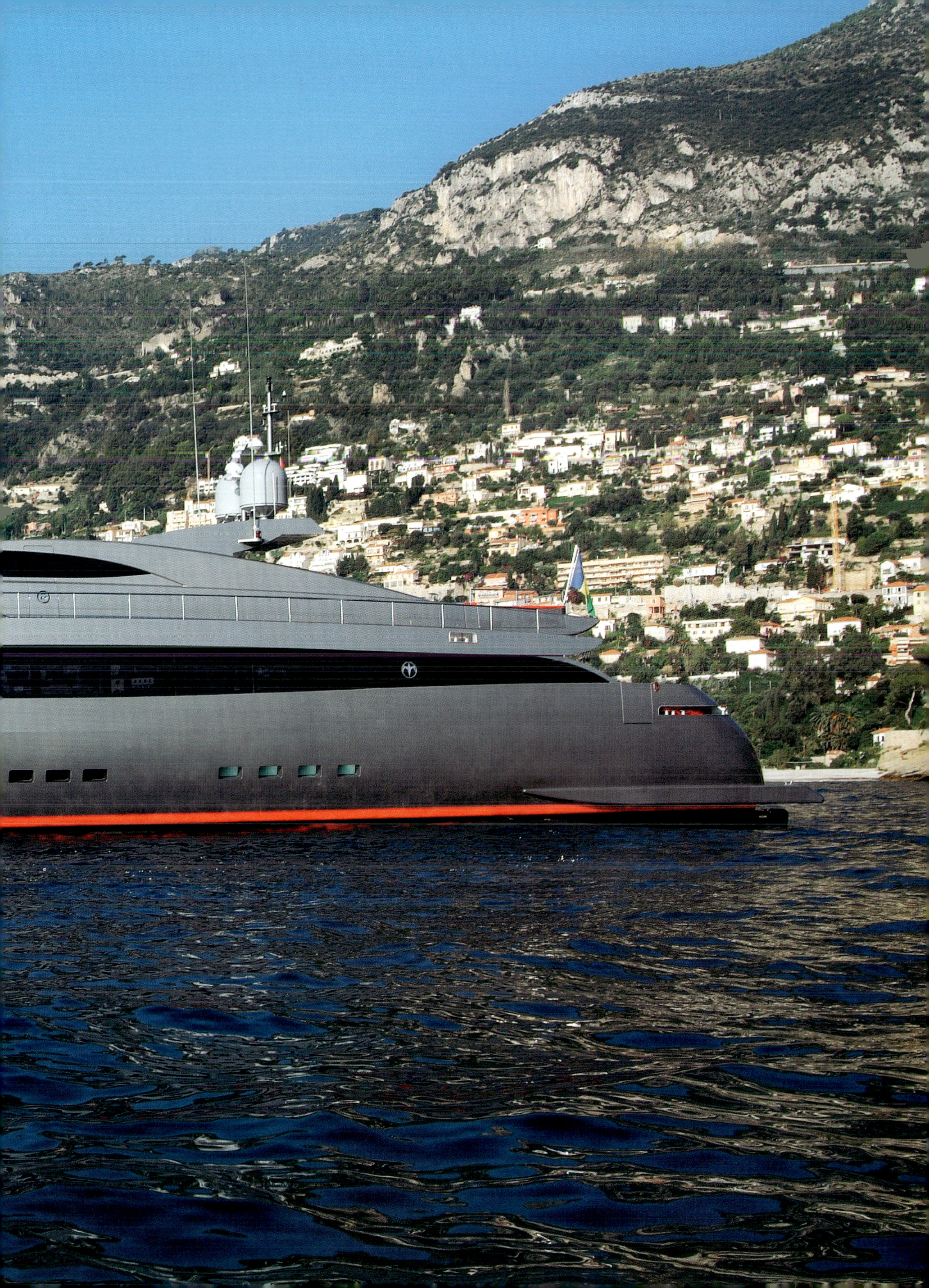

LEFT: *The upper deck, looking forward toward the glass doors of the owner's study.*

ABOVE: *The study is appointed with Arne Jacobsen and Marcel Breuer furniture. The tongue-and-groove, sanded-teak floor extends from the study to the deck, blurring the indoor/outdoor boundary.*

ety of textures underfoot provides sensuous pleasures. Leather walls contribute another textural element. The glass doors on either side of the living garden contain a liquid-crystal technology that allows them to change from clear to opaque. When clear, there is an unobstructed view from front to back. The bulkheads, partitions, and some of the built-in furniture are treated with a chalk-based plaster that can easily be updated and repainted. The ceiling has a stressed, metallic palladium finish on top of a red primer that reflects natural light during the day and artificial light at night. Again, in keeping with the motif of bringing the outside in, the highly polished stainless-steel window frames are angled to capture light reflecting off the sea.

The saloon's theme of light and texture is continued in

the owner's suite, located forward of the saloon. Light floods in through the skylight and side windows, but roll-up shades can modify, diffuse, or block it out. Bed coverings of linen, cashmere, fur, and suede afford great textural variety. A flat-screen TV is housed behind a tinted panel. Two side doors open to private, fold-out balconies, again bringing the outside in. In the stunning master bathroom, the washbasin and tub are made from 150-year-old Japanese hinoky wood, which exudes a delicate perfume when wet, providing an inexhaustible source of aromatherapy. Porfiri says this wood, which comes from a forest near Kyoto, is the most expensive in the world.

Aft on the lower deck—reached by a very tactile staircase—is the VIP stateroom, which can be either a full-beam suite with his-and-hers bathrooms, or two cabins with en suite bathrooms separated by a screen that slides out of the closet. Each of the two identical double guest cabins features Pullman berths and inventive ladders to reach them. All the closets are fitted with a series of compartments that Porfiri likens to a Louis Vuitton travel trunk. In these cabins, the curved structure of the yacht is fully revealed.

On the flying bridge level of the top deck is the owner's clean-lined, wood-panelled study, featuring yet another skylight and Arne Jacobsen and Marcel Breuer furniture. The tongue-and-groove, sanded-teak floor extends from the study to the outside deck, where a portable awning can be rolled out and unfurled to shade the long, sanded-teak dining table. Inside, outside—the boundaries blur here, as everywhere on this boat.

The overall effect of *Nina J* is eclectic: modern, contemporary, casual chic, with an antique here, an important piece of furniture there. For the most part, the interior is light and white, although blocks of reds and lime greens accent the saloon. The palette of the owner's stateroom is a bit earthier with its rust, parchment, and sand tones, cooled by the splash of turquoise that can be viewed through the windows.

ABOVE: *A portable awning can be rolled out and unfurled to shade the aft deck's long, sanded-teak dining table. A large sun pad sits aft.*

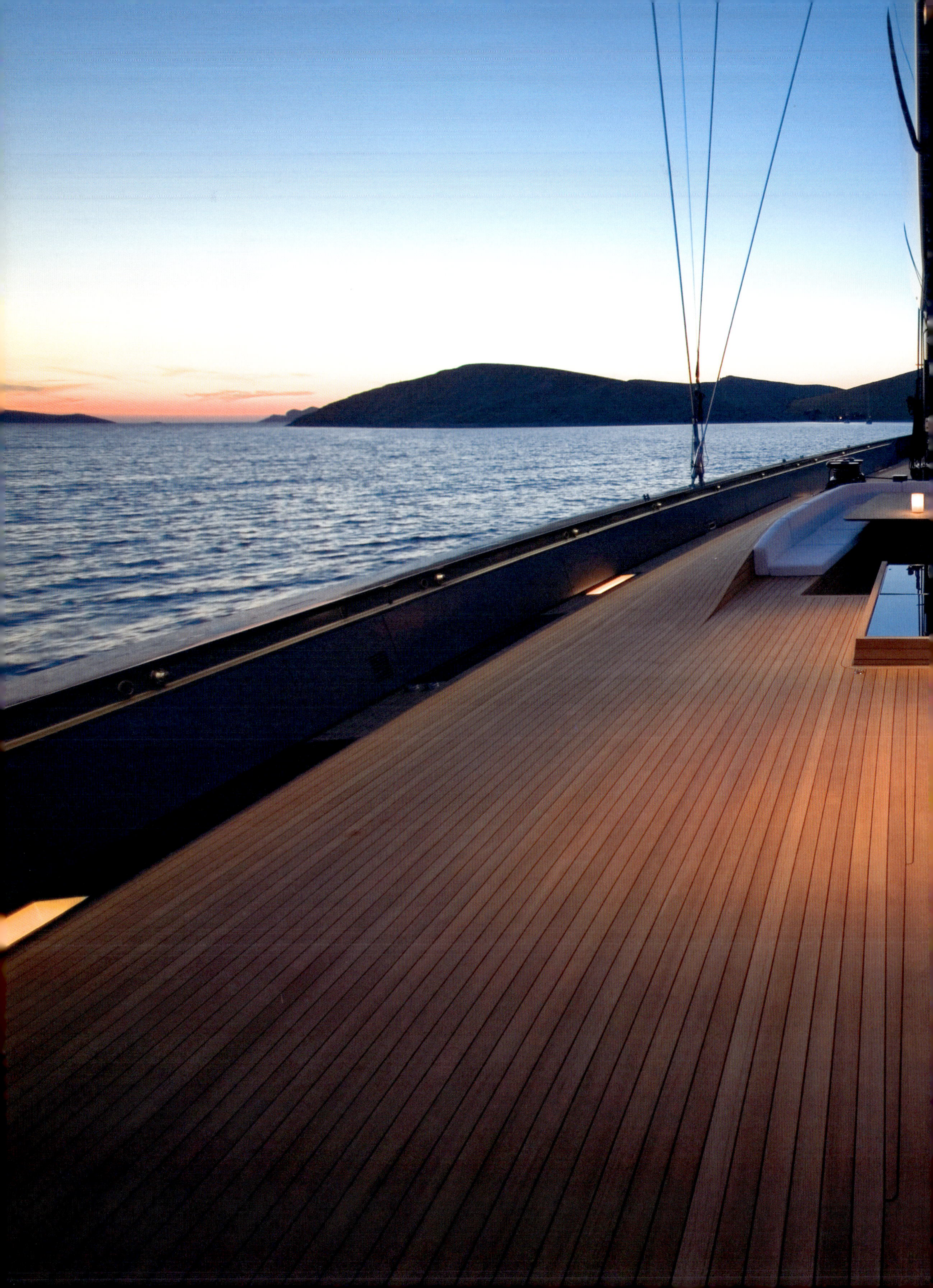

Wally 143
Esense

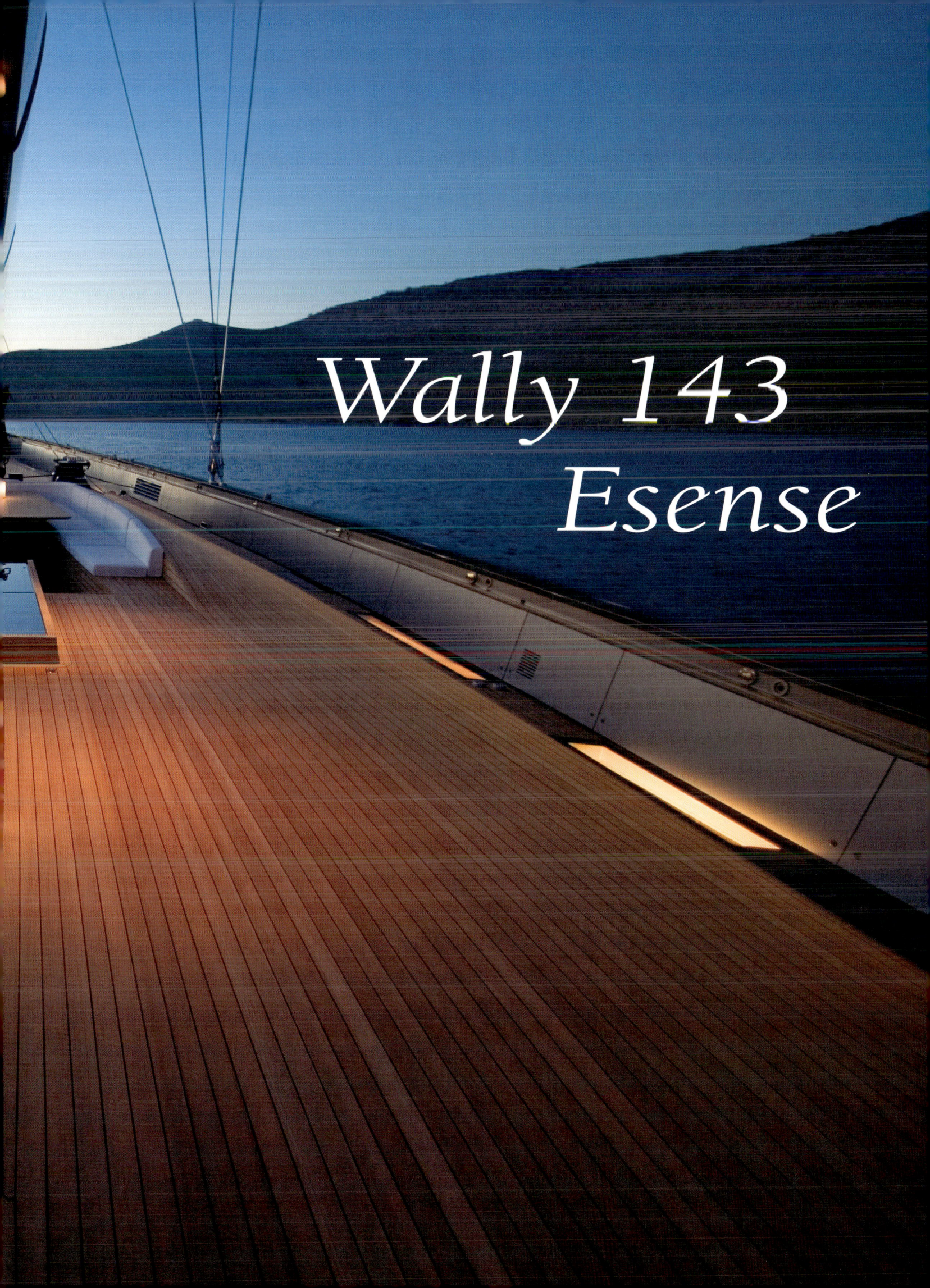

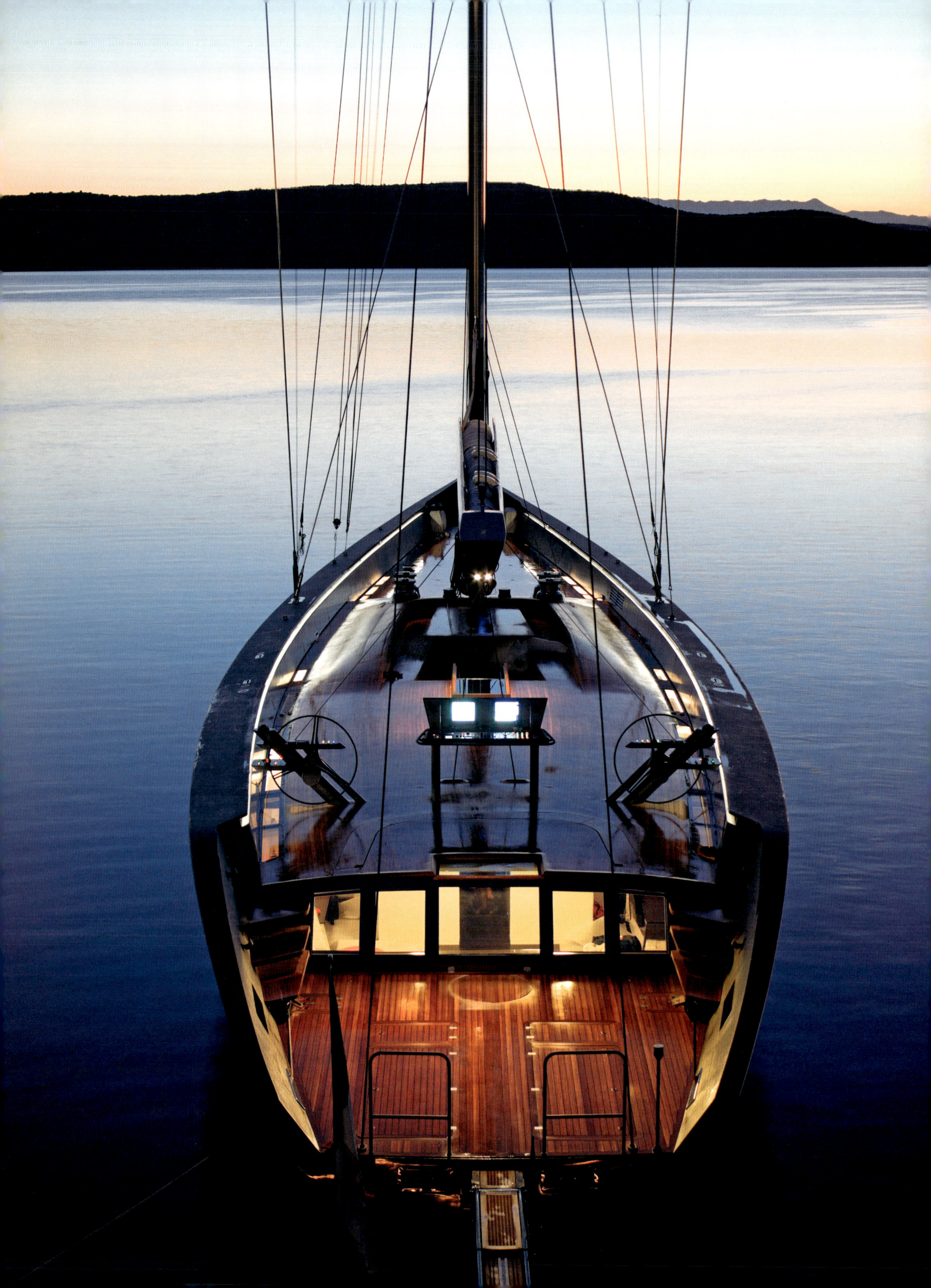

RIGHT: *The forward cockpit provides maximum interface with the elements while sailing, dining, or socializing.*

No yacht afloat exudes greater style than a Wally. In the eyes of many, Wallys are simply the sexiest sailing yachts on the water. Their impossibly uncluttered decks, sublimely simple yet elegant interiors, and aggressive exterior profiles place them in a class unto themselves. Descriptors like "classic" and "traditional" are not part of the program. Company founder Luca Bassani is a mould breaker of the first order. Guided by his enlightened vision, Wally has rocked the mores and conventions of yacht design and construction since the early 1990s.

The 143-foot (43.6-metre) *Esense,* launched in late 2006 at the Wally Europe yard in Fano, Italy, won the prestigious ShowBoats International Award for Outstanding Achievement in a Sailing Yacht. She furthered the evolution of the Wally brand in ways large and small. At the time of her launch, she was some thirty-five feet longer than any Wally sailing yacht ever built. She was also the first Wally built with an eye toward serious world cruising. To attain that goal, she was equipped with hearty electrical and mechanical systems suitable for long ocean passages away from civilization. Her fuel capacity gives her transatlantic range under power.

Her naval architect was American Bill Tripp, who endowed her with underbody shapes intended to generate superior sailing performance. Despite her size, the simplicity of her sailing systems enables her to be operated by a crew of exactly one, although, as with any large yacht, it's much more pleasurable to let a full crew do the sailing.

Superb sailing performance is a central component of all Wallys, but the brand's signature element is style—unearthly shapes and expansive spaces on deck and cutting-edge design below. The deck of *Esense* comprises some 2,000 square feet (186 square meters) of nearly hardware-free, barefoot-friendly teak. This sprawl of hardwood is bordered by wide, flat bulwarks that

PRECEDING PAGES AND OPPOSITE: *The decks of the Wally 143* Esense *epitomize the builder's signature commitment to uncluttered spaces. Sails are controlled from the helm.*

double nicely as seating while the yacht is in port. Reduce her scale to one-tenth, and she might easily be mistaken for a high-performance sailing dinghy. Her "terrace-on-the-sea" aft deck places guests in close contact with the water and provides access to the saloon, which, atypically for most sailboats, is positioned aft. Few motoryachts and even fewer sailing yachts are as beautifully designed for alfresco entertaining, which was a priority for her young Italian owners.

On the *Esense,* as on all Wallys, carbon fibre serves as both a high-tech, performance-enhancing building material and an aesthetic element. The distinctive black weave of this material can be seen in accents throughout the yacht. Her hull is made of a carbon-fibre composite that is light, strong, and stiff. Her 187-foot- (57-metre-) tall mast is also made of carbon fibre, which reduces weight aloft to improve sailing performance. Her North 3DL carbon mainsail furls into the boom.

Wallys' signature interior style is modern-minimalist-elegant. French designer Odile Decq's decor for *Esense*—her first yacht project—takes the look to new heights. The sharp, geometric shapes of the furniture and the starkly contrasting white and black colour scheme accented with bold splashes of orange suggest an aesthetic fusion of the 1950s and sometime far off in the future. Clutter is not part of a Wally's interior design vocabulary. Like the deck, the public spaces below are well suited to large-scale entertaining with intimate areas created by the general layout of corridors and media and utility stations, but few impediments tment.

The yacht has four staterooms. The master spans the full beam and features a queen-size bed, a writing desk/office, and an en suite head, shower and sink. The sunken bathtub—undoubtedly one of the sexiest ever created—is made of carbon fibre. It is situated beneath the removable teak decking of the shower-stall floor. Two of the guest cabins have twin beds and en suite heads and showers. The third guest cabin has two Pullman berths and an en suite head and shower. *Esense* accommodates a crew of six, including the captain, in three cabins.

Esense is the first of a new breed of Wally supersailers expected to eventually approach 200 feet (61 metres) in length.

TOP AND BOTTOM LEFT: Esense was conceived as a long-distance world cruiser, but naval architect Bill Tripp endowed her with high-performance sailing qualities as well. Her simplified controls allow her to be sailed by a small crew.

ABOVE: Ornate is not in the Wally design vocabulary. The main saloon of Esense is a striking example of the company's minimalist aesthetic, as well as that of the interior designer, Odile Decq. It was her first yacht project.

LOA: 143' (43.6 m)
Beam: 28' (8.5 m)
Draft: board up/down 13' 1"–19' 8" (4–6 m)
Naval architect: Tripp Design Naval Architect
Exterior styling: Wally
Interior design: Odile Decq
Builder / year: Wally, Fano, Italy / 2006
Hull construction: Carbon fibre

164 / OUTRAGEOUS YACHTS

LEFT, BELOW, AND BOTTOM: Throughout the interior, the geometric shapes of the furnishings and fixtures, in combination with the starkly contrasting white, black, and orange colour scheme, suggest an aesthetic fusion of the 1950s and sometime in the future.

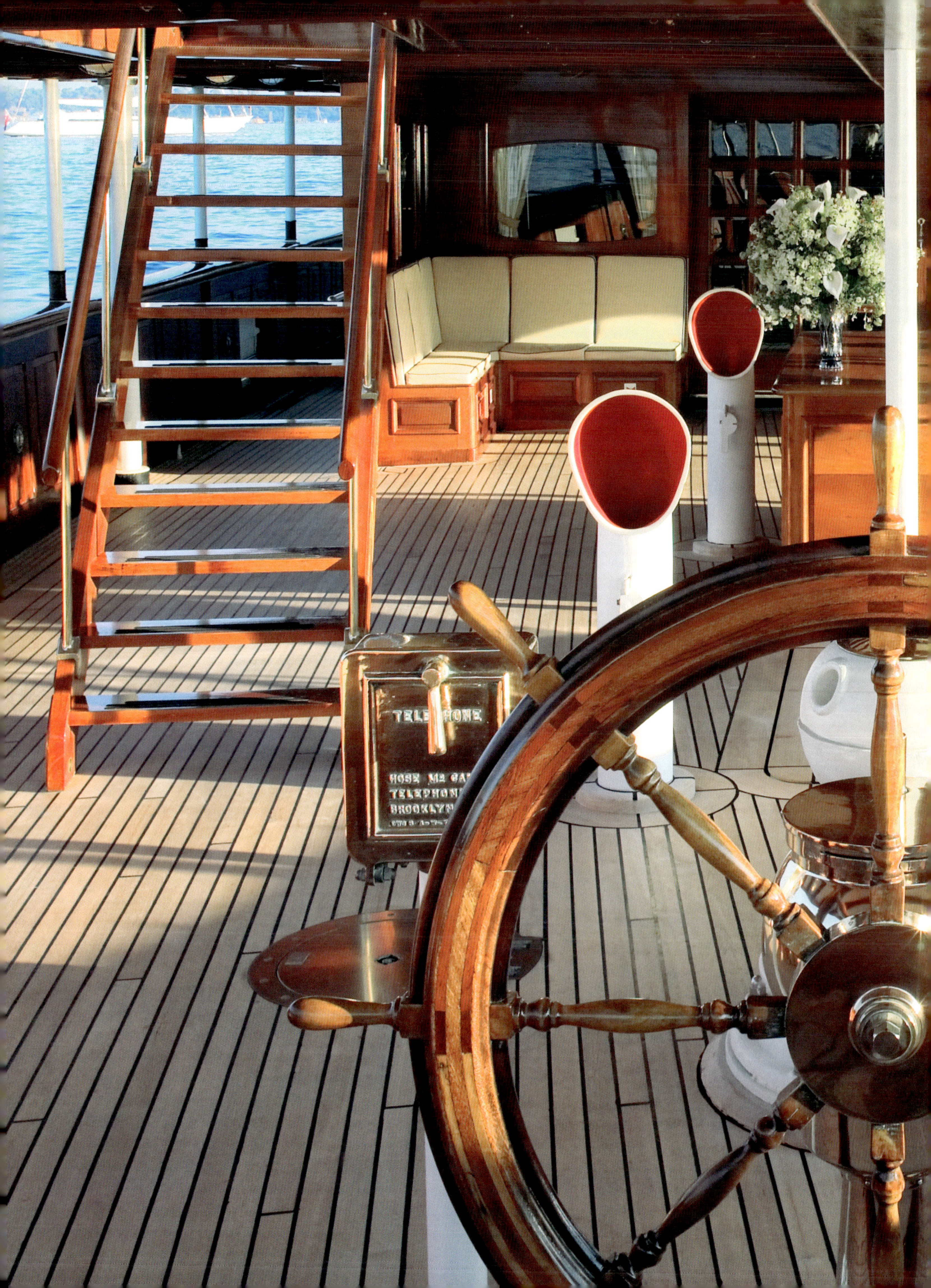

S.S. Delphine

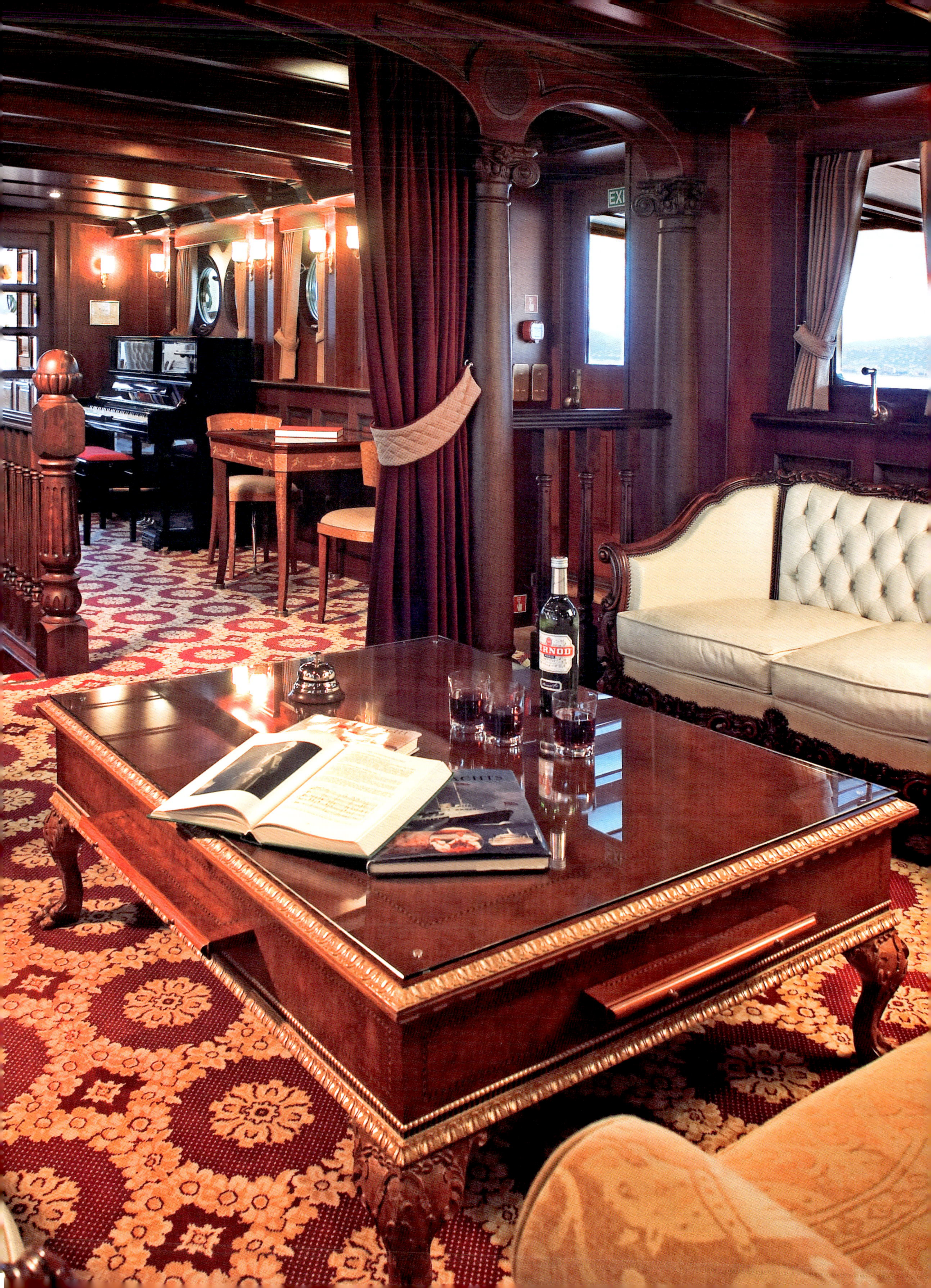

PRECEDING PAGES: *Delphine's main deck comprises a dining room, a lounge, a covered outside space, and three guest staterooms. Aft is the emergency steering wheel.*

In the rarefied worlds of thoroughbred racehorses, show dogs, and the social elite, pedigree means everything. In the yachting world, that term is reserved for yachts associated with exceptional designers, builders, or owners. The *S.S. Delphine* is such a yacht.

Delphine's pedigree is unassailable. Ordered in 1918 by automotive magnate Horace Dodge of Detroit and launched in 1921 shortly after his death, the 257-foot (78-metre) steam-powered (S.S. stands for steamship) yacht was designed by the renowned New York firm headed by Henry John Gielow. She was built at the Great Lakes Engineering Works in Michigan. At the time of her launch, she was the largest steam yacht in terms of tonnage in America and the largest yacht on the Great Lakes. The cost to build her in current U.S. dollars has been estimated at $160 million.

The breadth of *Delphine's* near century-long story is impossible to detail in brief, but there are a number of noteworthy milestones. After her launch, the yacht lived a mostly charmed life for decades in the hands of Dodge's widow, Anna. When she wasn't cruising, *Delphine* spent much of the time tied to a private pier off the Dodge compound in Grosse Pointe, Michigan. She was nearly lost in 1926 when she sank at a pier in the Hudson River in New York City after catching fire. The Dodge family had her raised and at great expense her badly damaged interior was rebuilt or replaced as required to restore her to her former glory.

OPPOSITE: *Corinthian columns and red curtains separate the aft part of the lounge, which houses a bar, a Yamaha Disklavier piano, and a game table, from the sitting area forward.*

RIGHT: *Her side decks possess the feel of an old cruise liner.*

Like many yachts, *Delphine* was requisitioned by the U.S. Navy during World War II. With her name changed to the *U.S.S. Dauntless*, she served as flagship of Admiral Ernest King, Commander in Chief of the U.S. Fleet and Chief of Naval Operations. There were unconfirmed rumours that Franklin D. Roosevelt, Winston Churchill, and other world leaders met on board the yacht, which was stationed in Washington D.C., in order to plan war strategy.

The Dodge family purchased her back after the war, reconverted her into a yacht, and kept her until 1968, when she was sold to the Lundberg Seamanship School in Maryland, to be used as a training vessel. In the mid-1980s she was sold to a company that planned to turn her into a cruise ship. But like so many "old ladies" *Delphine* eventually fell into disrepair. A subsequent series of owners attempted to restore her and keep her from the scrap yard before the Bruynooghe family of Belgium acquired her in 1997 in Marseilles and began a thorough restoration of the yacht and her precious engines that took five years to complete.

Much of her bronze and brass hardware had been removed over the years, but the Bruynooghes discovered that many important pieces had been saved simply because they'd been painted over. Besides sheer size and

LOA: 257' 10" (78.58 m)
Beam: 35' 5" (10.8 m)
Draft: 22' (6.7 m)
Naval architect: Henry John Gielow
Exterior styling: Great Lakes Engineering Works
Interior design / restoration: Ineke Bruynooghe
Builder / year: Great Lakes Engineering Works, Detroit, Michigan / 1921
Top speed: 11 knots
Hull construction: Steel

RIGHT: *The uppermost deck is completely outside. Its central attraction is a swim spa, which functions as a jacuzzi, a standard pool, and a current pool.*

TOP: *The S.S. Delphine in her early years. She was commissioned in 1919 by automobile magnate Horace Dodge and launched in 1921, shortly after his death.*

ABOVE: *Delphine as she appears today. She was saved from the scrap yard by the Bruynooghe family of Belgium. Her scrupulous restoration was directed by art historian Ineke Bruynooghe.*

sublimely elegant accommodations, two features stand out on this magnificent example of an early-twentieth-century pleasure craft. She has a striking "navy" bow, which, instead of tapering aft from the farthest forward point, rakes slightly forward toward the waterline. This design had several advantages over the clipper bow, which was more popular at the time: it reduced pitching in waves, maximized waterline length, thus increasing potential speed, and provided more space for interior accommodations. The navy bow can be seen on the ships of Teddy Roosevelt's Great White Fleet and other warships of the late nineteenth and early twentieth centuries.

The *Delphine*'s other standout feature is her steam power. She was built at a time when yachts and smaller ships were transitioning from steam power to diesel. It is ironic that a yacht commissioned by a twentieth-century automaker would have a steam engine, but Horace Dodge planned to take her around the world and her designers felt it would be easier to find skilled service for steam engines than diesel engines in faraway ports. Her quadruple-expansion steam engines can propel her to a top speed of 11 knots. They were completely refurbished during her recent refit.

Unlike modern yachts, which have engines that start with the push of a button, *Delphine*'s engines take time and special care to get going. First her oil-fired boilers must be ignited. As steam pressure builds to the

OPPOSITE: *Her rare, quadruple-expansion steam engines turn at a quiet 80–100 rpm and propel the yacht to a 10-knot top speed. She is the only steam yacht of her size available for charter.*

170 / OUTRAGEOUS YACHTS

No 578
GREAT LAKES
ENGINEERING WORKS,
DETROIT, MICHIGAN.
1921
ASTERN
AHEAD
FULL
HALF
SLOW
STAND BY
STOP
WITH
ENGINES

OPPOSITE: *Forward on the main deck is the dining room. Its three large round tables and two small tables seat twenty-six comfortably. All the interior spaces were restored in compliance with rigorous modern safety standards.*

TOP: *The lounge bar serves guests both in the lounge itself and on the promenade deck.*

ABOVE: *The music room is the largest public space on board and sports the largest bar, at which nine people can be accommodated easily. Three sitting areas are arranged around the Steinway piano. Together they can seat fourteen people.*

appropriate level, the machinery slowly begins to turn. And unlike modern diesel yachts, which may have just one engineer and an assistant to monitor operation, *Delphine* requires a whole team, including "oilers" who continuously move around the complex machinery lubricating various moving parts.

Whereas on modern yachts the helmsman has direct, instantaneous control over engine speed, on the *Delphine* the engines are controlled by telegraphs—mechanical controls on the bridge that let the engineer know the desired speed for each engine. Such systems make manoeuvering in tight quarters extremely difficult. To improve her manoeuverability, the Bruynooghes refitted her with a modern bow and stern thrusters.

Delphine's restoration was directed by Ineke Bruynooghe, an art historian who conducted extensive research into the yacht's history and construction. She was rechristened in 2003 by H.S.H. Princess Stephanie of Monaco.

In her current configuration, she accommodates twenty-six guests in twelve staterooms, including a spectacular owner's suite, and carries a crew of twenty-seven. Her interior was not only painstakingly recreated but also updated to comply with the highest commercial safety standards. She sports numerous modern amenities, including a gym, a hair salon, a large sauna, a jacuzzi and a mosaic Turkish bath. Her navigation and entertainment systems were retrofitted to meet current standards.

Yacht restorations on this scale are rare; every one preserves valuable elements of world maritime heritage that are more often than not lost to the scrap yard or wood pile.

Delphine is now available for charter in the Mediterranean.

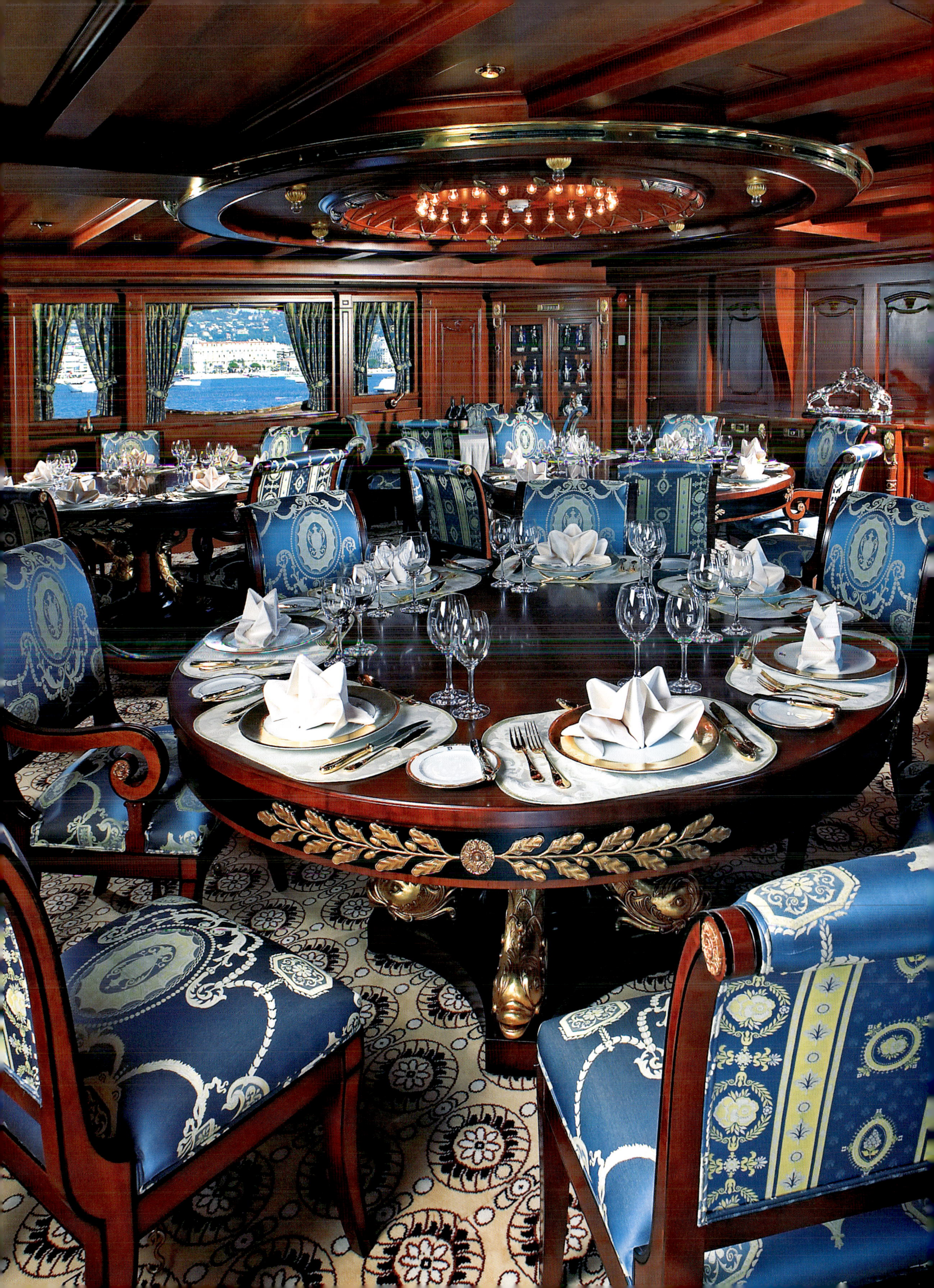

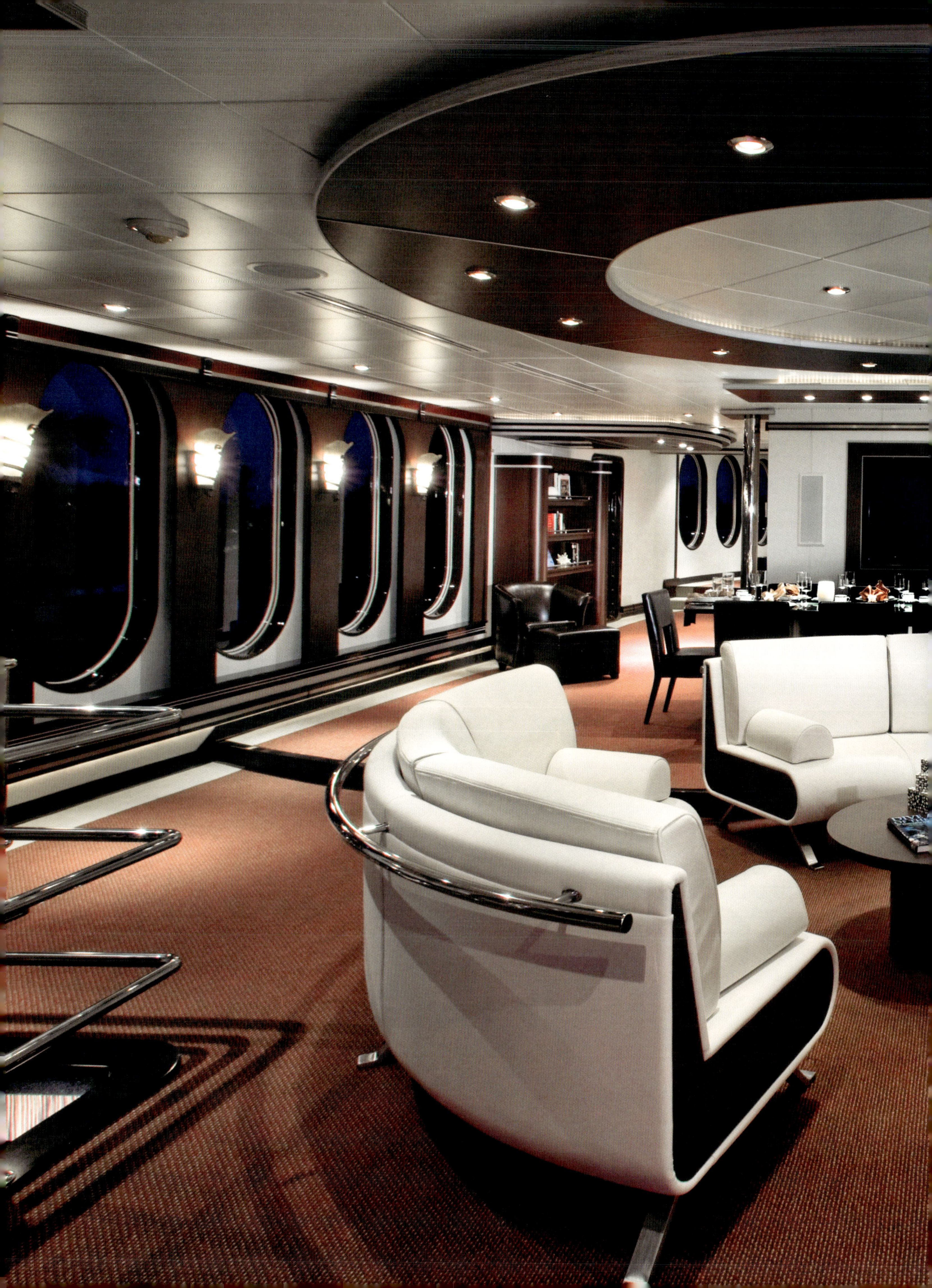

Allure Shadow

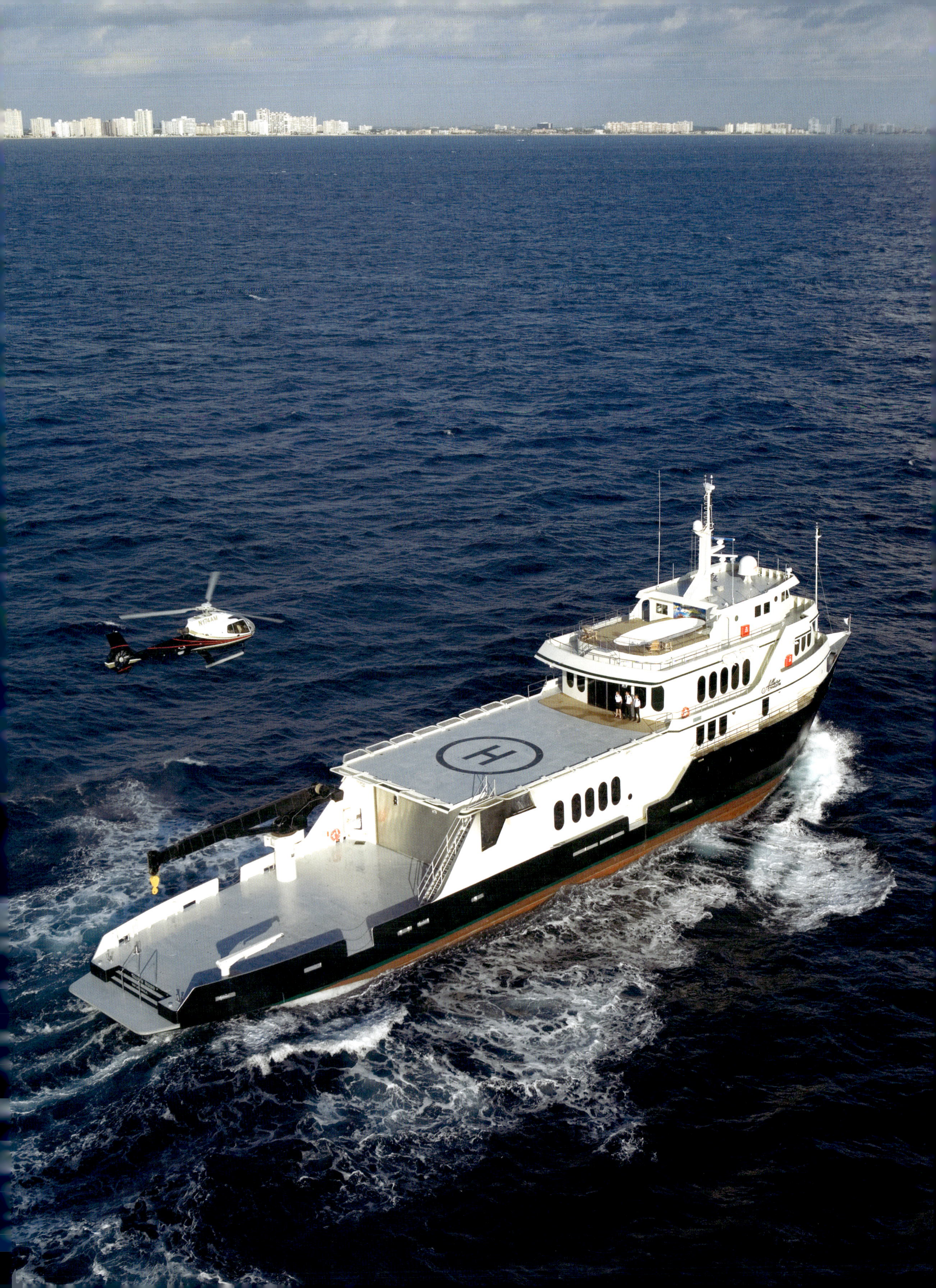

PRECEDING PAGES: *As befits an escort boat,* Allure Shadow's *interior decor is tastefully functional, and more typical of cruise-ship decor than that of most luxury yachts.*

It's a tanker. It's a freighter. It's an airport. It's a parking garage. It's everything the typical superyacht isn't, which is good news for yachtsmen who don't believe in travelling light.

An axiom of the yachting world is that all yachts represent compromise. Allocating more space for one thing often means taking away space from something else or leaving something behind. Unlike land-based structures, yachts cannot be built out or added onto. Yet more and more yachtsmen want to take small boats, dive gear, helicopters, or their favourite motor vehicles cruising with them.

In the past, virtually the only option for yacht owners who found themselves short on space was to build a larger boat. But recently, enterprising builders have developed a new class of vessel commonly called a "shadow" or "escort" boat. These boats are designed to carry small craft, water toys, additional crew, aircraft, or the owner's personal staff without compromising space on the mothership. The 220-foot (67-metre) *Allure Shadow* from Shadow Marine is a brawny example of this new breed of seagoing garage.

To develop its line of shadow boats, Shadow Marine obtained access to a fleet of decommissioned oil-industry vessels on the U.S. Gulf Coast. They selected the hulls that were most seaworthy and had the greatest structural integrity. A typical Shadow conversion involves cutting off the entire superstructure, removing the electrical and mechanical systems, and rebuilding the boats from the hull up, adding appropriate equipment and accommodations. The vessels are begun on spec, but are customized for an owner's needs when they are sold. Although all the Shadow Marine refits have been customized to some degree, two standard features have been incorporated into each hull: a full-scale helicopter landing area and a hangar.

Allure Shadow's helipad measures 50 x 34 feet (15.2 x 10.4 metres) and, unlike the typical yacht helipad, it can accommodate even the heaviest private helicopters. Positioned on the hangar deck below, a 35-ton crane with a 58-foot (17.7-metre) reach can lift the helicopter off the pad and move it down into the climate-controlled hangar, where it is protected from the corrosive salt air. The air-conditioned hangar is fitted with tie-downs to secure vessels and vehicles of any type, from Land Rovers and sports cars to mini-submarines. When an owner is cruising, *Allure Shadow* can be sent ahead of the main yacht to launch toys on a remote beach or be anchored some distance from a congested, restricted harbour, such as Monaco or St. Tropez, to serve as a landing pad for guests ferrying in by helicopter.

Functionality is the prevailing theme of all Shadow conversions. That applies to the accommodations as well. A buyer may find the arrangement and decor suitable for his needs, but he may also choose to upgrade, particularly if he plans to use the vessel as a primary yacht.

Allure Shadow has six staterooms with private baths and balconies on the guest deck; an expansive sky lounge and entertainment area on the helideck; and a game room, gym/spa, and theatre/library on the main deck. A pool shares the top deck with the bridge. The yacht's decor is tasteful, but more typical of that found

OPPOSITE: *Her exterior, while devoid of the rust and grime found on commercial vessels, is still all business.*

RIGHT: *Shadow Marine's initial conversion of* Allure *from oil-rig service vessel to yacht included the installation of luxury amenities. An outdoor pool with an all-weather flat-screen TV was part of the upgrade.*

Allure Shadow's *combined saloon/dining room is tastefully, if not opulently, decorated. The conversion was intended to create a tag-along vessel to carry gear, staff, and overflow guests.*

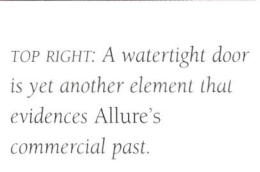

TOP RIGHT: A watertight door is yet another element that evidences Allure's commercial past.

BOTTOM RIGHT: The bar is in keeping with the utilitarian spirit of the interior.

ABOVE: Allure Shadow has TVs in nearly every space. The screening room has a 65-inch (165-centimetre) model and thundering surround sound.

LOA: 220' (67 m)
Beam: 40' (12.2 m)
Draft: 8' / 12' (2.4 m / 3.7 m)
Naval architect: Shadow Marine
Exterior styling: Lay Pittman & Associates
Interior design: Kimberly Gonzales
Builder / year: Shadow Marine, Florida / 2007
Top speed: 12 knots
Hull construction: Steel

on cruise ships than that of most luxury yachts. The interior, installed by Shadow, though functional, is done with subtle elegance. The custom furniture and cabinets are covered with mahogany and Fineline veneers on the guest decks and clean plastic laminates on the crew decks. The custom sofas and settees are upholstered in Majalite, a strong, durable synthetic leather, with wood veneer and stainless-steel appointments. The easy-maintenance, fire-resistant suspended overheads are by Dampa Marine Ceiling Systems, and the countertops are Corian and stainless steel.

Instead of marble or exotic wood, the floors are covered in Stratica, an eco-friendly material simulating wood and tile, and the carpeting is low-maintenance wool. The colour scheme throughout is white for overheads, walls, and upholstery, a dark veneer for furniture, and burgundy for carpeting. Art Deco-style sconces provide soft lighting throughout the guest areas.

Allure Shadow is equipped with a Kaleidescape entertainment system that holds thousands of songs and movies, and there are flat screens in nearly every space on board. The cinema has the feel of a mogul's private screening room, with a 65-inch (165-centimetre) flat screen and a thundering audio system. The sky lounge is also equipped with a 65-inch flat-screen. Each bunk in the children's suite has its own screen as well.

Functioning as a tender to another yacht, *Allure Shadow* can serve as a portable fueling station for an owner's main yacht. She has a fuel capacity of 100,000 gallons, as well as tanks for aviation fuel and gasoline for small boats and personal watercraft. Her engines are industrial-strength, bulletproof, 16-cylinder Caterpillar 399 diesels that generate 1,225 horsepower each and produce a top speed of 12 knots. They've been stripped down and completely rebuilt. Her plumbing, HVAC, and water-treatment systems are commercial in scale.

Nearly every yacht today is equipped with some sort of at-anchor stabilization system. *Allure* relies on a time-tested fin-less system known as a Flume tank to reduce rolling. The Flume system comprises a large, baffled water tank, oriented athwartships, which fills up on the side opposite the direction toward which the ship is rolling. Essentially a passive system, it requires little maintenance and also works well at anchor.

Adventurers who climb high peaks focus on getting themselves to the top, while bearers haul the gear. For adventurous yachtsmen who prefer to sail with all the luxuries they love, *Allure Shadow* is the ultimate seagoing sherpa.

TOP: *In the spirit of cruise ships, each guest stateroom has its own full bathroom and private balcony.*

ABOVE: *The gym has a markedly commercial feel.*

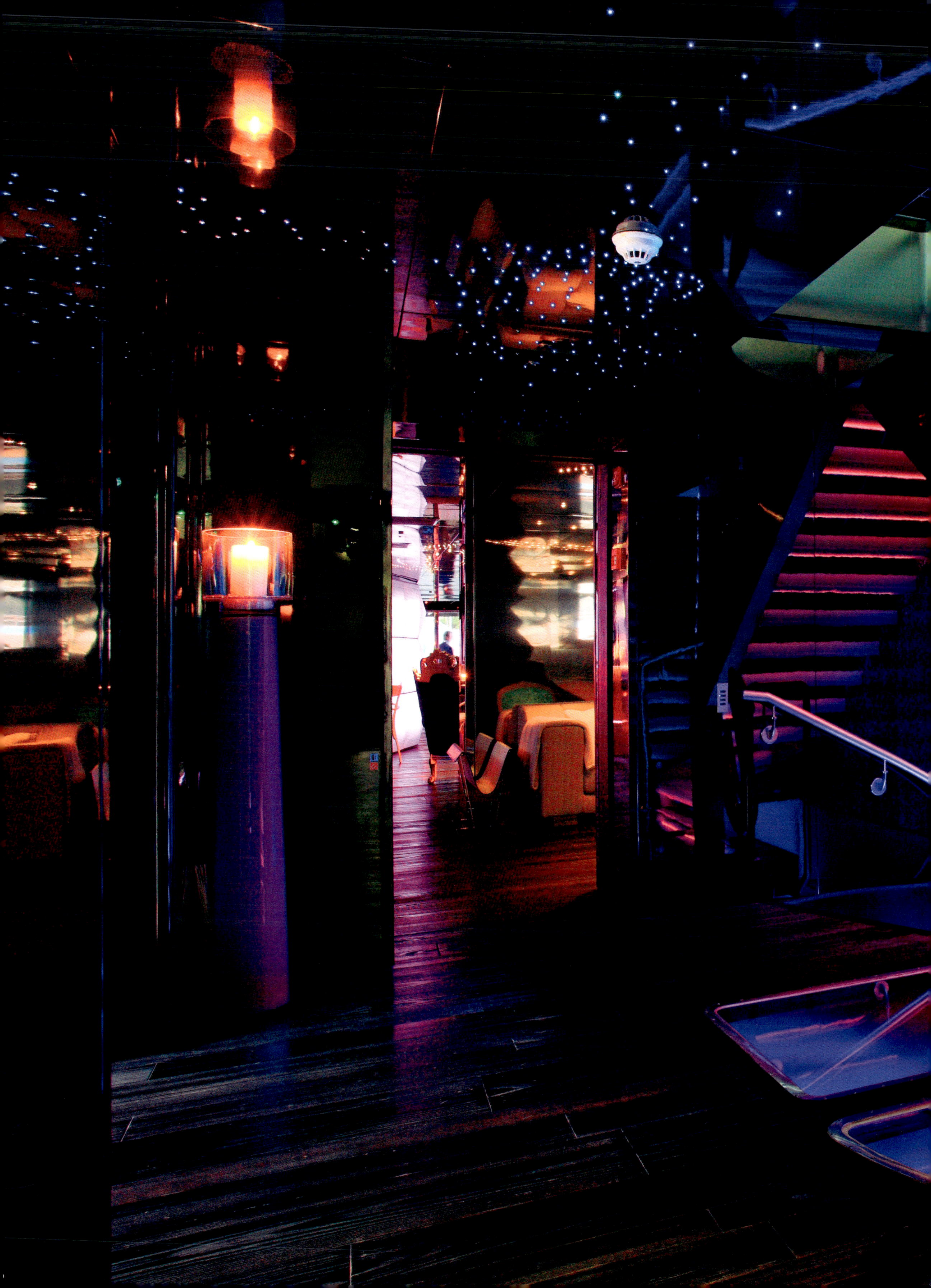

Sea Force One

PRECEDING PAGES: *The interior is filled with theatrical symbolism. For instance, prominently displayed on the main landing of the Plexiglas-and-steel central staircase is a bronze sculpture of the owner's personal icon—a fishhook that he always wears around his neck.*

LEFT: As one enters the main saloon, the hypnotic video art of Fabrizio Plessi dazzles the senses.

In 2008, at the prestigious Monaco Yacht Show, which annually showcases the world's finest superyachts, Prince Albert II personally toured a select handful of the year's most exceptional yachts. His tour of *Sea Force One* (the name is a take-off on Air Force One) turned out to be his longest. There is much to absorb on this highly unusual yacht, and it requires time to take it all in. The typical reaction upon entry is disbelief that one is on a boat. The experience is more theatrical than nautical, and the deeper one delves into her interior spaces, the greater the wow factor. The decor is deliberately suggestive of *Pirates of the Caribbean* and *Phantom of the Opera* staged at an art space in Chelsea in New York City. All of this is purely by design. The young European owner of *Sea Force One* was very involved in her conception. He unashamedly explains that the boat is all about himself and his alter ego, Captain Magic, a character who is part pirate and part warrior. The boat's logo, which is depicted on the transom, is half skull and half mask. This yin and yang of romance and contradiction is a theme that carries through the entire boat.

Admiral Mariotti Yachts built the 177-foot (54-metre) *Sea Force One* in conjunction with Cantieri Navali Lavagna in Genoa and naval architect Luca Dini. Typical of other modern motoryachts of her size, she has ample living quarters, sleeps ten guests in five cabins, and op-

RIGHT: The owner, who calls himself Captain Magic, designed much of the furniture, including the hammock that hangs in the main saloon.

OPPOSITE: *Sliding glass doors make it possible to dine alfresco in the sky-deck dining area.*

ABOVE: *Luca Dini's design for the exterior of* Sea Force One *is aggressive and military looking, with no-nonsense styling.*

LOA: 176' 6" (53.8 m)
Beam: 34' 5" (10.5 m)
Draft: 9' 6" (2.9 m)
Naval architect: Luca Dini Design
Exterior styling: Luca Dini / Admiral Mariotti Yachts
Interior design: Owner
Builder / year: Admiral Mariotti Yachts, Milan, Italy / Cantieri Navali Lavagna, Genoa, Italy / 2008
Top speed: 18 knots
Hull construction: Steel

erates with up to twelve crew. Her appointments, however, are completely unconventional and unboatlike. For starters, she is not a "white" boat; the dynamically shaped hull is painted a polished black and the superstructure is steely silver. *Sea Force One* is the second yacht that the yard built for the owner. (Unusually, the boat was constructed more like a ship than a traditional yacht. Instead of the plating-over-frames construction typical of steel yachts, the hull was built in seventeen discrete sections that were then joined together. Similarly, the superstructure was fabricated from seven aluminium sections.) Incorporated into the hull are three hydraulic terraces, one off the main foyer and one on either side of the master stateroom. Today, it is more and more common for yachts to have balconies or beach terraces, but when the boat was conceived in 2004, open balconies were rather revolutionary. The aggressive exterior shape is even more dramatic at night, when light is projected from the main deck and strip lighting illuminates the hull. High-tech lighting, fibre optics, and automation are all key to this yacht. In fact there are more than 49 miles (80 kilometres) of wiring aboard.

Although the exterior is impressive, it is not until you step aboard that you feel transported to Captain Magic's world. The main saloon entryway is flanked by white pyramid-like protrusions. No raised-and-fielded mahogany panelling here; instead, the material is barrisol—a stretchy synthetic fabric used occasionally by avant-garde architects and artists. Those familiar with the modern dance troupe Pilobolus might recall their use of this sensual fabric in their choreography. On *Sea Force One* the white translucent material is backlit, creating a light show of ever-changing colours. The entrance to the main saloon also features Mai-Thu Perret's sculpture *Big Golden Rock*. The furniture in the saloon is equally whimsical; a white fur sofa, a black fur swing suspended from the ceiling, and a large white leather table in which Kiki Smith's work *The Bones* is encased. The owner designed much of the furniture himself.

The bulkhead dividing the main saloon and the media room is a steel partition with hypnotic video art by Fabrizio Plessi consisting of multicoloured spheres

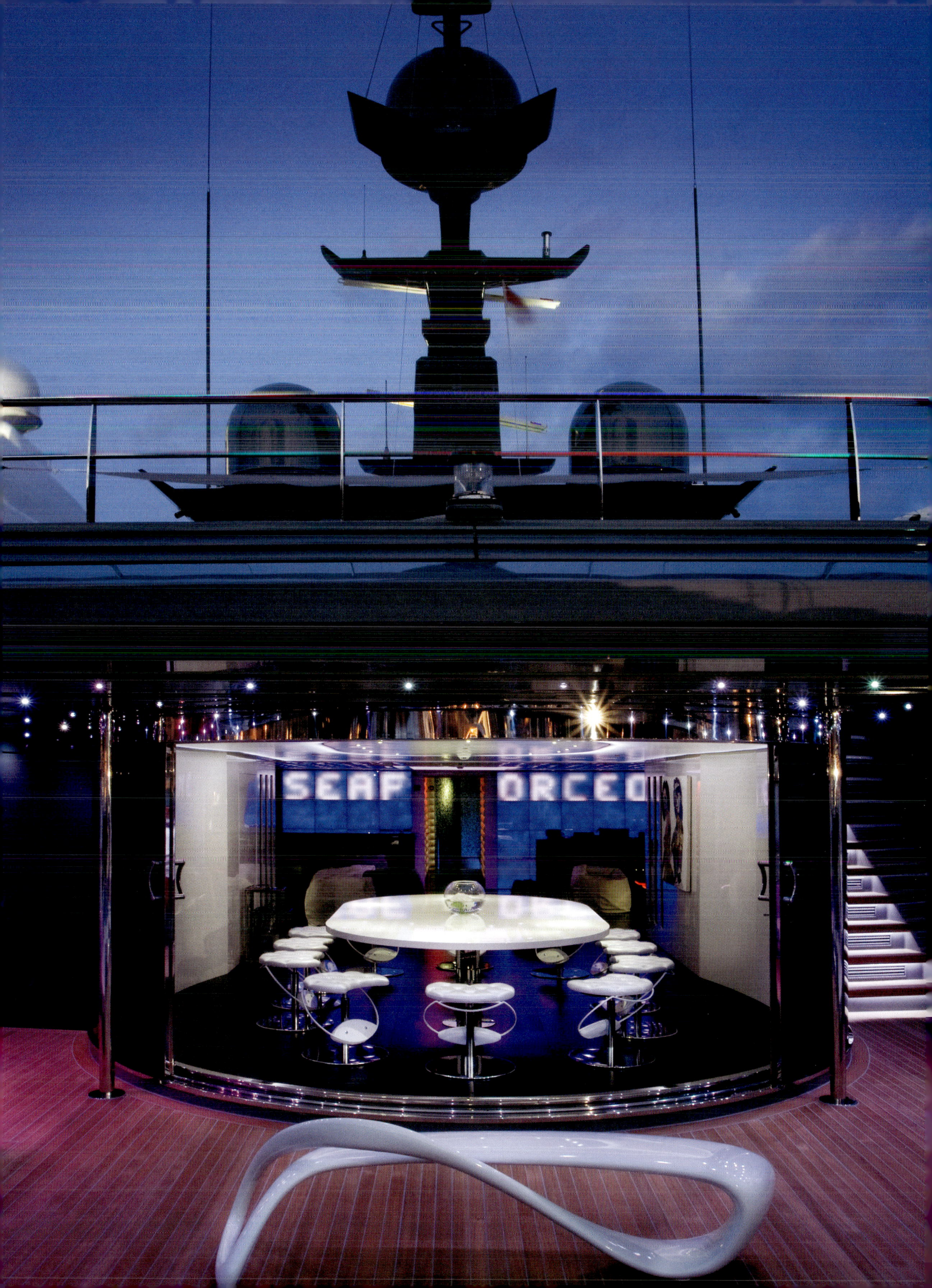

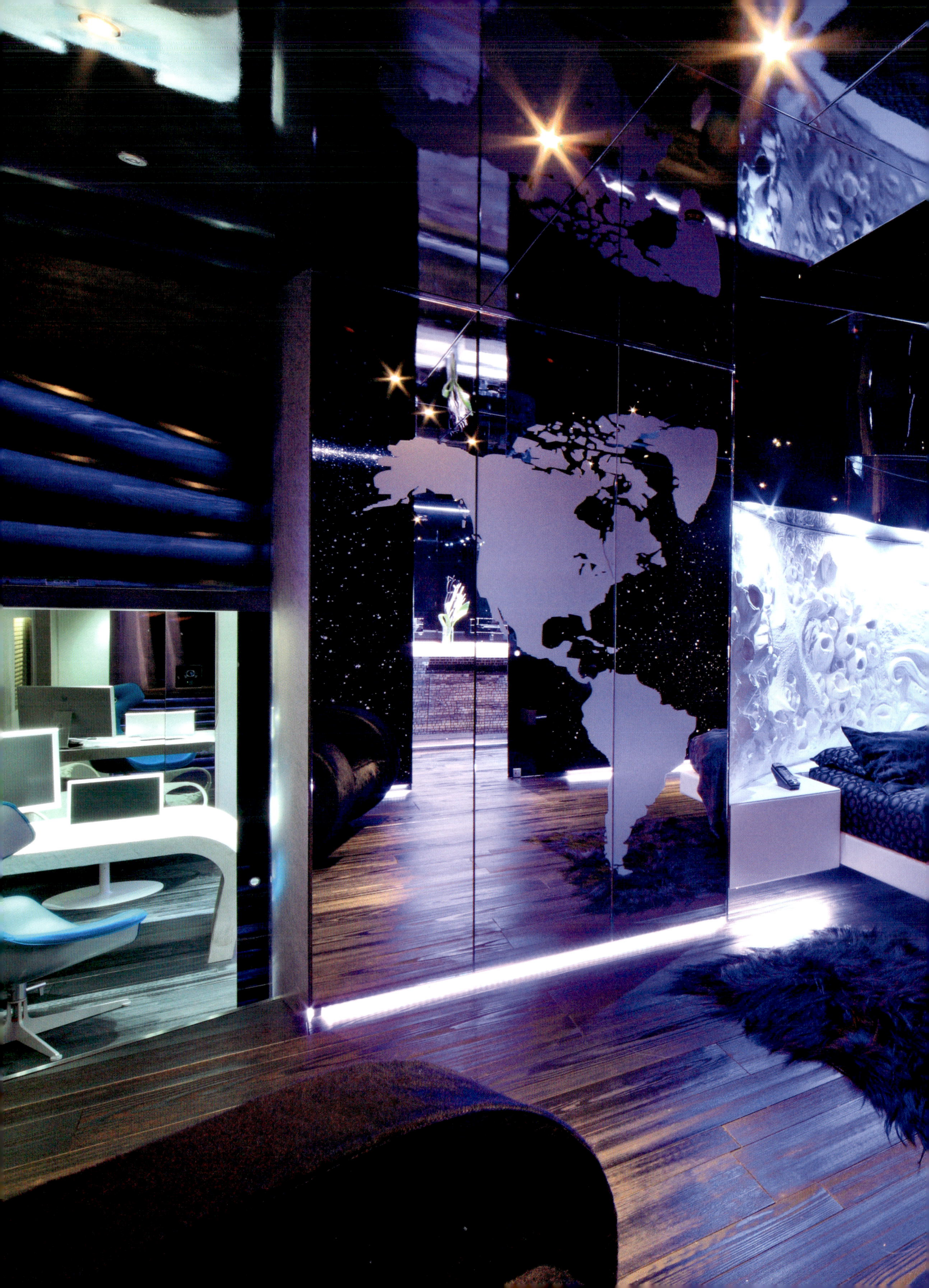

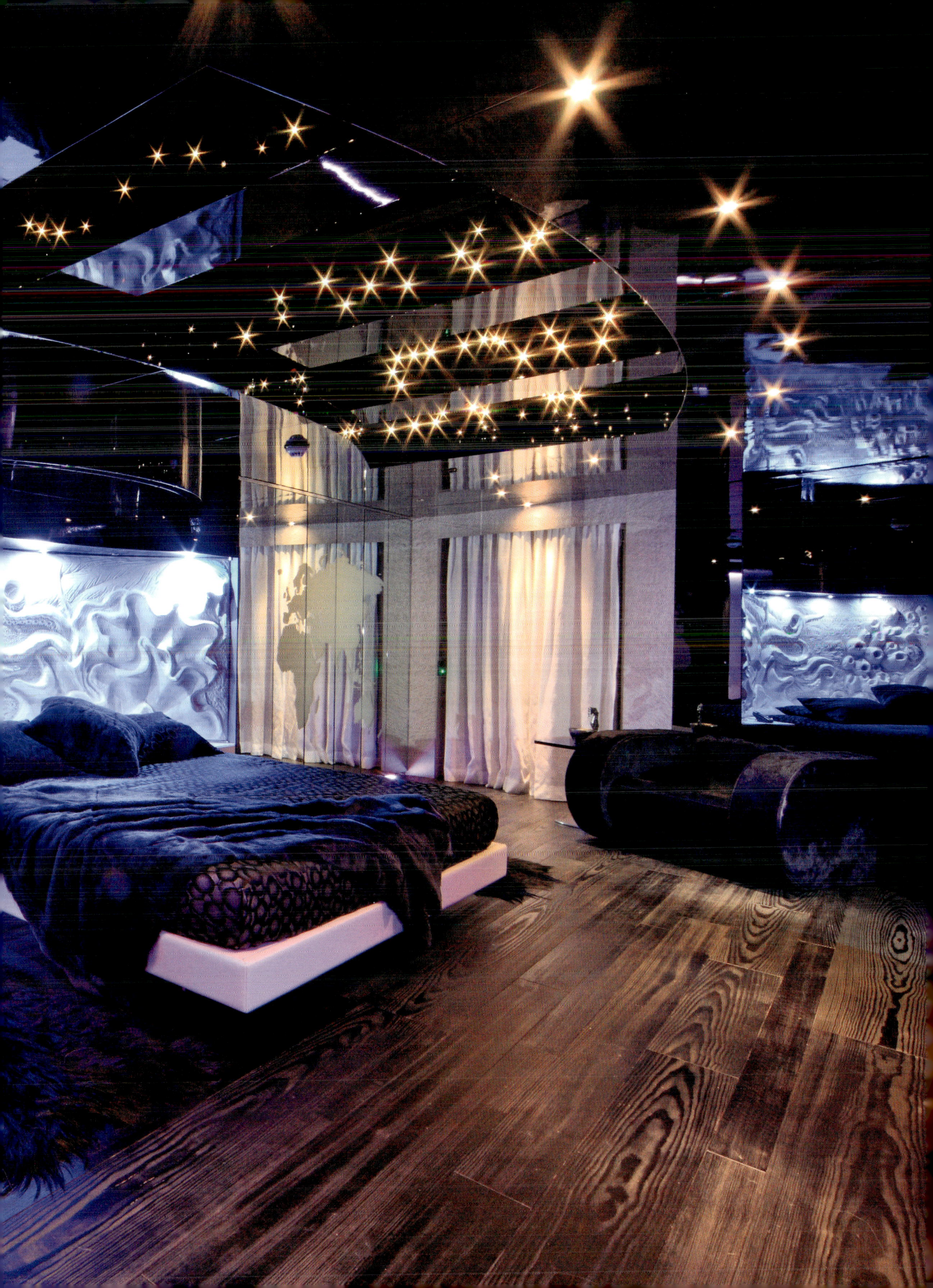

PRECEDING PAGES: The mystical master stateroom features a coral-reef-inspired headboard designed by Carlo Lombardi. The mirrored closets are covered with a special film layer depicting a map of the world.

TOP AND ABOVE: Each of the five guest cabins has a unique decor and a name signifying its theme, such as Earth, Cubist, and Jet Lag. The lighting makes the furniture appear to be floating.

through which wild scenes are projected. The media room has a viewing couch and a large TV hidden behind a mirror. In keeping with the pirate theme, Roberto Vannucci's sculpture *The Piratess* is showcased here.

The floorboards are a dark stained wood, but portions of the floor on the main and upper decks are transparent so that light can radiate from one deck level to another. A cascading Plexiglas staircase with illuminated risers extends from the upper sky lounge to the lower accommodation deck. The wall of the stairwell is a shimmering mosaic made of mother-of-pearl.

In the master stateroom, forward on the main deck, you first enter a study with a swooping, built-in white desk. The port-side wall is covered in white leather and has an oblong nook, tucked into which is a black, tufted leather sofa. Moving forward to the bedroom, the bulkhead opposite the king-size bed is covered in black velvet that has been painted a fluorescent blue. In the dark, it twinkles with a galaxy of stars and planets. A TV screen slides down from the ceiling, and two televisions are hidden behind side mirrors. The bed itself has an amazing papier-mâché headboard depicting an underwater relief by Carlo Lombardi. The mirrored wardrobes are covered with a special film on wich appears a map of the world. Two balconies—one to port, the other to starboard—open off the master suite. In the master bathroom the shower and bathtub are made of pietra luna slate, and the walls and cabinets are covered in a mosaic of mirror pieces. The silicon sinks are reminiscent of horse troughs, long and deep.

The guest accommodations include four en suite staterooms. There are two doubles with leather walls and black ceilings, and two VIP staterooms, one with a predominantly blue colour scheme, the other primarily burgundy. The latter features an ultramodern version of a four-poster bed, sporting steel columns instead of wooden posts. The cabins' names are tied to their individual personalities: Treasure, Earth, Cubist, Jet Lag, and Space. All guests aboard must certainly feel like major participants in the Captain Magic mystique.

The sky lounge, with its black leather floor, shiny white-lacquered walls, and a ceiling that is partly barrisol and partly woven fabric, doubles as a disco. The DJ console and the bar are of black glass with black Corian tops. The bar encompasses a mirror that conceals a TV. A couple of white leather lounge sofas and beanbag chairs add to the seventies disco ambience. Aft is a powder room tiled in silver-leaf mosaic and a

TOP: *A backlit water stream from a tap tickles the visual appeal of a guest bathroom.*

ABOVE: *Steel cables replace wooden posts on this updated four-poster in the VIP cabin.*

OVERLEAF: *A bulkhead separates the media room from the main saloon.*

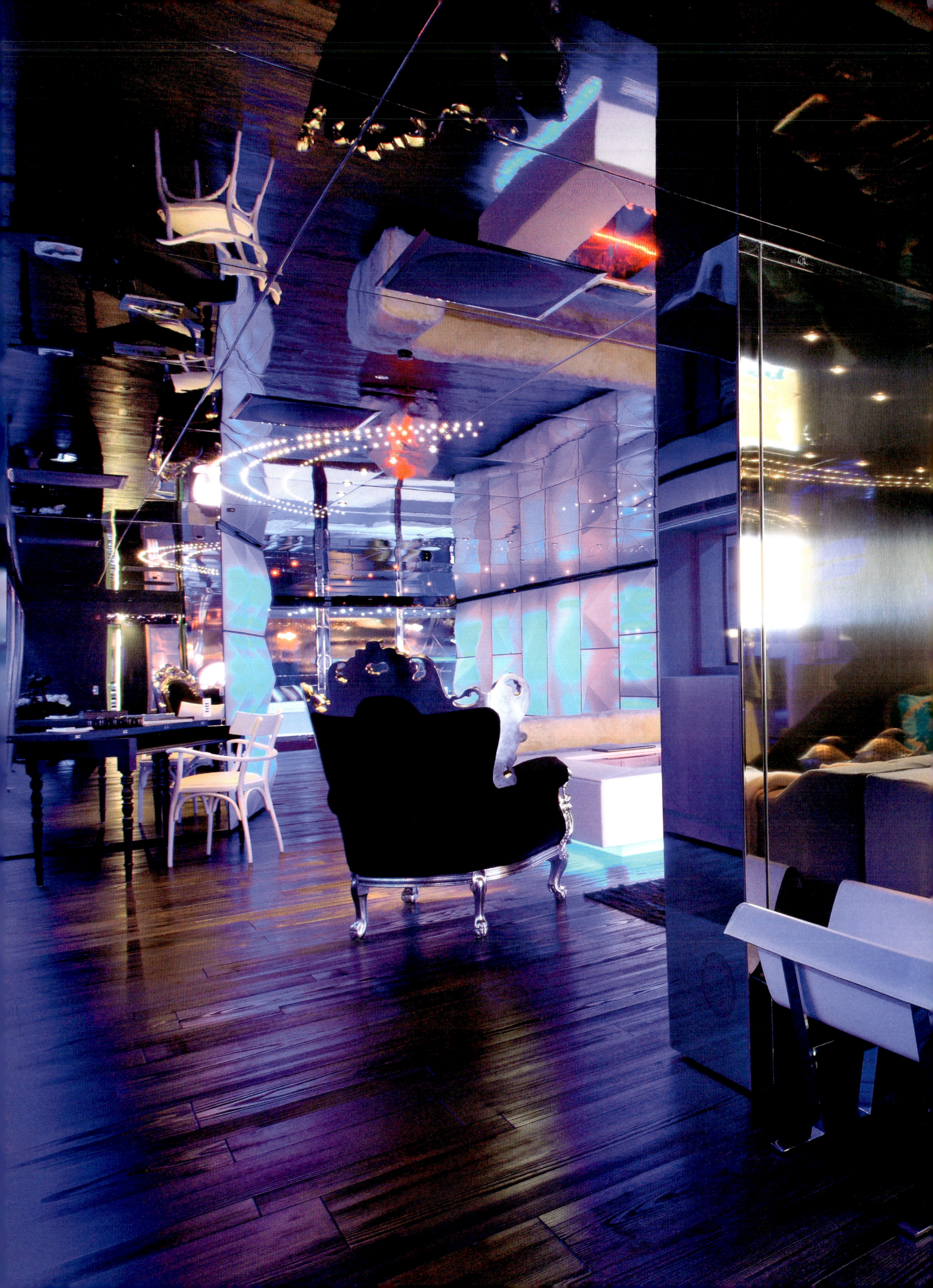

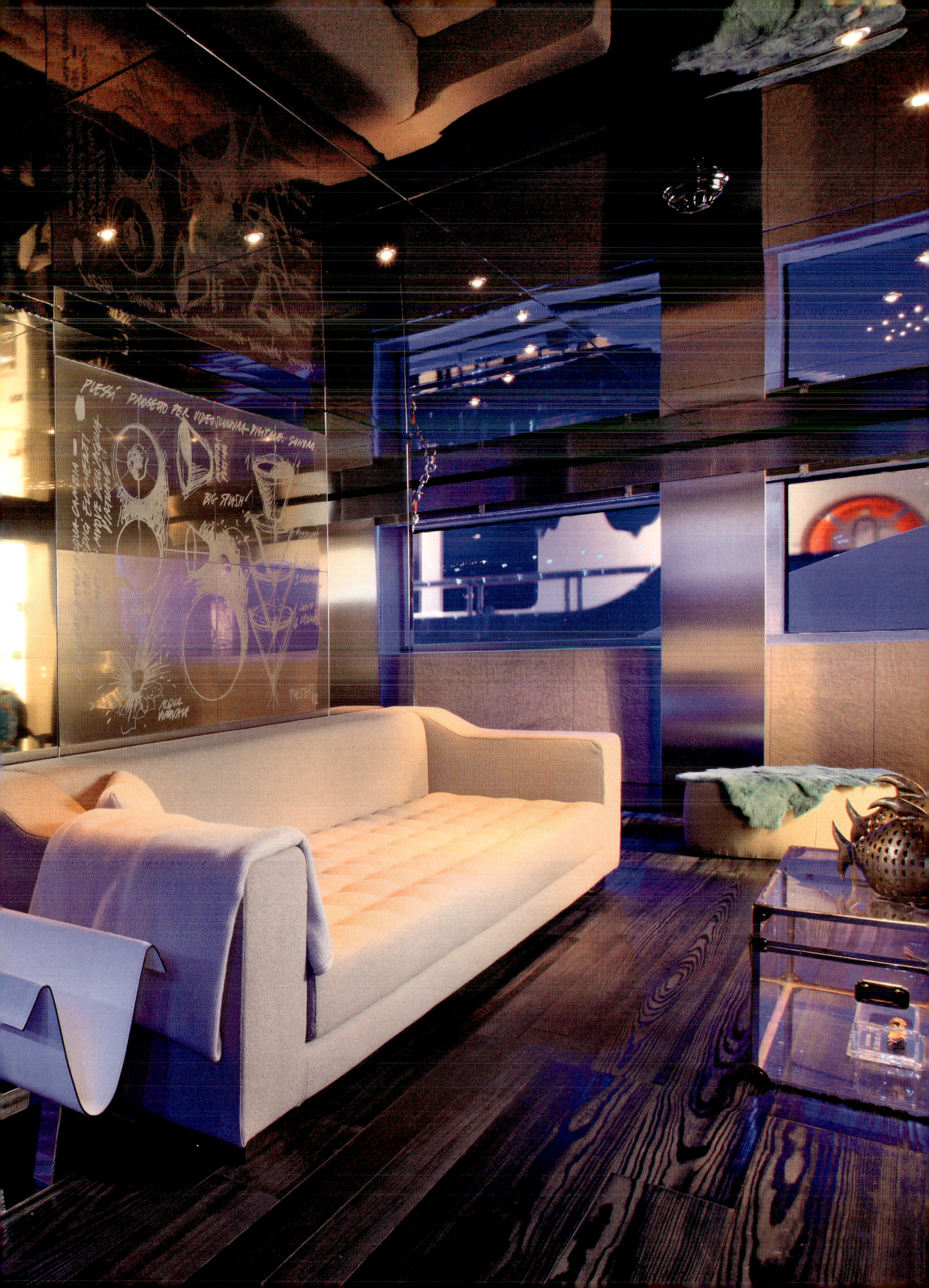
BIG SPLASH!

gymnasium provided by Technogym with a black leather floor. The stern wall is covered with a mirror that hides a TV screen, but its most interesting feature is a laser indicator that projects the position of Mecca on request. Outside, on the aft deck right behind the sky lounge, is an oval table that seats up to twenty people. The sundeck at the very top of the boat has a sushi bar, plenty of sun-bathing space, and a hot tub that incorporates two waterfalls.

The wheelhouse is black with leather floor, walls, and ceiling. The ship's instrumentation is highly sophisticated. Two Caterpillar 3516B engines power the boat, reaching 17.5 knots and achieving around 5,000 nautical miles at a more economical speed of 11 knots. There are also two Caterpillar generators (200 KW) and an emergency 80 KW generator.

In addition to being wildly exceptional in terms of looks, *Sea Force One* boasts both ABS (American Bureau of Shipping) and RINA (Registro Italiano Navale) certifications. An additional distinction is that she merits RINA GREEN STAR, indicating that she is in compliance with strict environmental-protection regulations. She is also the first yacht to qualify for the RINA SECURE YACHT classification, which means that she has a monitoring system of all onboard areas, access ways and outside areas around the yacht. This system helps assure maximum safety and privacy for the guests on board. Whether pirates are imagined or real, this is a yacht that is both highly imaginative and very real.

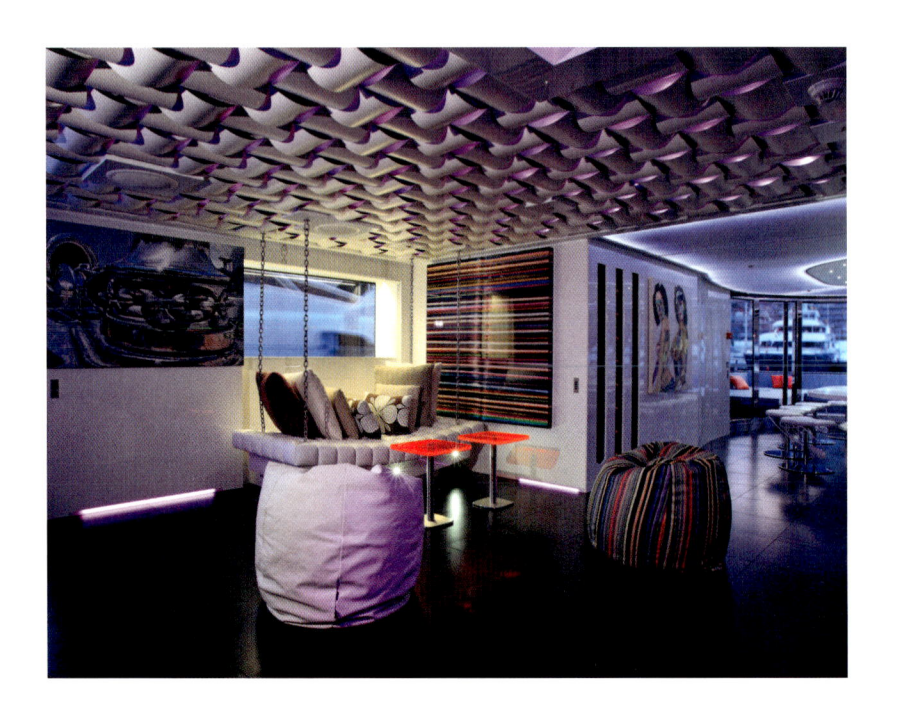

LEFT: *Like all the spaces aboard* Sea Force One, *the sky lounge is a riot of colours and textures. Its ceiling is made of woven polycarbonate strips that create patterned light. Beanbag chairs and contemporary art add a pop feel to the room.*

ABOVE: *Both inside and out,* Sea Force One *is a visual expression of Captain Magic's buccaneering spirit.*

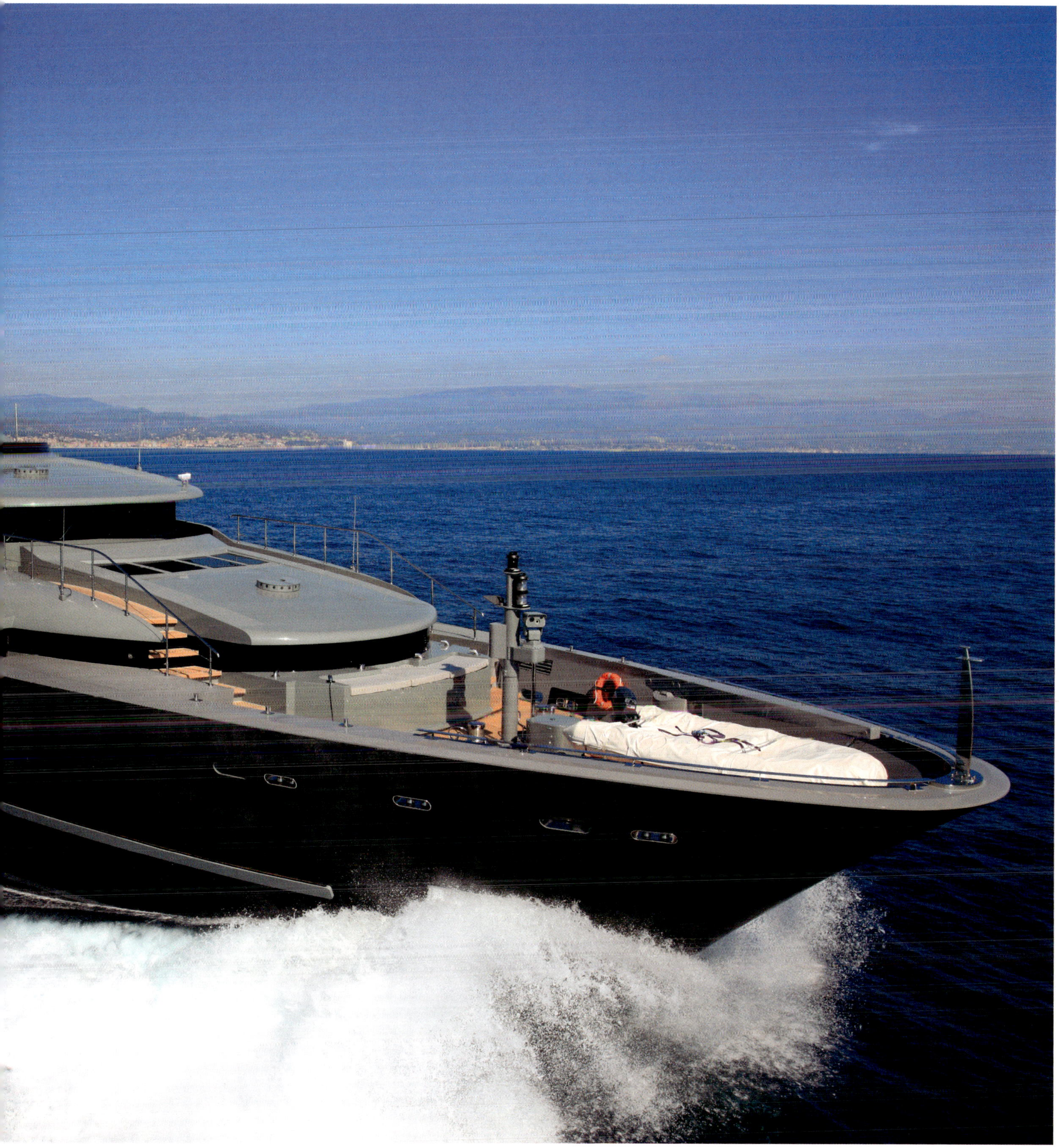

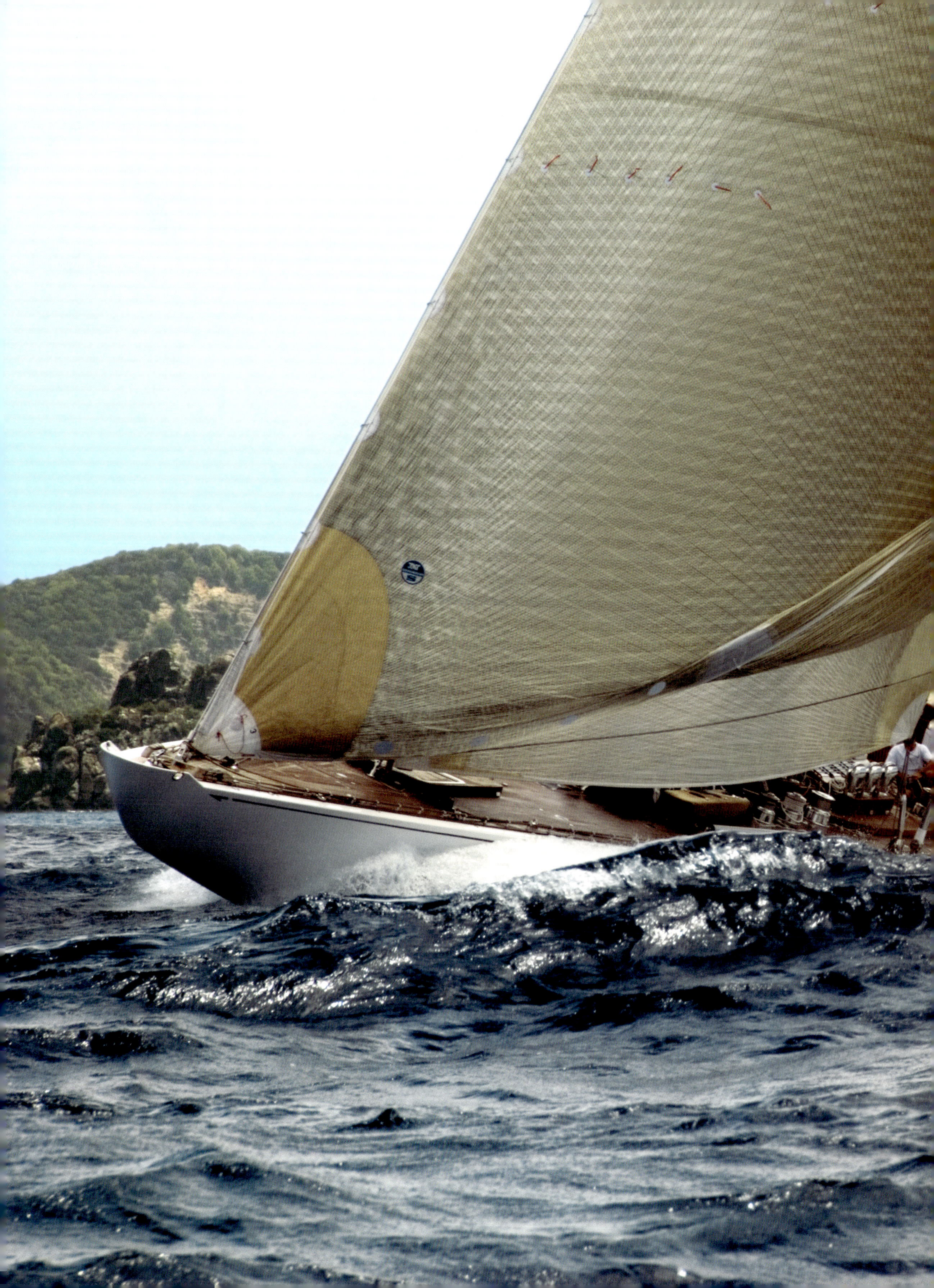

Ranger

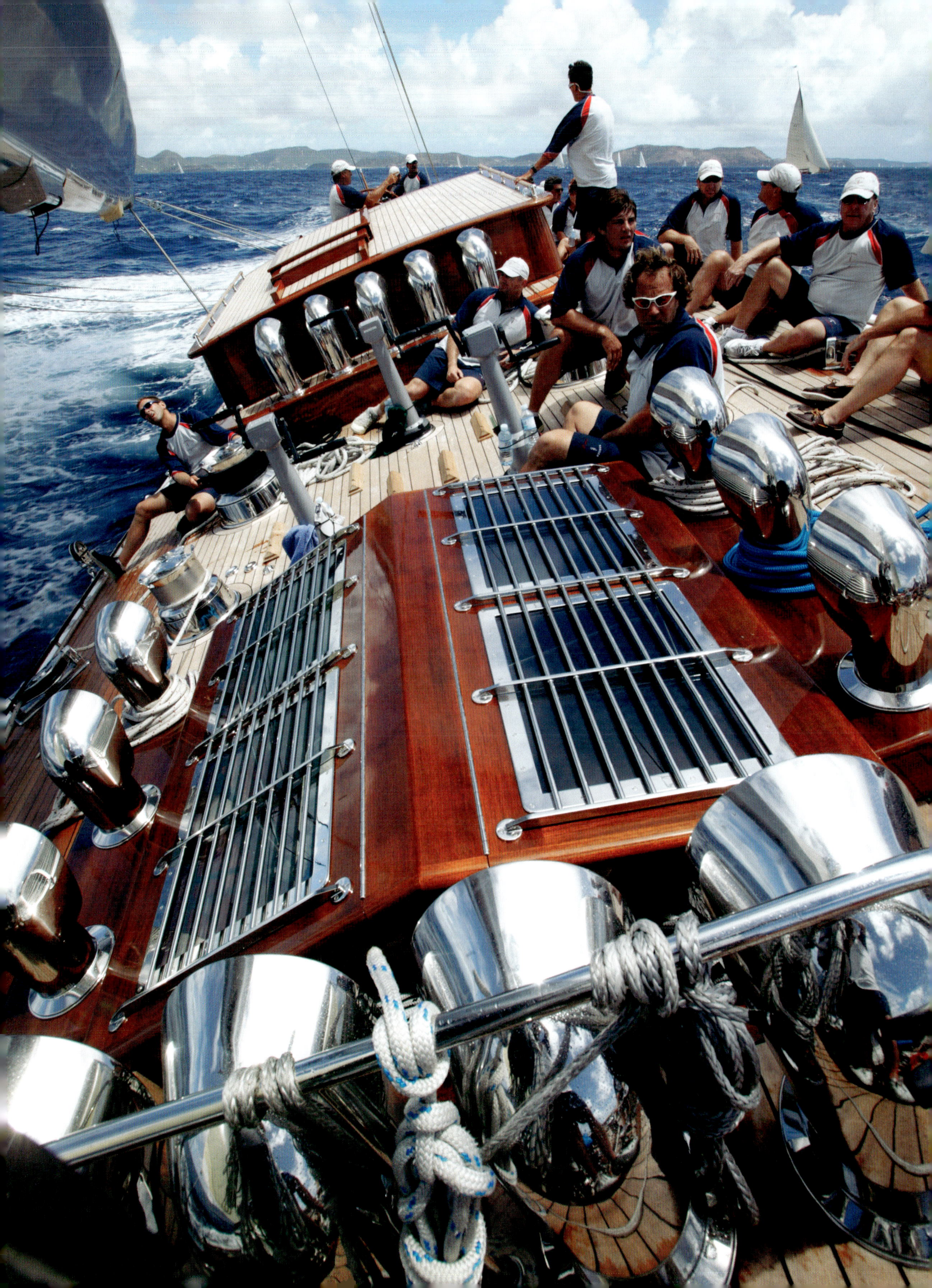

PRECEDING PAGES: Ranger *presses toward a mark during the Antigua Classic Yacht Regatta.*

OPPOSITE: Her deck is adorned with stainless steel. Mostly professional sailors comprise her race crew.

ABOVE: Winches are often underwater when the yacht is heeled hard and going for it.

They are the pure embodiment of power, grace, and aesthetics under sail. To watch them race is to be transported back in time. To sail aboard one with as many as thirty crew is to experience the ultimate waterborne ballet.

Few sailing craft stir the hearts of sailors as do the mighty J-Class racing yachts of the 1930s. Built to specifications consistent with the New York Yacht Club's Universal Rule, these powerful, magnificent craft were sailed in the America's Cup regattas of 1930, 1934, and 1937. A mere ten were built and only three of the originals survive today. But thanks in part to the audacity and vision of yachtsman John A. Williams, who in 2003 took delivery of a close approximation of the 1937 Cup defender *Ranger*, a new age of J-Class racing has taken root, and several near-replicas have been built and launched.

The last of the originals, *Ranger* has often been called the "Super J," having been what many believe was the consummate expression of the type. Created by legendary designers Olin J. Stephens II and Starling Burgess, the yacht went on to win thirty-five of her thirty-seven starts, including four straight against the British J boat *Endeavour II,* to successfully defend the 1937 America's Cup.

Stephens and Burgess worked on a number of hull designs, from which the final design was chosen. Models were made and subjected to tank-testing; the design deemed fastest for the conditions off Newport, Rhode Island, in summer was the one selected. Stephens and Burgess famously made a pact not to reveal which of them was responsible for the eventual winner until after the other's death. After Burgess died in 1947, Stephens credited him with being responsible for the successful *Ranger*'s lines. Stephens died in 2008 at the age of 100.

The idea to build a new *Ranger* came to Williams during the 1999 Antigua Classic Yacht Regatta. He had chartered *Endeavour*—one of the three surviving originals—and had organized a J-Class regatta as part of the event. The regatta brought together for the first time *Endeavour*, which had been extensively and stunningly restored in the 1980s; *Shamrock V*, which had been restored earlier to her J-Class specifications; and the recently restored *Velsheda*. Hanging in *Endeavour*'s saloon was the transom of the original *Ranger*, which, Williams wrote later, inspired him to learn more about her.

Within a year Williams had assembled a team of key people, most of whom had worked on one or both of his previous yachts, *Atlanta* and *Georgia*. He hired Italian naval architect Paolo Scanu, a veteran of the *Georgia* project, to design a new *Ranger,* which he wanted to be not only competitive on the race course but fitted out as a luxury cruising yacht. She would not be a precise replica but would conform to modern J-Class rules. Among the differences from the original, the new *Ranger* would have a slightly longer waterline than the original's 87 feet (26.5 metres; the maximum under the Universal Rule for the J-Class) and would carry a modern carbon-fibre rig, as opposed to the original's Duralumin.

The Universal Rule required yachts to be built to Lloyd's scantlings so that they could be sailed across oceans. Like all the original Js, the original *Ranger* was built to these specifications and was eminently seaworthy, but having no engine or modern mechanical systems, and with correspondingly austere accommodations, she was essentially a day racer. Unlike the British Cup challengers, she never had to cross an ocean on her own bottom.

Williams had worked with interior designer Glade Johnson on yachts before and hired him to take on the accommodations of the new *Ranger*. Danish Yacht in Skagen, Denmark, was selected as builder. Other designers and architects pitched in as well under the direction of project manager Bill Sanderson.

Nearly three years later the yacht was complete. Instead of the Spartan interior of its namesake, the new *Ranger* was fitted out with sparkling, varnished, luxury-yacht accommodations. She sleeps eight in four cabins (ten if the Pullman berths are used), including a spectacular owner's suite. Her interior may be smallish for her 136-foot (41.5-metre) overall length, but it had to fit within the long overhangs and narrow beam of a classic racing yacht. The interior style is classically American; the walls are panelled in glossy, raised mahogany with crotch-cut flamed mahogany centers. The interior was built in Sardinia and shipped to Skagen for installation.

One of the engineering challenges the designers faced was to find a way to isolate the interior from the vibration of the engine and the hardware noise generated by the massive loads handled on deck. The solution? The entire interior structure "floats" on foam. Many of the interior elements (built-in furniture and so on) are cored rather than solid wood, to reduce the weight. She was built to British Maritime and Coastguard Agency (MCA) safety standards to make her suitable for charter.

She left Skagen in winter for the transatlantic crossing to the Caribbean, where Williams and his crew christened the new *Ranger's* racing career at the 2004 St. Barths Bucket Regatta, laden—appropriately—with America's Cup veterans as crew. Following soon thereafter was her debut at the Antigua Classic Yacht Regatta that same year. She has since had great success on the international big boat racing circuit, often beating her older rival *Velsheda* on straight time. Like many yachtsmen, Williams greatly enjoys designing and building new boats. He put *Ranger* on the market in 2008, planning to commission another racing yacht. He can take great pride in his contribution to the reinvigoration of this magnificent racing class.

LOA: 136' 5" (41.5 m)
Beam: 21' (6.4 m)
Draft: 15' 11" (4.7 m)
Naval architect: Paolo Scanu
Exterior styling: Paolo Scanu
Interior design: Glade Johnson Design
Builder / year: Danish Yacht, Skagen, Denmark / 2003
Hull construction: Steel

LEFT: *Many consider the sight of a stately J-Class yacht working aggressively in a race one of the finest images in sailing.*

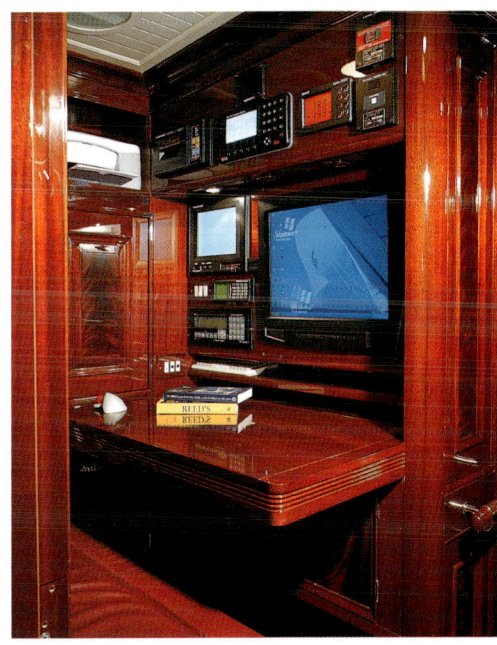

CLOCKWISE FROM TOP: Highly varnished crotch-cut flame mahogany panelling accents the dining area on the starboard side of the main saloon. The nav station is tucked under the stairs aft, by the master cabin. A gleaming staircase descends into the main saloon. The companionway from the pilothouse to the main saloon.

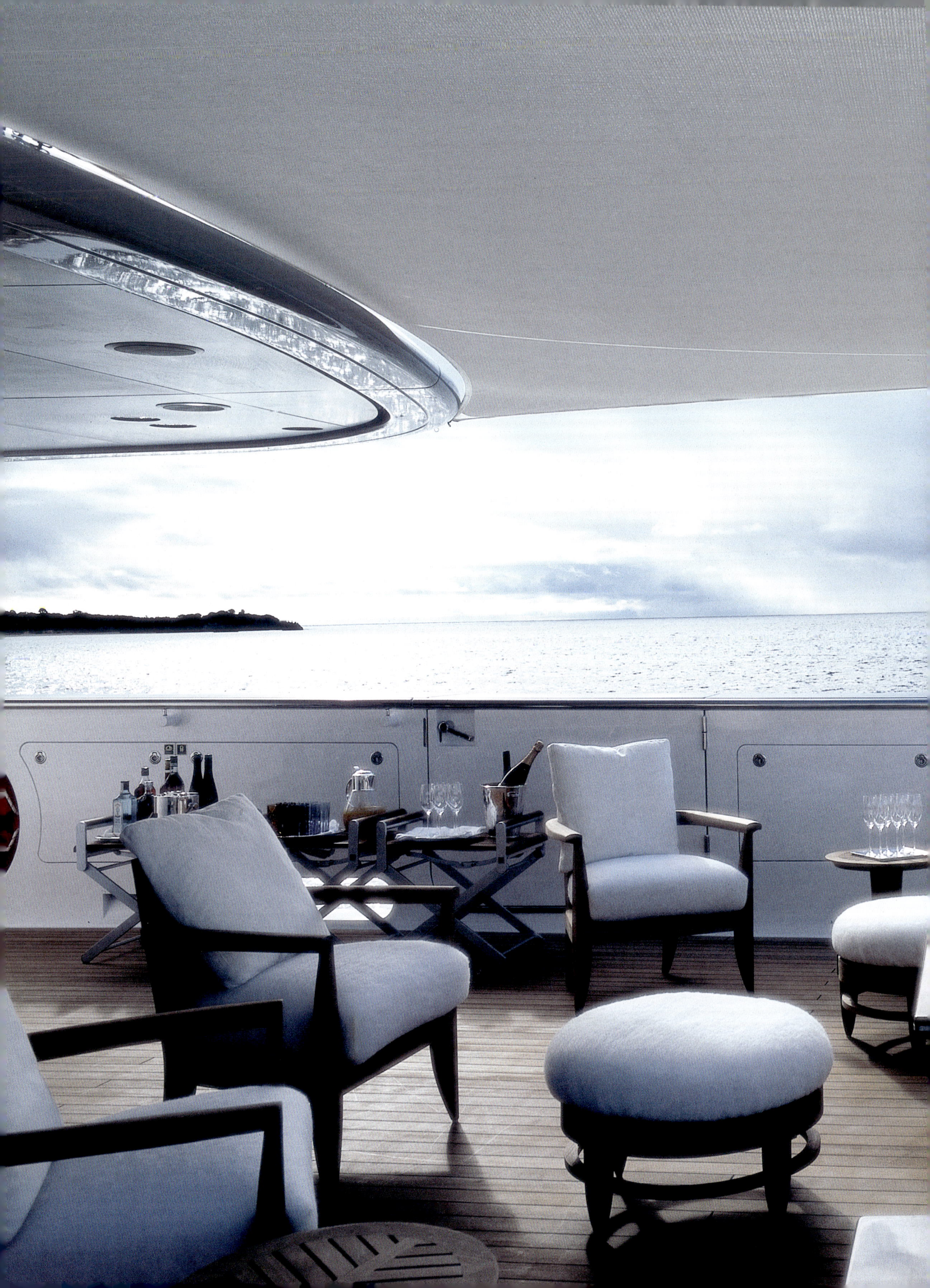

Silver

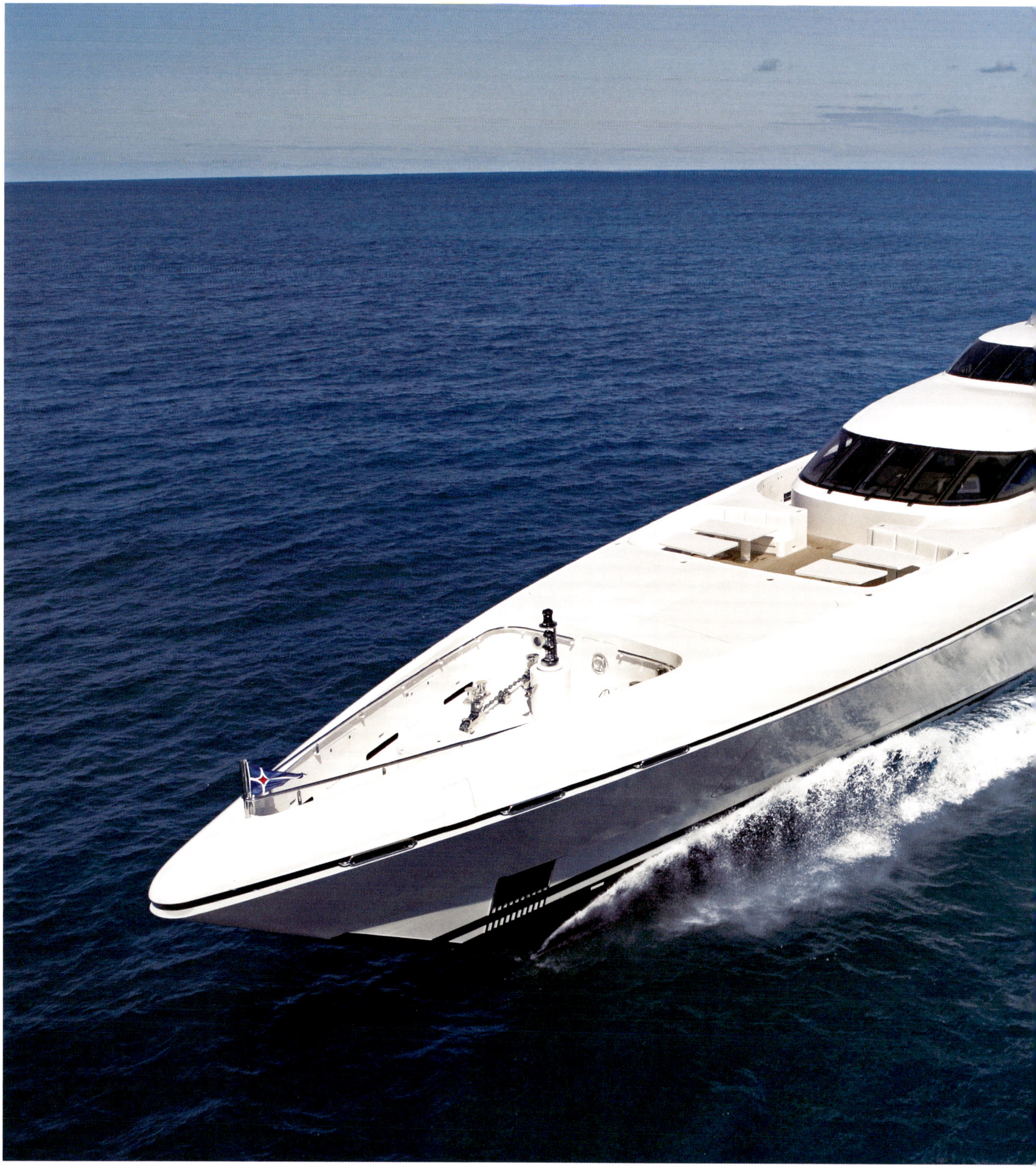

PRECEDING PAGES: *The main deck aft is one of Silver's primary outdoor living areas. Its covered spaces can be used for lounging, dancing, or alfresco dining.*

The power of passion can carry an idea a long way. European entrepreneur Guido Krass had long admired the fast commuters that ferried the American titans of industry from their homes in Connecticut and Long Island to New York City in the 1930s. Those boats were long and narrow—and fast. Krass had also admired the aluminium crew boats servicing the oil platforms in the Gulf of Mexico that operated at high speed for many hours and days on end. In Krass's view, today's superyachts are too beamy with excessive draft, volume, and displacement—concessions to accommodate amenities at the expense of efficiency. He wondered whether a superyacht could be created that would have extended range, be fuel-efficient, carry at least eighteen guests, and be fast—goals that are often mutually exclusive.

In the 1990s Krass had worked with naval architect Espen Øino on modifications to a yacht Krass owned. On a ski trip in 2000, the two men began serious discussions about the high-speed concept Krass envisioned. Soon thereafter, the project began to pick up steam. Drawings were done and eventually models were built and tank-tested in Russia and Sweden. Unable to find a shipyard able to build exactly what he wanted, Krass established a yard of his own in Western Australia. In 2007 Hanseatic Marine launched the 240-foot (73-metre) *Silver*—as close an approximation of Krass's ambitious goals as Øino could design, and, ultimately, one of the most interesting and innovative yachts ever to part the waves.

ABOVE: *The sleek, slippery design of the 240-foot (73-metre) Silver is reminiscent of the fast, narrow commuter vessels that carried the American titans of industry from their homes on the shore into New York City in the 1930s.*

RIGHT: *Silver's tenders and toys launch from gull-wing doors forward near the bow. The areas aft are reserved for guest activities.*

LEFT: Unlike the typical yacht swim platform, Silver's "beach club" was designed to allow guests to lounge in complete comfort close to the water. It has a bar, a TV, a sauna, and a gym.

OPPOSITE, TOP: Silver's main deck aft is set up for casual outdoor dining.

OPPOSITE, BOTTOM: Designed by German Danilo Silvestrin, the main saloon is modern and simple, yet elegant, as is the decor throughout the yacht.

LOA: 240' (73 m)
Beam: 32' 10" (10 m)
Draft: 8' 2" (2.5 m)
Naval architect: Espen Øino Naval Architects Inc.
Exterior styling: Espen Øino Naval Architects Inc.
Interior design: Danilo Silvestrin
Builder/year: Hanseatic Marine, Henderson, Western Australia / 2008
Top speed: 25 knots
Hull construction: Aluminium

Generally, high speed and long range are not happy bedfellows, so weight was a consideration from the beginning. Built of steel, a yacht the size of Silver would be neither fast nor fuel-efficient, and her size also excluded fibreglass as an option. It was clear to both men that aluminium was the building material of choice. As it turned out, Silver became the longest aluminium yacht ever built.

To reduce resistance and, consequently, the amount of power needed to push the yacht to the speeds Krass desired and achieve the range he envisioned, an efficient hull shape was essential. By the end of 2001 Krass and Øino had defined a hull shape, and they took a seven-metre model to the Krylov Shipbuilding Research Centre in St. Petersburg, Russia, for further refinement. They were the first Westerners to use the facility, which housed the largest testing tank in the world. Then they took another model to SSPA in Göteborg, Sweden, to cross-check the data they had received from Russia. The whole process took about a year.

Meanwhile, Krass had begun to shop around for a suitable shipbuilding yard. He visited several yards that either didn't understand what he was trying to do or were in poor financial shape. He ended up buying land and setting up his own yard in Henderson, Western Australia, south of Perth. The yard started cutting metal for Silver five years—and, Krass estimates, some 100 man years of development work—after his initial discussions with Øino on the ski trip.

One of Krass's goals was to make Silver suitable for charter. He observed that many of today's charter clients are busy and impatient and want to get to their leisure destinations quickly, so speed was imperative. Most charter yachts today are classed under the British Maritime and Coastguard Agency (MCA) to carry a maximum of twelve guests. Krass felt, however, that those who were in a position to charter Silver at the rate she would command would want accommodations for more than twelve guests. Meeting the design and construction requirements of the MCA rules for charter yachts has become onerous in recent years. But making a yacht legal to carry more passengers—the eighteen Krass wanted—meant adhering to even more rigorous design and construction regulations in accordance with the Safety Of Life At Sea (SOLAS) convention, requirements generally aimed at cruise ships. Krass and company had to invent some innovative ways to incorporate the SOLAS requirements into a superyacht without making it look like a cruise ship.

Silver's exceptional range, speed, and fuel efficiency—4,500 nautical miles at 18 knots, consuming a mere 500 litres of fuel per hour, or transatlantic at 22 knots—are the result of several factors. First is her efficient hull shape, which features a relatively narrow beam, a relatively shallow draft and a bow with a fine entry. Second is her comparatively light weight, which, along with her hull shape, permits the use of engines generally found on smaller yachts. Her low profile, though not directly contributing much to her performance, enhances her aesthetic appeal in ways reminiscent of the design of the commuters of old.

Operating on the assumption that yacht guests generally spend as little time as possible inside, Silver's

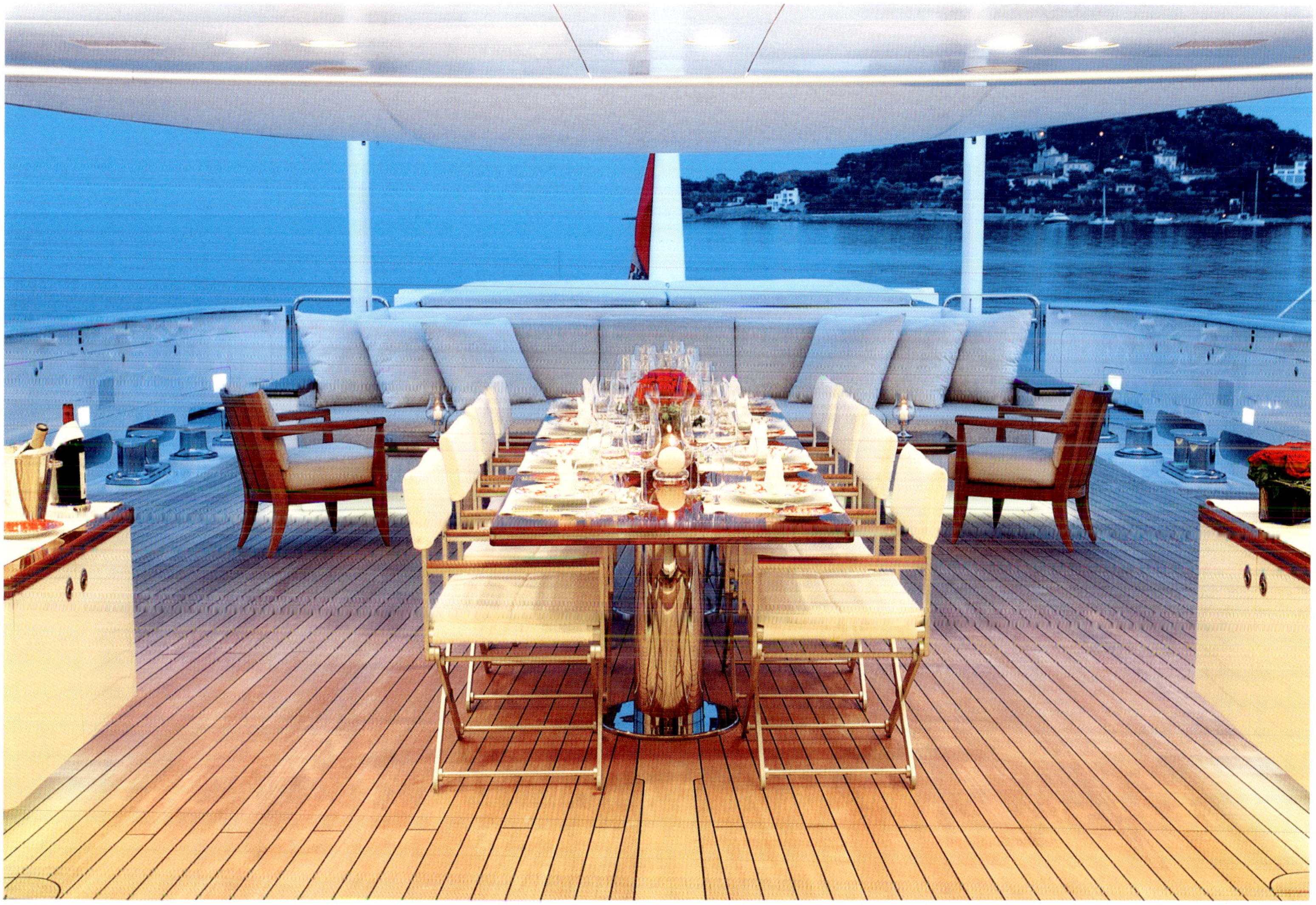

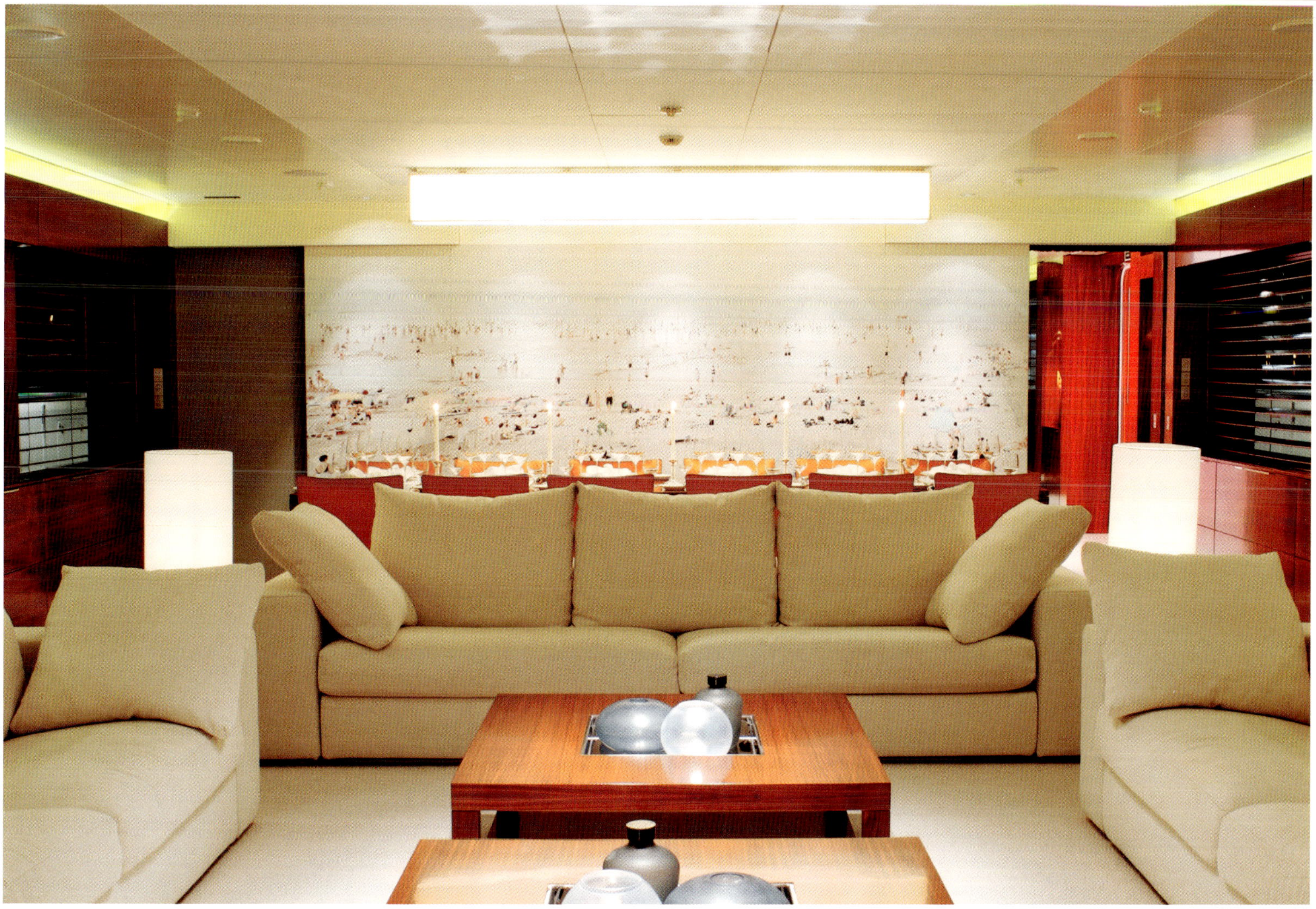

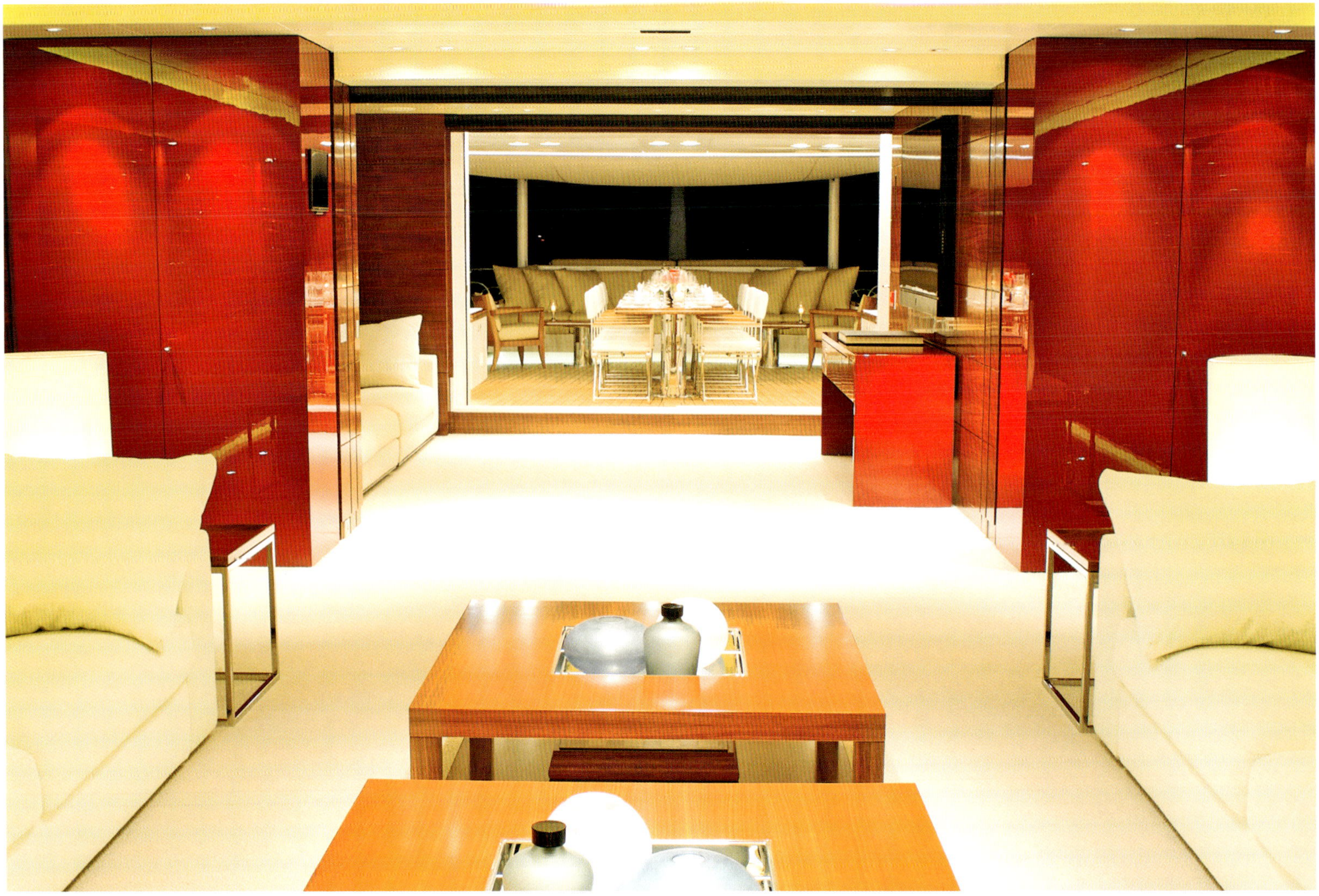

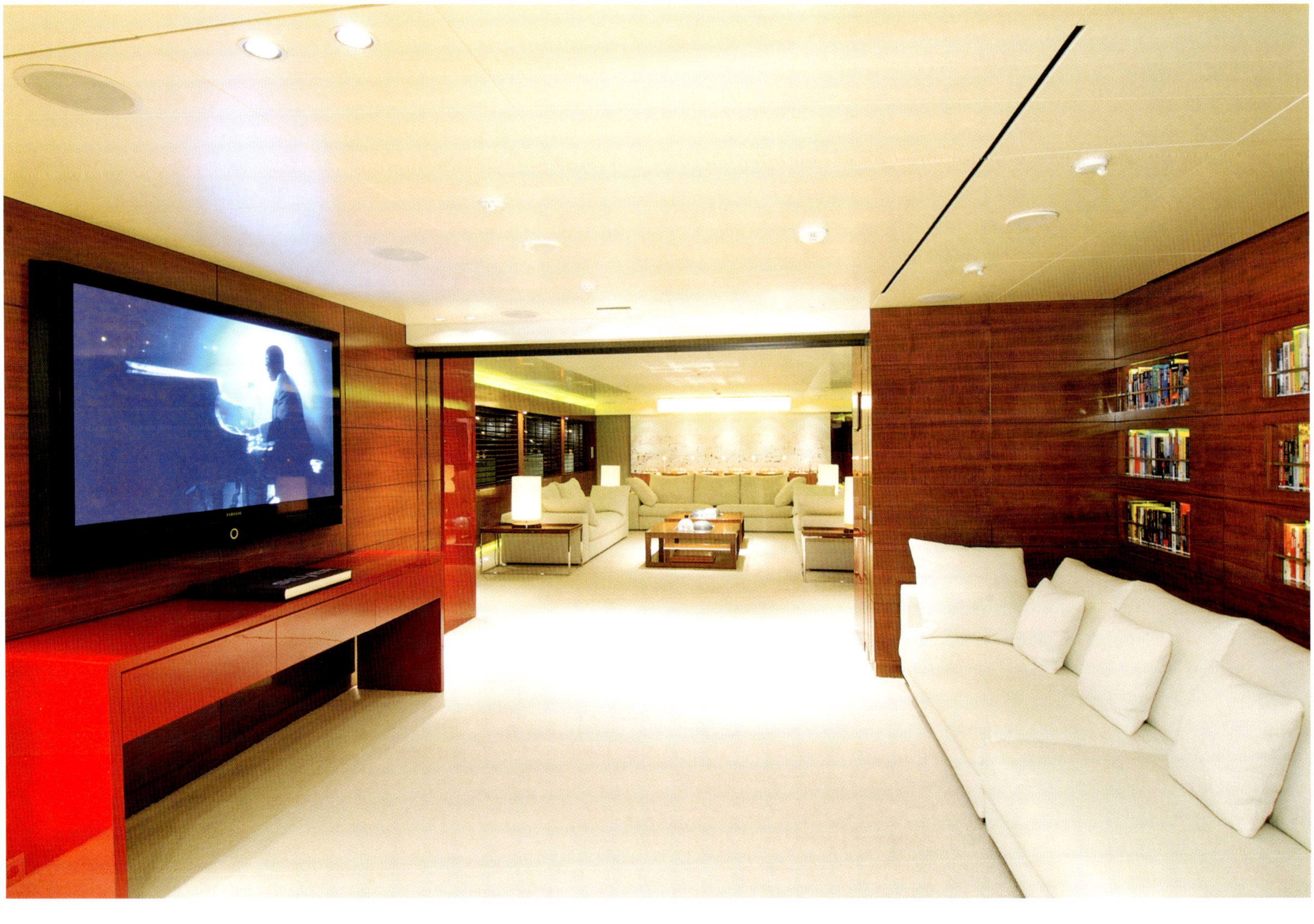

OPPOSITE, TOP: *The view from the saloon to the main deck aft shows that Silver's large platform consists of an aggregation of intimate spaces.*

OPPOSITE, BOTTOM: *In an unusual arrangement, guests gain access to the main saloon from the aft deck through a cinema room.*

interior was kept understated compared with that of many modern superyachts. But with a thoughtful, simple, contemporary design by German Danilo Silvestrin, featuring versatile lighting and walnut veneers, the interior is comfortable and elegant and provides generous space for her eighteen guests and sixteen crew. Her tenders and toys are stored in innovative bays with gull-wing doors near her bow, thereby freeing up space on the aft decks and the "beach" facility on her swim platform. She is equipped with at-anchor and under-way stabilizers to maximize guest comfort.

Being aboard a 240-foot yacht sprinting along at more than 20 knots is a thrilling experience in itself. But more thrilling still is the ability to make it to the next port on the Riviera quicker than you can by crowded road—and in far greater luxury.

TOP: *The contemporary master suite occupies an entire deck. Its splendid accommodations include a private deck, several lounge areas, and his-and-hers bathrooms.*

ABOVE: *A sauna is part of the yacht's extended "beach club," housed in the transom.*

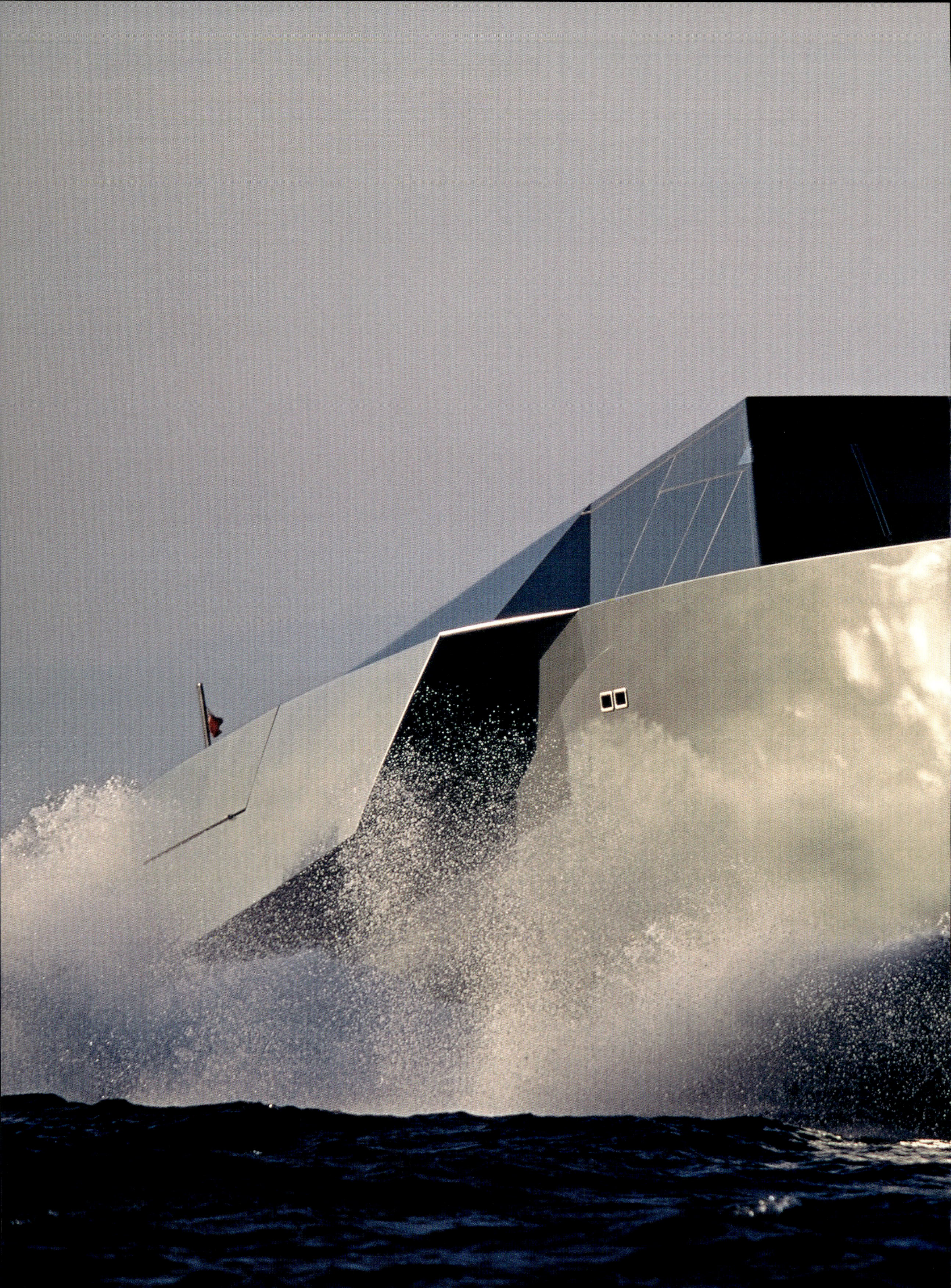

118 WallyPower

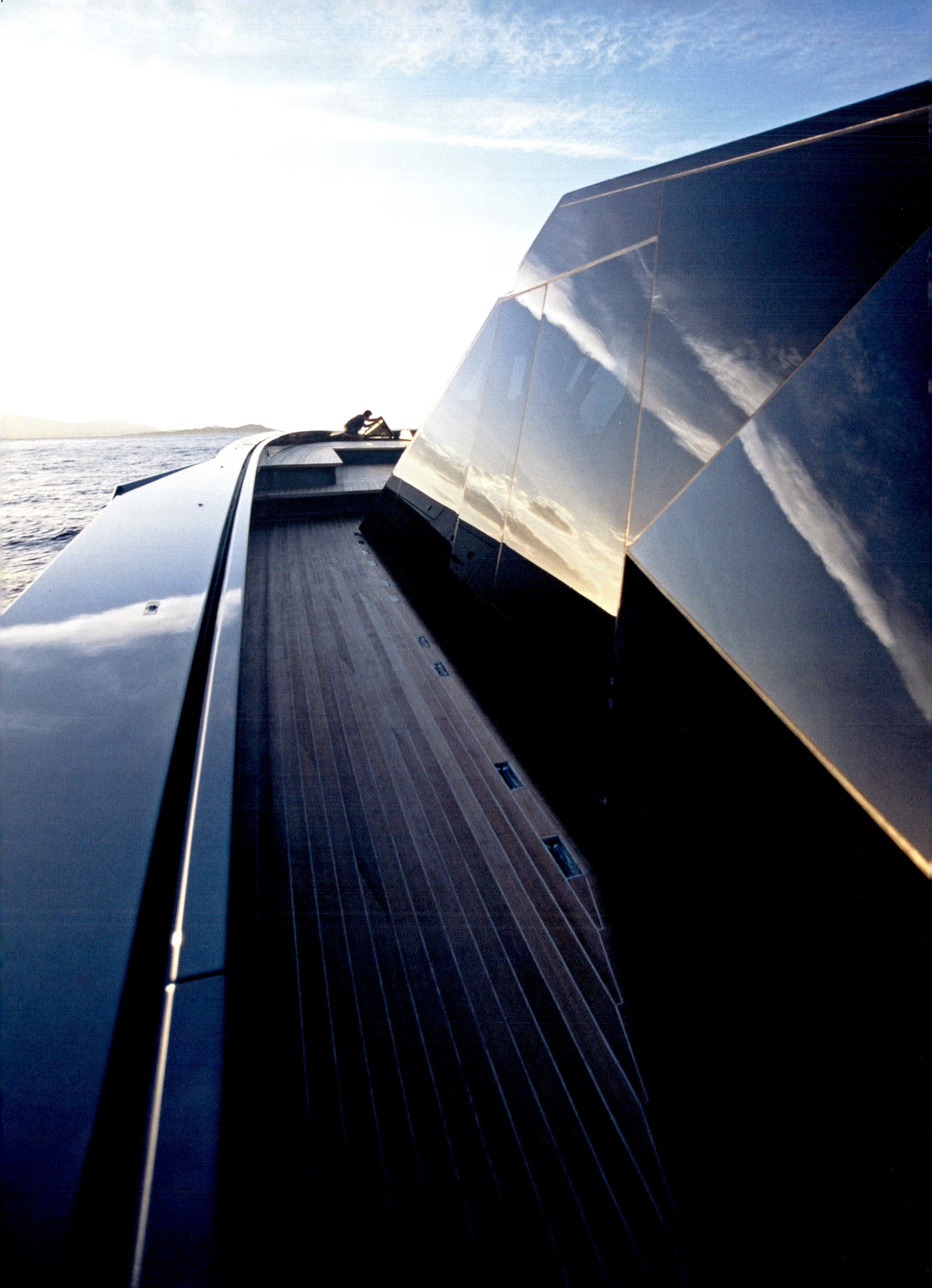

PRECEDING PAGES: *At speed, the* 118 WallyPower *resembles a modern stealth aircraft more than a luxury yacht. One almost expects her to lift off and soar away.*

RIGHT: *The* WallyPower's *helm is compact and spare for a 118-foot (36-metre) yacht, but it contains all the equipment necessary to navigate, communicate, and control the yacht's systems.*

Wally has long been synonymous with sublime, super sexy sailing yachts. So when the Monaco-based company announced that it was entering the motor-yacht market, no one expected it to produce a fleet of dowdy white boats.

Wally's first powerboat offering, the *118 WallyPower*, is a head-turner of the first order. She is a yacht unlike any ever launched—a bundle of innovation shaped like something from the future, a supremely styled, high-tech, high-speed vessel befitting a James Bond or a Captain Kirk.

Wally mastermind Luca Bassani, who rewrote the way sailors view sailboats in the 1990s, broke new ground in the powerboat segment when he unveiled the radical design of the *118 WallyPower* in 2002. First, the yacht looked unlike anything else afloat. First impressions evoke analogies more aeronautical than nautical. The unusual angles of her deckhouse, the air intakes along her topsides, and the hard chine that sweeps down from her near-plumb bow make one feel she shares more DNA with a stealth aircraft than a luxury motoryacht. Watching the *WallyPower* hiss across the water at speed, you half-expect her to break away and soar to another altitude.

OPPOSITE: *Like all Wally yachts, her decks are free of gear and clutter.*

OVERLEAF: *Despite nearly curve-free shapes, the* 118 WallyPower's *aft deck and saloon have a soft, inviting ambience.*

Enter her engine room and the analogy runs deeper. For propulsion, the first *118 WallyPower* relies on three DDC TF50 5,600-horsepower gas turbine engines connected to water-jet drives. The package propels the 95-ton vessel to speeds in excess of 60 knots—a number rarely heard of in the world of superyachts. In addition to the turbines, the engine room houses a pair of conventional 370-horsepower Cummins diesels, which are connected to the water jets for slower-speed operation. All-diesel power is an option on the model, but it won't produce nearly the speed the turbines do.

The yacht's relatively light, tank-tested hull is designed not only for speed but for a comfortable ride. It is fibreglass on the bottom and composite fibreglass/carbon fibre/balsa core on the sides. The bow is shaped to pierce through the waves. The yacht's grey-green exterior seems to change colour depending on the light and the hue of the water.

The aeronautical theme carries through to the helm, which in many ways feels more like that of a high-tech fighter jet than a conventional superyacht. The helm is integrated into the space in the superstructure occupied by the carbon-fibre dining table and the saloon.

Bassani and the teams of designers who contribute to his projects are never at a loss for innovation. As with most Wally sailboats, the *WallyPower's* teak decks are clean and flush, without clutter or impediments to moving about. Cleats, mooring winches, and a tender all stow out of sight, enabling safe on-deck movement and entertaining. The tender stows in the forepeak; to access it, a section of the deck rises up on hydraulic lifts.

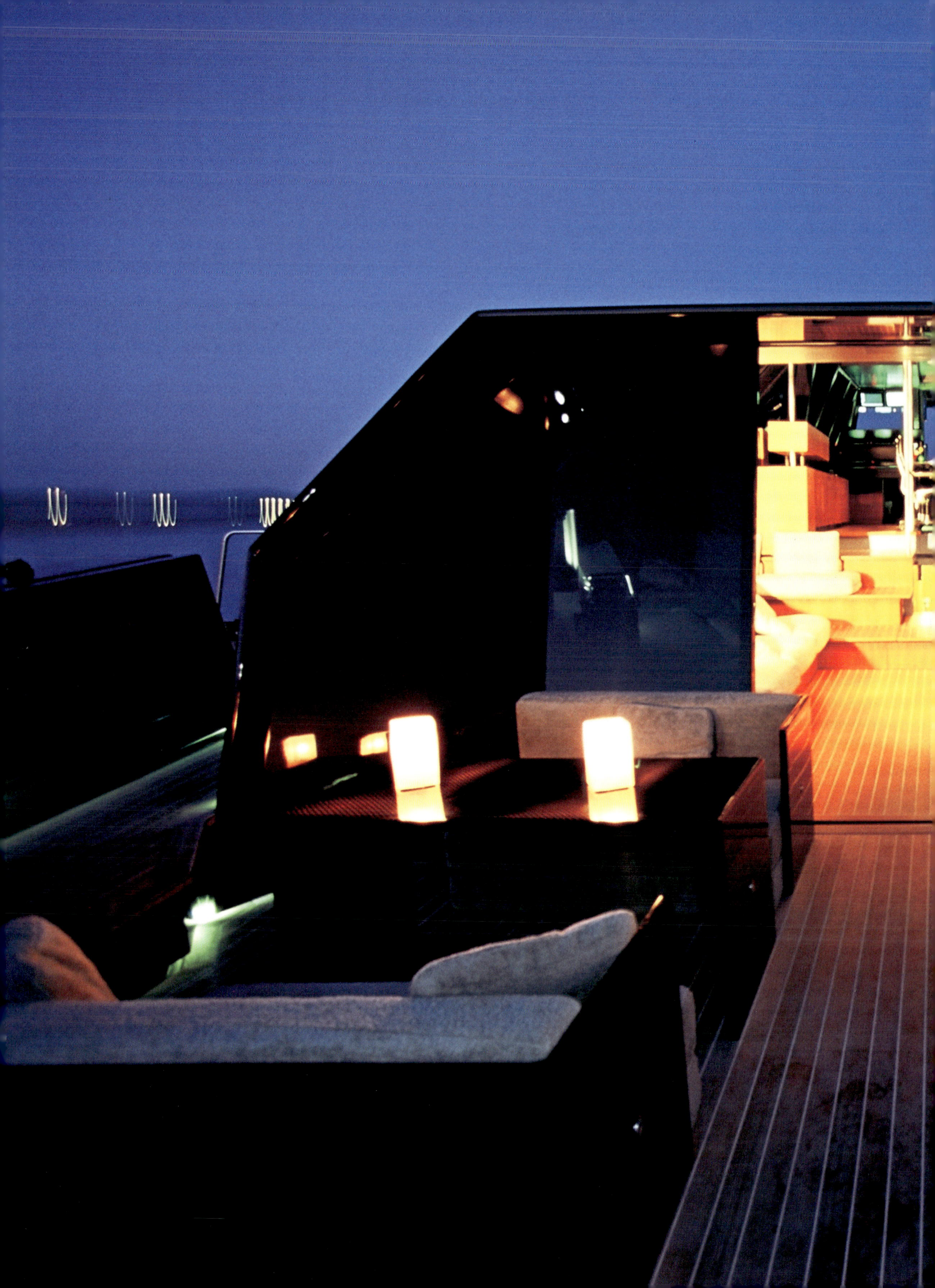

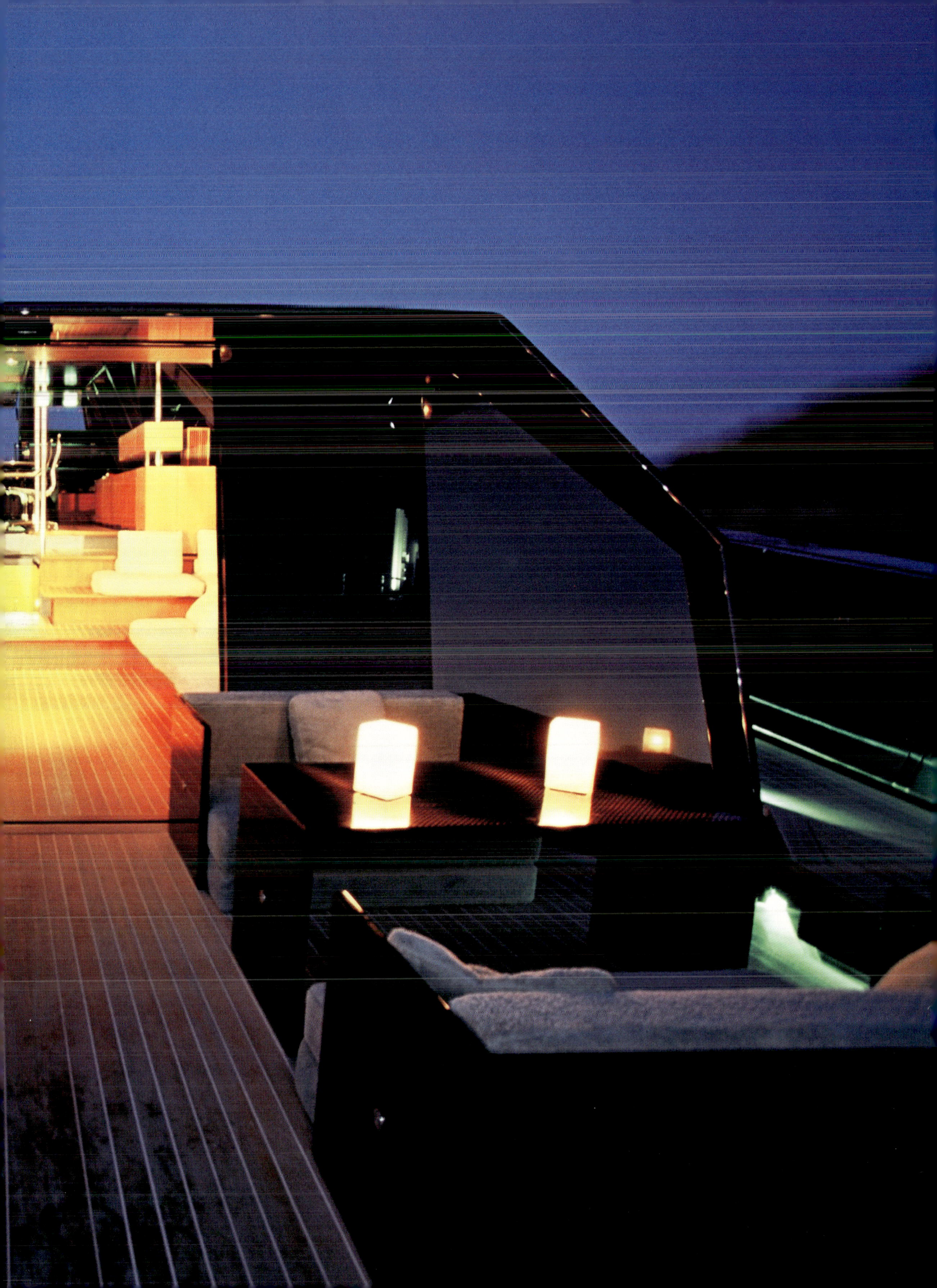

TOP AND ABOVE: *The decor of a guest cabin and bathroom typifies the minimalist approach to design and furnishings throughout the yacht. But the style serves a practical purpose as well. Keeping weight down is a key component in reaching the speeds to which the yacht aspires.*

A bimini made of North 3DL sailcloth covers the forward seating area. The aft gangway and swim platform extend out from the transom and down to near water level. A section of the portside bulwarks opens up to accommodate side boarding.

The interior area of the main deck also bucks superyacht convention. Unlike the interiors on most yachts, which let light in through windows or portholes, the indoor area of the *WallyPower*'s main deck is enclosed by a superstructure of laminated composite glass set in a carbon-fibre frame. As a result, each of the interior spaces has visibility in all directions and is bathed in ambient light. The greenhouse-like superstructure produces an almost organic connection to the world in which owners and guests cruise. Wally designs typically aim to integrate the indoor and outdoor environments as much as possible. The aft deck, which can be equipped with movable furniture, is on the same level as the saloon, which is just inside the superstructure. The saloon is set up much like a casual living room with facing sofas and abundant cushions to maximize comfort and socializing. Up a few steps is the dining area, which evokes the boardroom of an ad agency or a high-tech company. The navigation area and the helm share the upper level.

Wally yachts typically exhibit lightweight, minimalist-chic interior design. The *WallyPower* is no exception. The palette of white upholstery, shiny grey stainless-steel chair frames, tan flooring, and black carbon-fibre accents leave guests feeling refreshed and upbeat, as if they'd just eaten salad rather than sirloin steak and potatoes. The design has little kinship with conventional yacht interiors.

The guest accommodations for six are on the lower deck. The stylish master stateroom with king-size bed and his-and-hers baths is farthest forward. Just abaft are two double guest cabins with queen-size baths, and the crew accommodations for six and the galley are amidships. The massive engine room occupies roughly half the space on the lower level, but is well insulated from the accommodations.

A yacht such as the *WallyPower* may not be for everyone, but it's not just for James Bond either. It's ideal for anyone who thinks fast and sexy is fun.

ABOVE: *The very notion of a 118-foot yacht moving in excess of 50 knots is paradoxical. Here the WallyPower could almost be mistaken for a model.*

LEFT: *The saloon is a premier party space. Its glass-walled, light-filled ambience is reminiscent of a city penthouse.*

LOA: 118' (36 m)
Beam: 29' 6 (9 m)
Draft: 4' 6 (1.36 m)
Naval architect: Wally with Intermarine Italy
Exterior styling: Wally with Lazzarini Pickering Architects
Interior design: Wally with Lazzarini Pickering Architects
Builder / year: Wally Yachts, Monaco / 2002
Top speed: 60+ knots
Hull construction: fibreglass / carbon fibre / balsa core sides

118 WALLYPOWER / 217

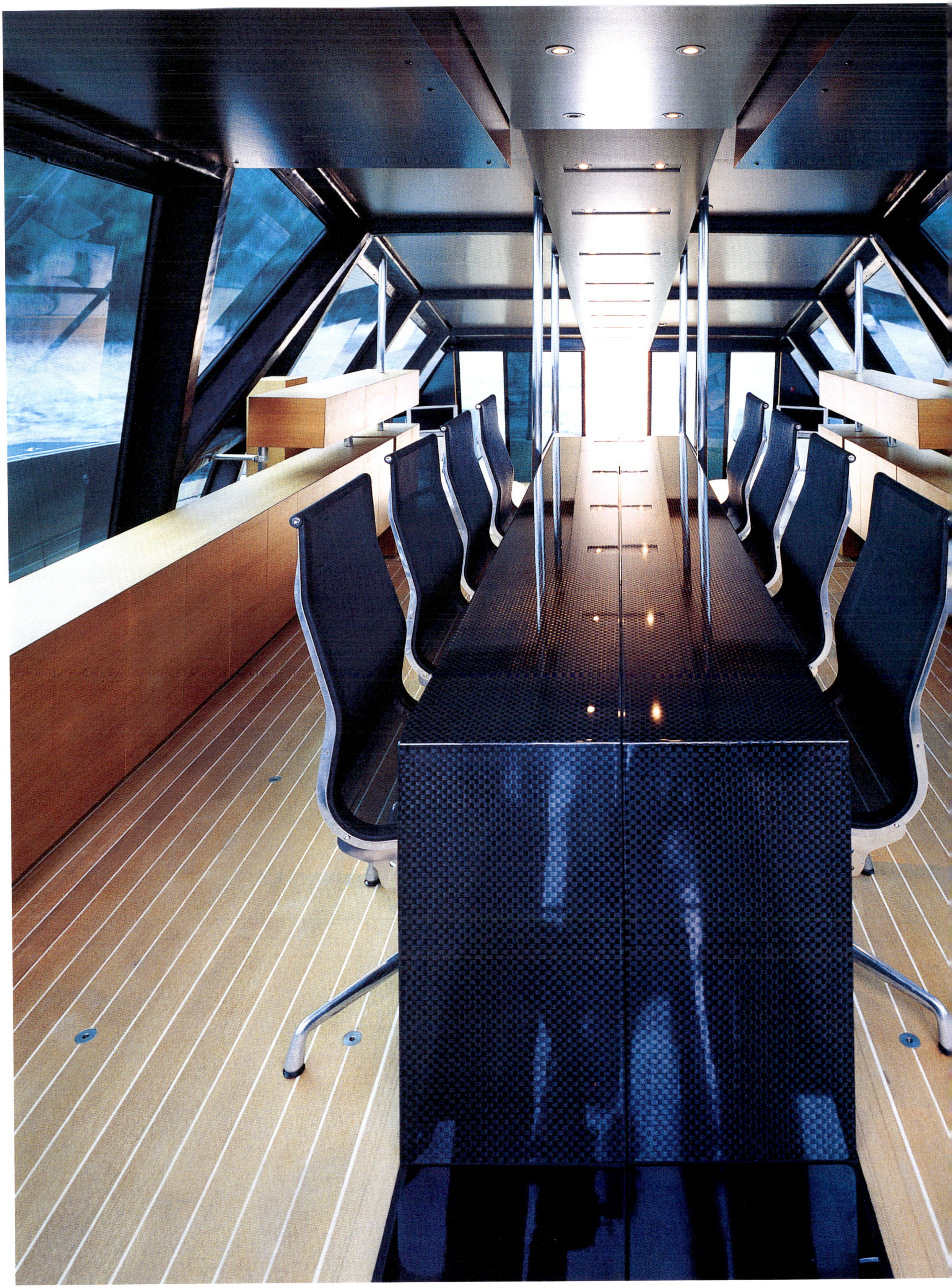

OPPOSITE: *The dining saloon could easily be mistaken for the boardroom of a modern office. The table is finished in carbon fibre with the weave exposed.*

ABOVE: *The foredeck converts from a sunning area during the day to an alfresco dining space in the evening.*

LEFT: *The galley is a study in stainless steel and 90-degree angles.*

OVERLEAF: *A canopy made of high-tech laminated sailcloth can cover the foredeck to shelter it from the elements.*

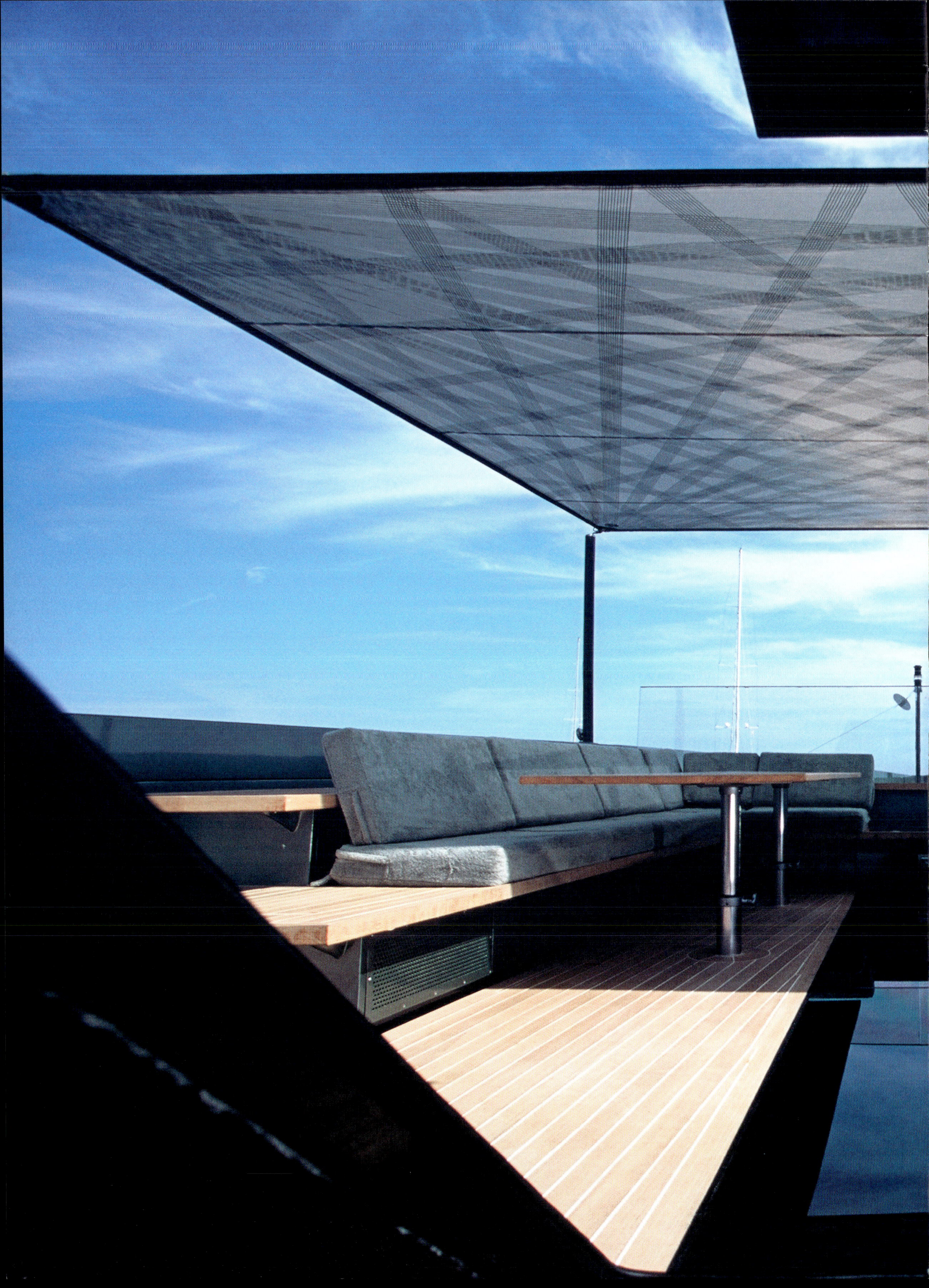

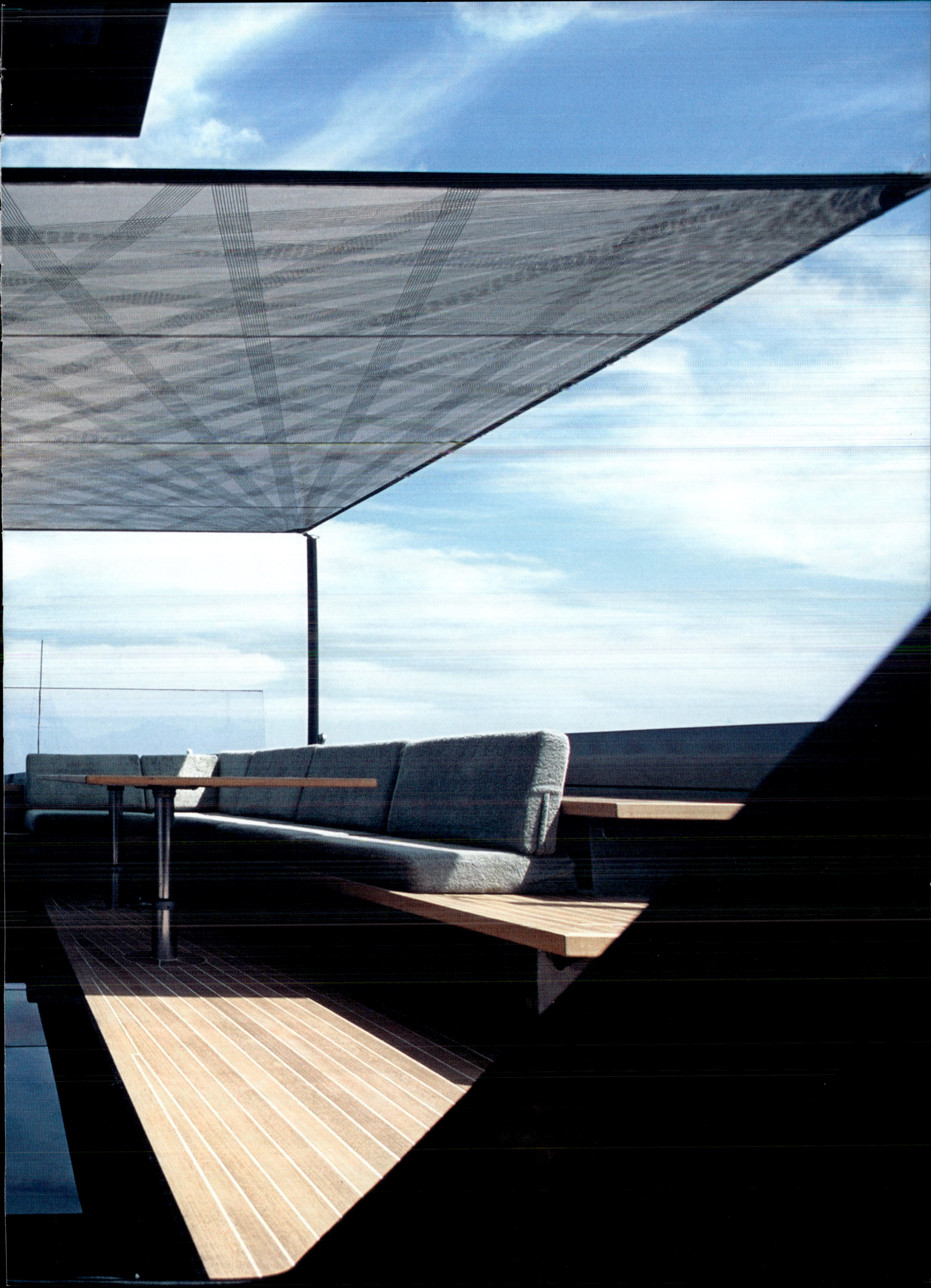

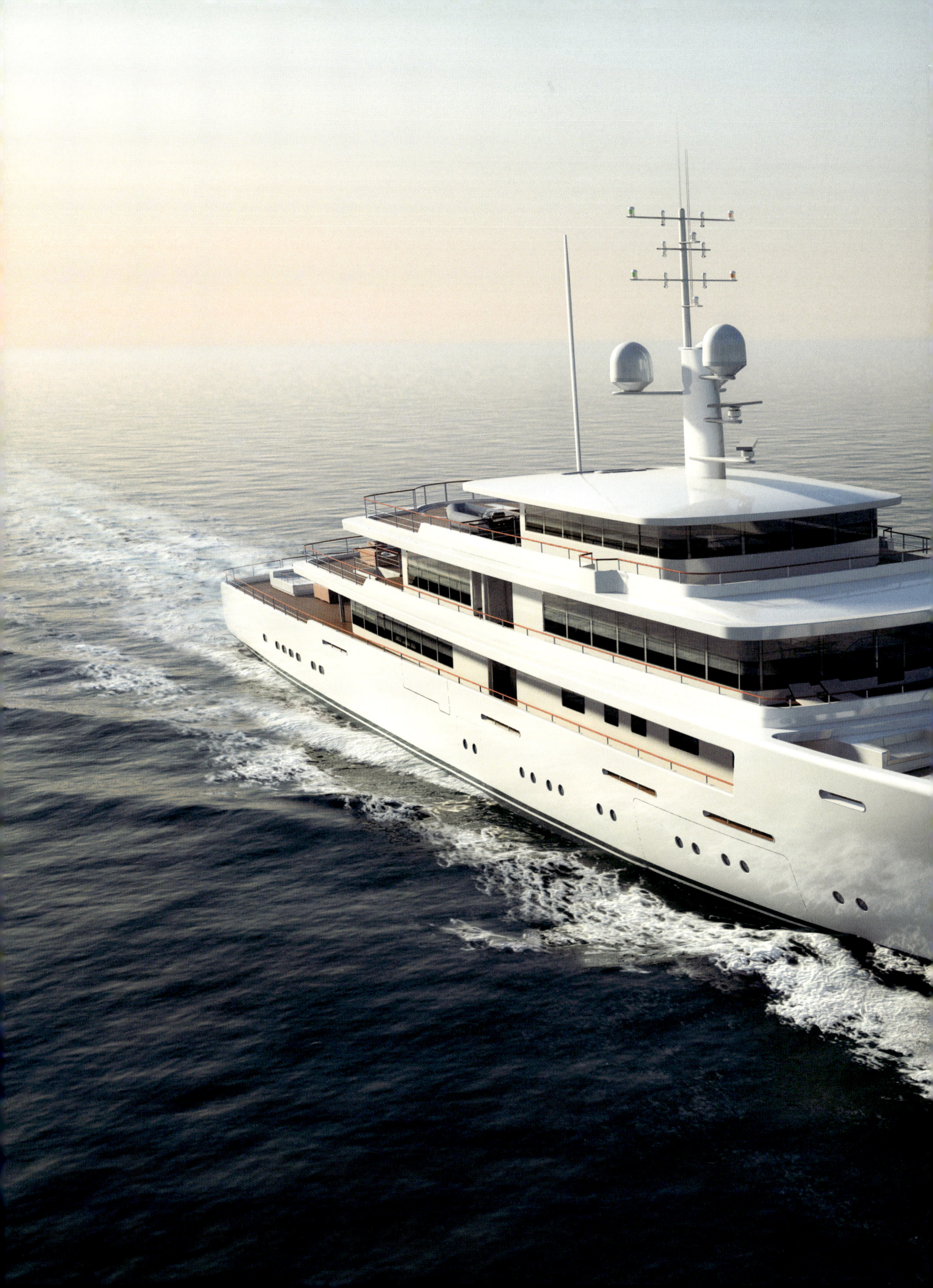

On the Horizon

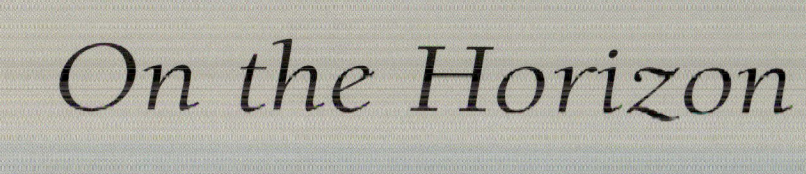

Today's outrageous yachts may seem downright tame compared to what's on the drawing boards of forward-thinking designers. Exciting designs with more efficient hulls, sexier superstructures, and power plants that use less fuel and generate less pollution are standing in the wings, awaiting clients willing to break away from the conventional.

Several forward-looking designs, such as Feadship's *Predator* (see pages 52–63), have already been built and more are queuing up. Here is a sampling of some of the most original concepts being developed by designers, both established and new to the scene.

PRECEDING PAGES: *Nauta Yachts design for "Project Light."*

BELOW: *Feadship design for the C-stream concept.*

ASHISH GUPTA

At first glance, the 492-foot (150-metre) "Maharaja" appears unbuildable. It looks more like a barge houseboat than a yacht. It is the brainchild of Ashish Gupta, a young Indian architect who heads a firm called Beyond Design. He is not a naval architect and refers to his project as yacht architecture, not yacht design. His only prior yacht design experiences are a 131¼-foot (40-metre) wooden yacht that was built in India and a refit of the interior of a large motoryacht. "Maharaja" includes a 49¼-foot (15-metre) infinity pool, a 59-foot (18-metre) beach lounge, a 98½-foot (30 metre) putting green, a large, open sundeck and a low profile. Gupta is convinced that his concept can be realized. Willem Stolk of the marine design and engineering consultancy Stolk Marimeks in The Netherlands agrees that with certain modifications this floating resort is doable.

IVAN ERDEVICKI

The "Kiss 250" is one of Ivan Erdevicki's Mediterranean Series designs. His intention in creating the series was to provide an alternative to the designs available from mainstream designers. "Kiss 250" is a simple, practical, elegant, and well-proportioned boat with modern appeal. Its design offers considerably more living area than is typical on yachts of the same size and places greater emphasis on open-air living.

The interior reflects the exterior styling of the yacht, which displays a distinct, if not dramatic, departure from the norm. The hull lines allow high speeds with minimum resistance, but without compromising comfort and safety. The styling and shapes of the exterior detail permit both metal and composite materials to be used in its construction.

COR D. ROVER DESIGN

Dutch designer Cor D. Rover's "Greenhouse" project incorporates his ideas about the direction he thinks the yachting market could move in coming years. Its organic, morphing shape has classic origins. Rover envisions greater use of structural glass on tomorrow's yachts, thanks to improvements in the chemical and structural characteristics of the material, as well as to advances in embedding chromatic shading and blinding within the glass itself. The abundance of glass, says Rover, will enhance guests' feeling of being close to the sea and the scenery.

FEADSHIP

The group of Dutch shipyards operating as Feadship produces some of the finest custom and semi-custom yachts in the world. Studio De Voogt, the group's central design agency, has responded to what Feadship foresees as the primary requirements in design briefs in years to come by creating a series of concepts called the "X-stream", the "F-stream" (left), and the "C-stream".

Each of the "streams" is intended to address the needs of the yacht owner of the future. The company predicts that he will be an eco-conscious person who enjoys using his yacht in a casual way, spends a lot of time outdoors, and rarely retires to a traditional dining room. He wants greater speeds, reduced fuel consumption, brighter interiors, higher ceilings, more water-sports equipment, and state-of-the-art technologies and design.

SETZER DESIGN GROUP

With its VL-66 design, Setzer Design Group addresses issues of both style and substance. In addition to its sweeping lines, the design features amenities such as an interior glass elevator, a sixteen-seat cinema, rounded windows that offer dramatic views and balconies off several of the staterooms that fold out over the sea. It has a highly efficient hull shape and would be powered by an efficient diesel-electric drive capable of producing cruising speeds of 15 knots.

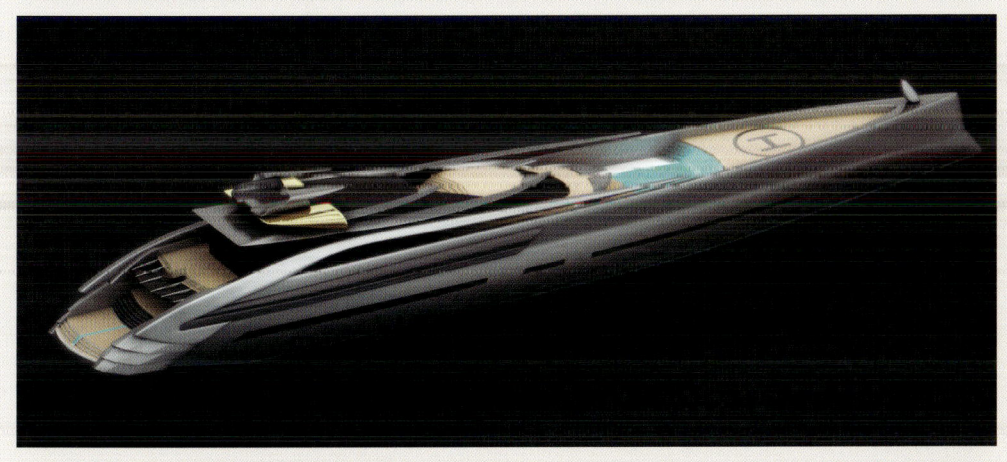

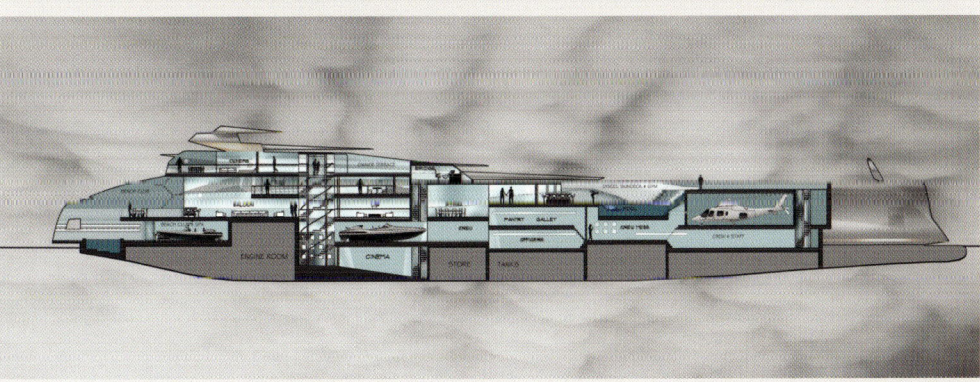

KEN FREIVOKH DESIGN

Ken Freivokh has been responsible for many innovative designs in recent years, including the mega-sailer *Maltese Falcon*. It is no surprise that the Freivokh team has generated a number of new concepts that diverge from the beaten path.

One of the latest projects is "Alien," an aggressive 367½-foot (112-metre) reverse-bow motoryacht for a young owner who has been keen to encourage innovation and lateral thinking. The yacht is a highly efficient, full-displacement, low-volume, long-waterline vessel capable of 24 knots with minimum wake. The interior concept departs from the normal practice of duplicating spaces such as salons on each deck, and instead offers a multilevel saloon with a mezzanine to accommodate a card room, library, and business center, and panoramic views of the terraces aft. The yacht includes a full helicopter hangar, a handsome spa-pool associated with the beach area, and a tidal pool and waterfall forward by the gymnasium and games room. There is also a cinema with underwater views and a six-deck-high glass atrium.

TONY CASTRO LTD

This 120-foot (36.6-metre) motor yacht is a minimalist concept inside and out. It is the brainchild of Tony Castro Ltd, a British company known for its innovative yacht design, and it represents a serious attempt to improve fuel efficiency—and still achieve a top speed of 35 knots. It will have half the normal horsepower and half the normal running costs for a vessel of its size. Power will come from a super-efficient six-engine system still in development.

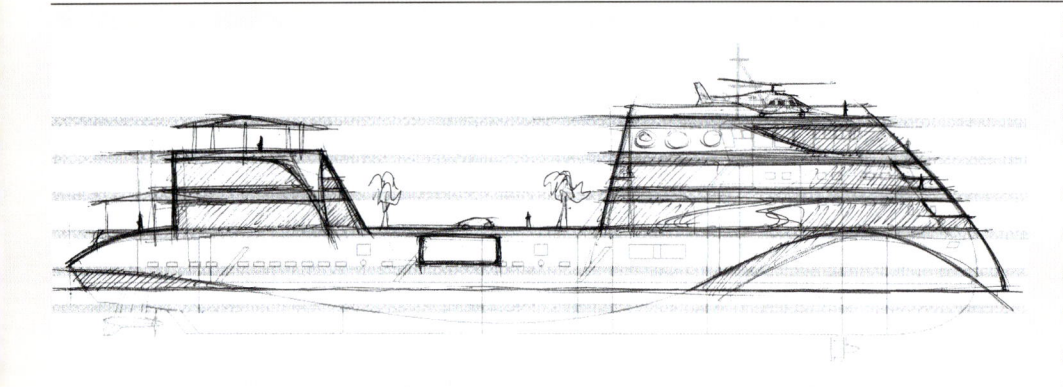

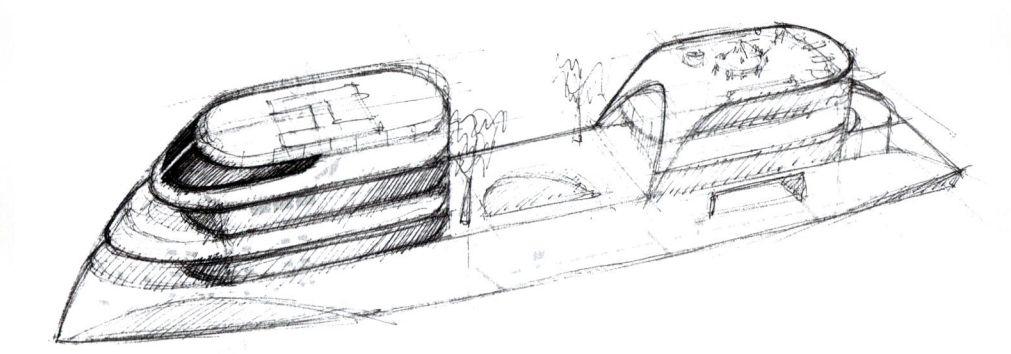

BANNENBERG YACHT DESIGNS

Bannenberg Yacht Designs was founded by the late Jon Bannenberg, an iconoclast and innovator in large yacht design. The firm is now led by his son, Dickie, and retains the forward-thinking creative edge synonymous with the name. This concept design is one of a number that the Bannenberg studio has developed around the established Ulstein commercial hull platform.

The Ulstein hull was developed to produce increased comfort and safety, lower fuel consumption and greater speed. The bow inclines aft and the hull has been significantly raised, while at the same time tolerating submersion. Bannenberg has given the yacht some attributes of explorer vessels, as well as the chiselled features and forms of military ships. The superstructure draws from modern architecture and breaks free of the bulwark/fashion-plate/full-height-window constraints typical of conventional new yacht projects. The blocks of accommodations forward and aft offer views in both directions and allow the amidships area to be used for a variety of purposes, including gardens.

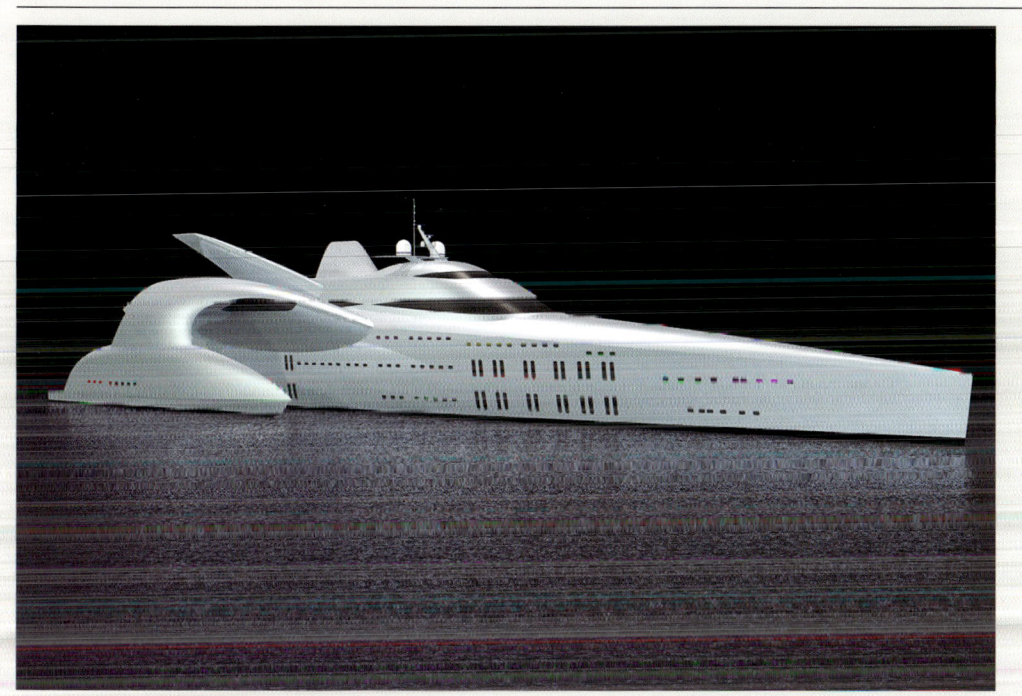

CRAIG LOOMES DESIGN GROUP

Most yachts and ships deal with waves by riding up one side and down the other. When the waves are small, the ride is easy. When they get larger, the ride obviously gets rougher. The Craig Loomes Design Group of New Zealand has created a multiple-hull form that pierces through the waves rather than riding over them, with the main hull actually semi-submerging.

The 486-foot (148.1-metre) design pictured has six duplex guest suites, each on two decks, and a private owner's suite on four decks, complete with its own elevator. The yacht would carry up to sixty crew and would be equipped with a helipad and viewing lounges in the beams that support the outer hulls.

WALLY

Monaco-based yacht builder Wally has rarely introduced a yacht model, power or sail, that has not left heads spinning. A feel for functionality, a flair for style and a fearless quest for innovation have placed the company in a peerless position in the yachting world.

The WallyIsland concept represents the company at its most audacious and creative. In a 2007 statement announcing the concept, Wally wrote, "What about a mega-yacht where you comfortably live on board as if it were your own estate? Where you have a piece of land that you can use to play your favourite sport, to grow your favourite plants, to enjoy your favourite outdoor activity?"

WallyIsland has all that, plus the amenities of a luxury yacht, and, with a fuel capacity of nearly 200,000 gallons, it can travel 15,000 miles at cruising speed.

ESPEN ØINO INTERNATIONAL

Developed by Espen Øino International in conjunction with the Nobiskrug Yard in Germany, "Freedom" is a 279-foot (85-metre) yacht featuring an enormous glass superstructure penetrated by a submarine-like conning tower that houses the wheelhouse. All the glass allows daylight to pour in and affords glorious views. At the same time, the external look of the boat is a bit ambiguous and menacing. The configuration of the hull creates substantial room below for big living spaces with generous headroom. Aft there is a spa/beach club combined with a drive-in dock/pool for tenders. With its cutting-edge naval architecture, "Freedom" promises to offer excellent seakeeping and high performance.

NAUTA YACHTS

Italy's Nauta Yachts and its chief designer, Mario Pedol, created the design for "Project Light" as a rethinking of the relationship between a superyacht and its environment. As of autumn 2008, more than 18,000 man-hours have gone into the project. Her length is 262½ feet (80 metres), and she has some 8,288 square feet (770 square metres) of luxury accommodations, including a deck for the exclusive use of the owner with private access to the pool on the foredeck. There are six additional guest cabins, two of which can be combined to create a full-beam VIP suite. With more than 2,140 square feet (200 square metres) of windows, this yacht will certainly have a portal to the world.

NUVOLARI & LENARD

The design team of Nuvolari & Lenard keeps working on bigger and bigger boats for Palmer Johnson Yachts. The latest, a 171-footer (52.1 metres), is a narrow semi-displacement hull with a vertical plumb bow. The whole boat has an aggressive military look, but the accommodations are as slick and luxurious as they come. The main saloon greets the main deck as one fluid inside outside space. Forward of the saloon is a private sitting room bathed in light. The owner's cabin has its own private study. Everything is clean and modern. The foredeck sports a swimming pool, not a hot tub!

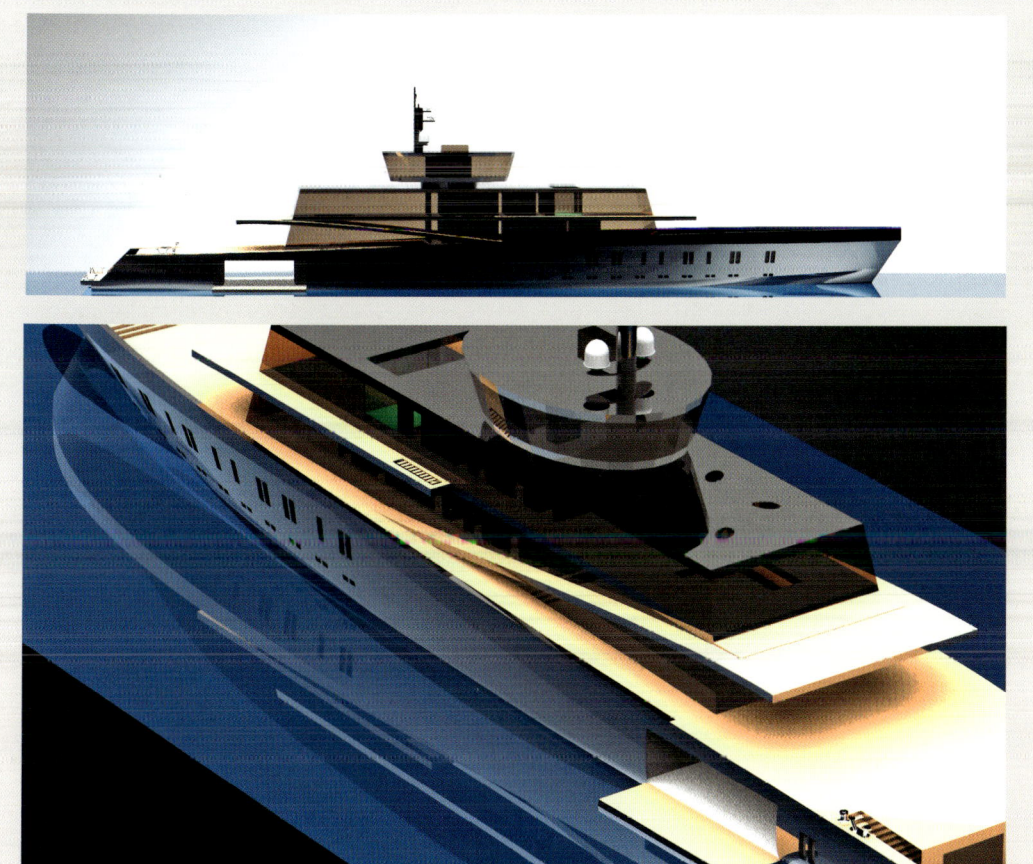

IVANA PORFIRI

Ivana Porfiri approaches all of her work in a very holistic manner and is concerned with the psychological and philosophical implications of her designs. When asked to describe the rendering she created for an "outrageous yacht," she says, "I am working on an idea for a boat without steps, where I imagine people running around with a dog or a bike, and where it would be possible to rest under a tree—perhaps not a palm tree, but an ancient olive tree, with the water and the sky always around, and the boat moving very slowly, somewhere else, even when it is raining or snowing."

ON THE HORIZON / 231

Acknowledgements

We would like to acknowledge all the yacht owners who allowed us to present their magnificent vessels in this book, as well as the builders, brokers and designers who supplied us with information, insights, photos and renderings. We would also like to thank Jacqueline Decter, our editor at Vendome Press, for her thorough fact checking and editing.

We are fortunate to be involved in the dynamic world of yachts and yachting. Each of us grew up with a passion for water and boats, and we have pursued careers that have kept us around both. We are grateful to all the other passionate travellers in this waterlogged world with whom we've shared countless memorable moments and great adventures afloat.

Jill Bobrow
Dana Jinkins
Kenny Wooton

All photos by Dana Jinkins, with the exception of the following:

Toni Meneguzzo, pp. 29, 163–65
Visions, pp. 52–53, 55 top, 57 bottom, 60 bottom, 61
Jainie Cowham: pp. 54, 55 bottom, 62–63
Bannenberg Designs/David Churchill, pp. 56–57 top, 58–59, 60 top
Shaw McCutcheon, pp. 68–69
Emilio Bianci and GiulianoSargentini, pp. 77 bottom, 82 top, 83
Simon McBride, pp. 78, 79 top, 82 bottom
Carlo Borlenghi, pp. 80–81
Courtesy of Liveras Yachts: pp. 84–93
Courtesy of Lulworth pp. 94–96, 99, 103 bottom
Rowhedge Heritage Trust, p. 97 top
Michele Menichini, p. 97 bottom
Irene Lucas, p. 98 top
Beken of Cowes, p. 98 bottom
Francesco Rastrelli, pp. 101–2, 103 bottom
Andrea Ferrari, pp. 104–13
Pam Jones, pp. 114–23
Matthieu Carlin, pp. 130—37
Martin Fine Photography, pp. 138–39, 141 bottom, 142–47, 201
Neil Rabinowitz, pp. 140, 141 top
Gilles Martin-Raget, pp. 158–62, 210–12, 214–15, 217 top, 219 top, 220–21
Courtesy of SS Delphine, pp. 166–73
Courtesy of Allure Shadow, pp. 174–81
Maurizio Paradisi, pp. 182–95
Rod Taylor, pp.202–5
Klaus Jordan: pp. 206–9
Guido Grugnola, pp. 213, 216, 217 bottom, 218, 219 bottom
"On the Horizon" designs courtesy of respective designers, pp. 222–29

First published in the United Kingdom by
Adlard Coles Nautical
an imprint of A&C Black Publishers Ltd
36 Soho Square, London
W1D 3QY
www.adlardcoles.com

First published in the United States of America by
The Vendome Press

Copyright © 2009 The Vendome Press
Text copyright © 2009 Jill Bobrow and Kenny Wooton
Images copyright © 2009 Dana Jinkins (except where noted at left)

First edition published 2009

ISBN 978-1-4081-2052-1

All rights reserved. No part of the contents of this book may be reproduced in any form or by any means – graphic, electronic or mechanical, including photocopying, recording, taping or information storage and retrieval systems – without the prior permission in writing of the publishers.

A CIP catalogue record for this book is available from the British Library.

Printed in Singapore by Imago